A Brief History of the United States Since 1945

A BRIEF HISTORY OF THE UNITED STATES SINCE 1945

ROBERT D. MARCUS

State University of New York at Stony Brook

St. Martin's Press / New York

Library of Congress Catalog Card Number: 74-24978
Copyright © 1975 by St. Martin's Press, Inc.
All Rights Reserved.
Manufactured in the United States of America.
For information, write: St. Martin's Press, Inc.,
175 Fifth Avenue, New York, N.Y. 10010

Cover illustration: Jasper Johns, "Three Flags," 1958.
Encaustic on canvas (three levels), 30⅞" x 48½" x 5".
Collection Mr. and Mrs. Burton Tremaine, Meriden, Connecticut.
Ektachrome courtesy of Harry N. Abrams, Inc., New York.

Excerpt from "Howl," from *Howl and Other Poems* by Allen Ginsberg.
Copyright © 1956, 1959 by Allen Ginsberg.
Reprinted by permission of City Lights Books.

To Mr. and Mrs. Henry Clay Anton

PREFACE

HISTORIANS SHOULD be cautious in writing about their own country in their own time: contemporary history presents the writer with unique problems of fact and interpretation. In writing this book, I have sought to be as scrupulously accurate as possible and have tried to provide a coherent framework for the tumultuous events of the postwar years. In short, I have tried to apply a historian's standards to events that my profession has yet to digest. My principle justification for the task must be that the history of the United States since 1945 is, quite simply, a tale worthy of the telling.

Many people aided me in this project. John W. Chambers, Jr., of Barnard College read the manuscript with great care, and much to my profit. James Moore of Hofstra University gave helpful counsel, particularly in matters of American foreign policy. Terry Cooney, Hardy Green, and Amy Srebnick, graduate students at the State University of New York at Stony Brook, aided me in my research. David and Sandra Burner straightened out some of the twistings of my prose. Norman Rosenberg read and made suggestions about several portions of the manuscript. Chilton Williamson, Jr., and Nancy Perry of St. Martin's Press met their responsibilities with exactitude and dispatch.

CONTENTS

TWO: 1960–1975

INTRODUCTION

THE UNITED STATES seemed to dominate the world in 1945. While Europe lay in ruins and the non-European world was only beginning its rise from Western tutelage, the United States was growing in economic, military, and cultural influence. The Second World War had jolted the country out of economic depression by expanding its factories, improving its technology, and upgrading and enlarging its labor force. Military demands had spawned immense manufacturing efforts; thousands of new enterprises made the United States the world's most powerful industrial state. The needs of modern warfare accelerated developments in computers, electronics, plastics, antibiotics, and the management of large-scale research and operations—all areas that would make possible the coming economic boom. And the war economy brought millions of new people into the work force, including large numbers of women and blacks.

America owned most of the known supplies of gold, so the American dollar, alone of the great currencies, remained stable. As a primary source of capital for reconstruction, New York City supplanted London as the financial center of the world. The United States also came out of battle with a strong and well-equipped army, the greatest navy and air force in history, and a monopoly (soon to be lost) in nuclear technology.

In retrospect, other assets appear equally impressive. The growth in both federal and private bureaucracies, generally lamented at the time, provided the human resources to manage the new economy—larger and more complex than any in the past. The spirit of sacrifice and the near unanimity of feeling spurred by the war effort eased the transition to a peacetime world. The nation was thereby spared the sharp divisions that other societies encountered, although the opportunities for change that healthy controversy might have produced were also curtailed. The G.I. Bill subsidized higher education for millions of veterans. High wages, overtime, thrift, and the dearth of consumer goods during the war had built up a backlog of savings that provided markets for the peacetime economy. Americans by 1945 had experienced fifteen years of shortages—of income during depression and of goods during war. During that time few schools, offices, and homes had been built to meet the needs of the population. Adding to this pressure, the birth rate rose suddenly after the war. The market for goods and services appeared endless.

The United States had also become the cultural capital of the world by 1945. After a long history of being a cultural province of Europe, the nation found itself harboring a large proportion of the world's intellectuals and leaders in the fine arts. Beginning in the 1930s, scholars in every field fled the totalitarian regimes to seek refuge and jobs in America.

International science was clearly centered in the United States by the end of the thirties; one by one, most of the creators of modern physics —Albert Einstein, Enrico Fermi, Niels Bohr, and others—moved to American universities and institutes that offered them a means to pursue their work without political interference. Similarly, major figures in the social sciences and the humanities—writers like Thomas Mann and architects like Walter Gropius—emigrated to America.

At the same time as the New World was draining the creative energies of Europe, America's own writers, artists, and scholars were discovering ever greater opportunities to develop their talents and gain remuneration and fame from a newly receptive culture. The result in nearly every field was an American cultural hegemony, at least in the immediate postwar world. New York City replaced Paris as the center both for artists and for the art market. Americans had once completed their educations by exposure to foreign cultures; now "American studies" programs sprang up abroad. The country's popular culture, especially jazz, attracted young people in many parts of the world.

In some, the overall American dominance bred heady visions of an "American Century" to succeed the vanished "Pax Britannica." Woodrow

Wilson's dream of a world ordered on the American model seemed able to be realized. And indeed, it hardly seemed strange to call for ideological dominance to match the nation's economic and military might. Visions of exporting our goods, our culture, and our institutions could easily arise from the special circumstances of the world at the end of a long war.

Paradoxically, these images of power carried with them impelling views of a world in confusion and faced with indefinite threats. Somehow America's power was more potential than actual, vanishing at the very suggestion of its use. The United States had the atom bomb, but did it dare use it again? The magnificent army swiftly demobilized, and most of the navy rusted in "mothballs." The huge industrial plant had been built for war production; could it be converted to peacetime use? Would the potential demand for goods result in large sales, or would the dislocations of the war's end induce people to hold onto their money? Would America's advantages turn to liabilities if its factories could find no overseas markets in bankrupt Europe and Japan? The future, as always, hazed into uncertainty. The indefinite tasks of peace stirred doubts after four years of clear-cut war needs. Many feared the return of depression.

In April 1945, in the midst of such hopes and doubts, the nation's leader, Franklin D. Roosevelt, slumped over in a chair while having his portrait painted at the Little White House in Warm Springs, Georgia. A massive cerebral hemorrhage took the life of the calm, steady figure who had guided Americans for so long. His successor, Harry S. Truman, was a former Kansas City haberdasher and a relatively unknown politician inexperienced in national leadership. Could he continue Roosevelt's legacy of an aggressive presidency? Or would he return the White House to the drab days of Presidents Harding and Coolidge?

With their new leader and an uncertain future, most Americans believed they were entering a new age. Throughout the war they had postponed their wants "for the duration," meaning until whatever date the war ended. When the fighting stopped in 1945, they virtually willed a fresh era; they demanded demobilization, an end to wartime controls, and the widespread availability of consumer goods even if it meant serious inflation. Youngsters longed for bubble gum and bicycle tires, both of which had vanished during the war. Men wanted new cars, women nylon stockings, and both new houses and appliances. A willingness to borrow accompanied these demands. The volume of consumer credit multiplied fivefold in the dozen years after the war, and the federal government financed mortgages for millions of veterans.

By the late 1950s, characterizations of American society all came to rest on one fact: high mass consumption of goods and services. The historian David M. Potter interpreted all of the country's past in a portrait of Americans as "people of plenty." The Harvard economist John Kenneth Galbraith, leafing through a small dictionary in search of synonyms for the idea of wealth, lighted on the phrase that Americans took to define themselves: "the affluent society." This described the life of most Americans, though not all, for millions were poor. Middle-class affluence connoted not the power and solidity of those with entrenched wealth; it referred to people only recently inundated by a cascade of goods and services and caught up in a bubbling stream of evanescent income, disposable goods, and short-lived "consumer durables."

It is possible to visualize the history of the years since 1945 as a series of triumphs for an affluent society gaining in wealth and steadily shrinking the pockets of poverty and neglect. This "Fourth of July image" of the nation is not wholly false. Yet one could with equal ease view these years as an age of American decline, of a nation moving from dominance to parity with the rest of the world, from stability to chaos, from unity to fragmentation, from clarity to confusion. But this view underestimates the travail and uncertainty of the world three decades ago and forgets the successes of the intervening years. The situation of 1945 could not endure and cannot be taken as a standard against which to measure the era. America intact amidst a world in ruins is hardly a reasonable ideal: America's share in the resources of the world, its productive capacity, and its military strength clearly could not and ought not to have remained at the level of 1945. American policy, for example, created its two main trade rivals, Japan and the European Common Market.

The story of these years is neither one of decline nor one of triumph, but rather is a mosaic of power and people. What did the nation do with its power at the beginning of this era and how have American lives and institutions changed during the last thirty years? To answer these questions this book will look selectively at the way American political and economic institutions have operated and examine their public policy to see how the configuration of power in the society has shifted over time. It will also examine in some detail the country's relationship with the rest of the world, which had a formidable impact on domestic life. Not since the Revolutionary Era have the lives of Americans been so affected by what went on in the rest of the world and by their responses to such events.

Finally, this book will search for the sinuous strands of American society in a period of rapid change. Large trends common to the nation as a whole may be seen to emerge: population growth; urban decay; movement to suburbs and to the Far West; rising levels of education; the proliferation of credit cards, branch stores, and condensed books; the ubiquity of television. But restlessness and a quest for leisure are far from the whole story. The flow of American life since 1945 has been rich, cutting through many new channels. Beneath surface similarities, the roots of diverse subcultures have flourished. Economic abundance has multiplied the range of choices available to a population diverse in its origins, varied in its surroundings and its circumstances. Young people began to discover their own culture with its particular heroes, products, music. An enormously expanded college population found itself large enough to support a separate set of institutions and styles. After generations of seeking to assimilate into the WASP culture, many working-class and lower-middle-class Americans, often of immigrant backgrounds, suddenly found emotional value in reasserting their ethnic heritages. Blacks sought to distinguish their culture rather than to abandon it. American society accelerated its historical pluralism. Yet this collection of subcultures was more than the sum of its parts. A fruitful intercourse between a national culture and its various subgroups represents the core of our social history.

PART ONE

1945—1960

◄ 1 ►

THE TRUMAN ADMINISTRATION

HARRY S. TRUMAN, a direct, round-faced man from Missouri, contrasted vividly with his urbane, polished predecessor. An unsuccessful small businessman in Kansas City, then a country judge —whom some thought too closely tied to the party machine boss Thomas Pendergast—Truman's political career lacked distinction until he was elected Senator in 1934, again with Pendergast's help. Once in Washington, Truman exhibited an inordinate ability for hard work; a tenacious, widely respected intelligence; and, most characteristic of all, great courage. On acceding to the presidency, he faced up to his unaccustomed responsibilities. A sign on his desk proclaimed: "The buck stops here." When critics harped too loudly, as they often did during the difficult years of postwar readjustment, Truman told fainthearted advisors, "If you can't stand the heat, get out of the kitchen!"

Truman's approach to a problem was to solve it quickly. This approach was not appropriate in the Senate, where it was necessary to spin out a legislative consensus on most issues. Thus, after many frustrating years as a Senator, Truman readily accepted the challenge of White House leadership. The President, he thought, could

3

act decisively and quickly. He would soon discover, however, that vigorous action, couched in folksy aphorisms, could not always ease the convoluted problems America faced in 1945.

In his first important message to Congress in 1945, Truman outlined "a program of liberalism and progressivism which will be the foundation of my administration." He would consolidate the New Deal, protecting it from enemies and expanding its successes. Truman wanted Congress to boost the minimum wage from 40¢ to 65¢ an hour and "insure a decent standard of living for America's working class" by expanding social security benefits. He urged a national health insurance program to provide cradle-to-the-grave medical care. Regional development schemes like the Tennessee Valley Authority (TVA) would reclaim the southwest desert and harness the Missouri River.

Although an increasingly conservative Congress blocked all these projects, the legislators did approve a compromise version of Truman's call for government action to guarantee full employment. The Employment Act of 1946 recognized federal responsibility to manage the economy and established a Council of Economic Advisors to recommend measures of "stabilization." Truman had hoped to take up any slack in the American economy by boosting federal expenditures whenever private investment fell below the level necessary to ensure full employment. The act did not provide for this, but it did stake out government's role in planning for prosperity. As such, it institutionalized the lessons of Keynesian economic theory and the practices of wartime organization.

The most immediate issue, however, concerned demobilization and reconversion: mustering Americans and the American economy out of the war's artificial demands into peacetime production. This task, made more difficult by ideological jousting over the extension of wartime controls, soon dominated politics in Washington.

The Economics of Demobilization

The Second World War turned the American economy around by creating new industries and jobs. The enormous federal spending required to finance the war effort—about $321 billion—pulled the country out of a decade of depression. After 1945 the United States found itself in a situation far different from that of the other belligerents. France, Great Britain, Germany, and Japan all faced massive tasks of rebuilding; the United States had only to sustain its already burgeoning industries. Most economists, however, gloomily predicted that peace would end wartime prosperity. An abrupt cancellation of government contracts, together with the return of millions of demobilized veterans, might leave as many as eight million people jobless. Such fears never materialized. The economy rollercoastered through several hectic years, but reconversion did not bring financial collapse or massive unemployment.

New markets sustained American industry and American profits. Wartime austerity had created a shortage of consumer goods just when millions of Americans were earning good wages for the first time since the 1920s. After "V-J Day" (Victory over Japan), people spent their accumulated savings on everything from candy bars to houses. New consumer demand, coupled with Europe's enormous reconstruction needs, filled the void left by the termination of military production. Although the annual value of goods and services produced (the gross national product, or GNP) dropped to a low in early 1946, it climbed shortly thereafter; corporate profits reached an all-time high of $17 billion in 1947.

Employment levels also stayed relatively high, with over thirteen million veterans able to find work. The Serviceman's Readjustment Act of 1944, also known as "The G.I. Bill of Rights," provided money for educational stipends, job training, unemployment compensation, medical benefits, and even business ventures for former soldiers. But significant changes in the nature of the postwar labor force also kept unemployment under 4 percent. With the coming of peace, women, a substantial portion of the wartime work supply, returned to their homes in large numbers. Millions of veterans went back to school, and many older people retired. Unemployment went up less than 2 percent from 1945 to 1947.

The federal government only intermittently guided the reconversion. The sudden peace with Japan had caught Washington's bureaucracies off guard. Planners, anxious to end massive government spending, yet aware of the need to retain price ceilings to avoid inflation, ended up by introducing serious distortions into the economy. During the fall of 1945, they canceled thirty-two million war contracts and terminated manpower controls, raw material allocations, and most food rationing. Then the government quickly disposed of war surpluses and sold the plants it owned. Generous tax concessions and the lifting of excess profits taxes facilitated business adjustments. But the rigid price controls continued. No one wanted inflation to chip away at living standards, and most Americans felt that all the people, not just the rich, should share available consumer luxuries. The result, inevitably, was shortages and "black markets," in which scarce goods were sold to anxious consumers at illegally high prices.

The government moved to meet some of these economic dislocations. An acute lack of housing, owing in part to a scarcity of building materials, compelled Congress to pass an Emergency Housing Act to oversee a construction goal of almost three million homes for returning veterans. More mortgage loans, greater stimulus for the production of scarce building materials, and the lifting of rent controls combined to spur housing construction.

Other distortions remained that were demographical, more the result of people pressure than economic calculations. The influx of returning veterans and a spurt in the birth rate—the "baby boom" of the late forties—filled classrooms to capacity. Public schools lacked sufficient space, books, and teachers, especially in the lower grades. Colleges and universities were overwhelmed when almost two million veterans applied for educational benefits under the G.I. Bill. These institutions required immediate innovations in order to accommodate them. The University of Wisconsin, for example, established thirty-four centers around the state to provide the first two years of college instruction; the University of Illinois successfully transformed an amusement pier in Chicago into an instruction center.

Inflation and Labor Unrest

Everything about reconversion fed a stubborn inflation. The end of rationing did not ease continuing shortages in critical areas. During the first full year of demobilization, from mid-1945 to mid-1946, the Office of Price Administration (OPA), the chief presidential weapon against inflation since 1943, held price increases to just 7 percent annually. But ingenious black markets quickly belied official figures. Automobile dealers, for example, often sold cars with decorative hood ornaments that cost $500, explaining to customers that "the factory just makes the cars that way." Buyers put up with the charade, happy just to have the car that went with the expensive option. In about one year, such devices dropped real earnings—what wages actually could purchase—by one-eighth.

The shortages and rising prices provoked huge walkouts by labor during 1946, when wartime no-strike regulations ceased; a crippling total of 107,475,000 work days were lost. In January, 750,000 steelworkers went out on strike, joining electrical workers, auto workers, and meat packers. Four months later, in response to strikes in the coal fields and by transport workers, Truman seized the mines and then the railroads when rank and file union members refused the settlements offered them. He even threatened to draft railroad workers into the army. Ultimately labor unions forced Truman and business leaders to grant larger wage increases than they had anticipated, an average raise of 18½¢ an hour, and to yield other significant concessions, especially a cost-of-living escalator that automatically adjusted wages to prices.

Industry naturally wanted to pass these increased costs along to the consumer, but the OPA blocked such an avenue to profits. Together with conservatives long tired of government controls, businessmen pressed for an early removal of all price ceilings. They argued that the best way to boost production, thus ultimately reducing prices, was the lure of high profits. OPA leaders like Chester Bowles warned against "bonanza windfalls" and the dangers of a self-sustaining inflationary spiral if price controls ended suddenly. Caught between business and bureaucrats, Congress extended a watered-down version of the OPA on June 29, 1946. Truman angrily vetoed it, preferring to allow all controls to expire one day later. As he had calculated, prices skyrocketed wildly, climbing some 28 percent during the first sixteen days of July. So Congress restored price ceilings and rent controls, as Truman had hoped.

The price control machinery worked poorly, however, without the discipline of war. Farmers, for example, held beef off the market in an attempt to force a change in policy. Similar boycotts in other areas soon led the administration to admit the obvious: controls could not force producers to sell their goods. The government proceeded slowly to acquiesce. By mid-1947, controls remained only on sugar, rice, and rubber, while prices on other items soared. At the same time, however, reconstruction needs and federal spending for defense permitted productivity to climb with prices, thus avoiding a self-sustaining inflation and ensuring a degree of economic stability.

The demand for United States dollars for investment capital prevented a monetary crisis that otherwise might have developed from decontrol. Despite its internal tremors, the domestic American economy was the most stable in the world, a condition that guaranteed its prosperity.

Republican Congress, Democratic President

In the 1946 congressional elections, Republicans played on voter discontent with an inspired slogan, "Had enough?" Since the GOP had made steady gains in both houses of Congress since 1938, its victory in 1946 reflected a long-term trend away from Democratic dominance as well as a predictable disenchantment with Truman's policies. The President had alienated labor leaders and the progressive wing of his party by his economic policies. Moreover, suburban migration had weakened the political clout of urban, traditionally Democratic machines. Then, too, some new Congressmen, like Richard Nixon of California, accused their opponents of "Communist sympathies," a red herring that won many votes from worried citizens. But the Republicans of this eightieth Congress soon discovered that, although they might all oppose the Truman administration, they lacked sufficient internal unity to control administration policies.

One wing of the party, under Senator Arthur Vandenberg of Michigan, advocated a European-centered foreign policy of cooperation and pledged not to dismantle New Deal economic and social reforms. But perhaps the majority of Republicans were drawn toward a neoisolationism that gave priority to balanced budgets rather than an expansive globalism. Their lack of concern with global politics was rooted in the belief expressed by General Douglas MacArthur, now ruling Japan as America's proconsul: "The Communist bid for world power will play itself out in Asia." These conservative Republicans chafed to undo what "that man" Roosevelt had accomplished in the New Deal. Their leader, Senator Robert A. Taft of Ohio, wanted "to return to the traditional American heart of things, liberty." The New Deal had gone too far: "We have got to break with the corrupting idea that we can legislate prosperity, legislate equality, legislate opportunity." The Republicans also wanted to reduce government interference in the economy, although many approved federal incentives to private business. John

Taber, the new chairman of the House Appropriations Committee, vowed "to meat-axe government frills."

After cementing an enormously effective alliance with southern Democrats by promising to bottle up civil rights legislation, Republicans blocked funds for public housing, education, some farm programs, and social security increases. The conservative coalition passed, over Truman's veto, the Taft-Hartley Act, which weakened unions by restricting the right to strike and safeguarding an "open shop," thus limiting the prounion Wagner Act of 1935. Following wartime precedents, the new law revived the device of government injunction to prevent workers from leaving their jobs, instituted an eighty-day cooling-off period, and forbade secondary boycotts and jurisdictional strikes. The National Labor Relations Board gained new judicial and investigative powers for settling disputes. The law also required union members to sign affidavits disavowing Communist affiliation. In general, the bill favored employers and curtailed the freedom of unions. Truman predicted that the new labor regulations sowed "seeds of discord which would plague the nation for years to come."

The Taft-Hartley Act encouraged states to legislate "right to work" statutes that outlawed contracts requiring union membership as a condition of employment. The passage of the act also had long-range consequences: by allowing unprecedented government intervention in union affairs, it fathered additional restrictive policies later in the 1950s.

The rank and file protested the passage of the law with sporadic wildcat strikes, but union leadership objected only to certain features, especially section 14(b), which prohibited the closed shop. No leader challenged the right of government to curtail union activities or to limit the political rights of individual members, perhaps because the act did not curtail nationwide collective bargaining, labor's most potent weapon. So the unions moved to "clean house"—to rid themselves of known or suspected left-wing leaders and locals. The Congress of Industrial Organizations (CIO), during 1949 and 1950 alone, expelled eleven member unions charged with Communist domination. Yet some union leaders, like Philip Murray, vice-president of the United Mine Workers, attacked Taft-Hartley as "conceived in sin [by] diabolical men who, seething with hatred, designed the ugly measure for the purpose of imposing their wrath upon the workers." Such emotions sustained a vigorous drive by labor to repeal all or part of Taft-Hartley during 1948, but the Senate voted to sustain the use of injunctions. After this second defeat, labor lived with the law, content with discovering its loopholes.

The Eightieth Congress had pruned labor's power, but it also acted, this time with Truman's support, to streamline federal government and reduce bureaucratic expenses. The President appointed Herbert Hoover to head a prestigious commission on executive reorganization in 1947; two years later its report resulted in the consolidation of many government agencies to eliminate duplication and end outdated activities. The Presidential Succession Act of 1947 inserted the Speaker of the House and the president pro tempore of the Senate, both elected rather than appointed officials, before the cabinet offices in the line of presidential succession. During 1947, Congress also passed the Twenty-second Amendment to the Constitution, and the required three-fourths of the states ratified it by 1951. Spurred by the concern that Roosevelt's example might permanently aggrandize the presidency, Congress prohibited more than one reelection of a President or more than ten years in office.

The most important of the government changes during these years came as a result of the National Security Act of 1947, which unified the nation's armed services under one cabinet office, the Department of Defense, and relegated top military officers to an advisory institution, the Joint Chiefs of Staff. Civilian agencies, such as the Central Intelligence Agency and the National Security Council, now dominated strategic planning. The act was designed to reduce wasteful, interservice rivalry by putting the army, navy, and the new air force under one secretary, but the three branches still jostled one another for dwindling appropriations, though less publicly than before. Eventually, however, the ramshackle defense bureaucracy did become more efficient, and its goals became more consonant with America's overseas political objectives.

In the area of civil rights, Truman moved courageously to rectify some of the discrimination that degraded the country's black minority. The New Deal had revolutionized black political loyalties, persuading them to abandon the "party of Lincoln" and to become strongly Democratic. When blacks flooded northern industrial cities in search of more jobs and less discrimination during and after the war, they became a powerful political force. Clark Clifford, a shrewd campaign stragegist, and NAACP leader Roy Wilkins pointed out that Democratic presidential chances in 1948 depended on this black urban vote. Truman, like subsequent national Democratic candidates, acted to meet the desires of this new constituency. He appointed a distinguished multiracial committee on Civil Rights in 1946, which the following year released a report that recommended wide-ranging measures to outlaw America's caste system: federal laws against lynching and poll taxes, FBI investigations of civil rights violations, and a permanent Federal Employment Practices Commission (FEPC). Southern filibusters in Congress blocked such measures, but the President acted vigorously in areas of unquestioned presidential authority. He desegregated government offices and the armed services in 1948, appointed blacks to the federal judiciary and high administrative posts, and ordered the Justice Department to assist private petitioners in civil rights cases. It was as much as any President could do in the late 1940s. The Supreme Court would follow his example almost a decade later; the Congress, not until later still.

The 1948 Election

A long era dominated first by the social experimentation of the New Deal and then by the novel exigencies of mobilizing for total war had bred a cranky attitude toward further change. Even before the tensions of Cold War grew keen, observers and politicians sensed a climate of exhaustion. American voters seemed to have "had enough" not only of inflation, shortages, and international imbroglios, but also of their President, the man who had created, it seemed, more problems than he had solved.

Truman was unpopular even among Democratic leaders. His hard line toward the Soviet Union brought attacks from the party's left wing and from domestic radicals. Henry Wallace, an ardent "One World" advocate whom Truman dismissed from his post as Secretary of Commerce, formed a Progressive party that siphoned off liberal votes. Truman's support for civil rights alienated the party's right wing in the South and led to an independent Dixiecrat ticket headed by J. Strom Thurmond of South Carolina. With the Democrats badly split and the President standing low in the public opinion polls, Republican victory seemed assured. Virtually every political expert foresaw an easy win for New York Governor Thomas E. Dewey, and magazines began to speculate about the policies of his new Republican administration.

Truman countered by conducting an energetic, "whistle-stop" campaign, gleefully attacking Dewey when crowds yelled, "Give 'em hell, Harry!" The President dismissed the Republican-dominated legislature as "the Do-Nothing Eightieth Congress," as "errand boys of big business," and as "gluttons of privilege." Many came to admire Truman's pluck: they identified with him as the underdog out to clip Dewey's supercilious eastern manner. The split in the Democratic party actually aided Truman in the Midwest, where Wallace's extremism reassured many that the President was a moderate, not a socialist. And in urban areas, the Dixiecrat ticket served to highlight Truman's good record in civil rights. In spite of a remarkably low voter turnout, enough New Deal Democrats, especially in the large cities, rallied to the party to allow Truman to eke out a victory.

The President carried the populous states of the South, Midwest, and Far West, receiving slightly more than 24 million popular votes and 303 electoral votes. Dewey swept the East, except for Massachusetts, and won scattered support elsewhere, which brought his total to 22 million ballots and 189 electoral votes. Thurmond and Wallace each polled over a million popular votes; Thurmond carried four states in the Deep South. Political scientists have called 1948 a "maintaining election" because voting trends followed the pattern of previous contests since 1932 more than they reflected the specific tensions of 1948.

Truman's victory was a triumph for Roosevelt's New Deal coalition. Labor and ethnic groups feared the Republicans more than they disliked the President. Farmers liked the predictability of parity prices and feared Taft's prescriptions for a free market. Southerners and urban bosses realized that presidential patronage was more important than ideological spats. So the unlikely New Deal combination held together yet another national election for the Democrats.

The Fair Deal

The historian Eric Goldman has called 1949 "a year of shocks." At home, the economy behaved erratically: gross national product and capital investment dove sharply, and unemployment rose to 7 percent. The cost of living actually went down. Although the return of nickel beer delighted Manhattan bartenders, deflation slowed the

Pictorial Parade/EPA.

Even political experts incorrectly predicted the results of the 1948 presidential election. Here, on the morning following his victory over Thomas E. Dewey, Harry S. Truman displays an edition of the *Chicago Daily Tribune* that appeared before all the returns were in.

pace of business generally, for everyone was waiting for prices to drop even further. The long-expected postwar slump had finally come, but the federal government acted vigorously to prevent any slide into depression. Direct subsidies spurred new housing, and the Treasury and Federal Reserve Banks lowered interest rates. A new war—this time in Korea—brought large government spending, full employment, and federal controls to restore prosperity. In 1950, 30 percent of the budget went for military procurement: three years later, the figure stood at 62 percent. During this same period the gross national product increased by half, to $340 billion in 1953. But inflation rose along with the GNP, and price increases offset the gains of rising wages.

This gyrating domestic economy coincided with stunning reverses in foreign affairs. (Chapter 3, "The Cold War," deals with overseas developments more fully). The Soviet Union detonated its first nuclear weapon, and China fell to the Communists. The war in Korea mocked the country's hopes for peaceful containment of communism and its assumptions of omnipotence. Concern for national security and fears about domestic subversives provoked hysteria and grim "witch hunts." America's confident departures in foreign policy—the collective security arrangements of the North Atlantic Treaty Organization, the internationalist commercial policy of the Marshall Plan—stumbled across unsettling realities.

Anxiety about the future quickly submerged Truman's hopes to extend Roosevelt's social and economic programs. The President called for a "Fair Deal" in his 1949 State of the Union message, "greater economic opportunity for the mass of the people." His program abandoned the prescriptions of "frenetic, professional liberals," as Truman called those he thought too leftist, and moved instead with a "steady pace." Sobered by the President's upset victory in 1948 and the realization that most Americans wanted to continue reform, Congress quickly passed a much-needed public housing program, increased social security benefits again, boosted the minimum wage to 75¢ per hour, and extended rural electrification and public power. But on more dramatic, more emotional issues, Congress quickly earned its nickname, the "ho-hum Eighty-first." The legislators neither repealed the Taft-Hartley Act nor tampered with earlier New Deal measures. Southern legislators dubbed any bills that challenged the region's informal system of racial terror as "unwarranted federal interference with local customs." Congress politely debated Truman's plan for national health insurance, well aware that conservatives would block any decisive action on it. As the new decade began, an unnerving crisis of confidence—set off by reversals overseas—soon preoccupied the American people with vague fears of impending doom, instead of the search for a better future.

The Communist Issue and National Security

Ever since 1945, when the Grand Alliance between the Western powers and Stalin's totalitarian regime in Russia had ripped apart, Americans even remotely connected with the threatening forces of communism became suspect. As early as 1942 and 1943, President Roosevelt had instituted wartime loyalty checks, but no one panicked when several minor bureaucrats admitted their party membership. Only against the backdrop of deteriorating East-West relations in the late 1940s did several startling disclosures propel the security issue into prominence. Treasury agents raided the Communist-sponsored *Amerasia* magazine in 1945 and turned up a cache of classified documents taken by enemy spies. The next year, Canada announced that at least twenty-three trusted public employees had passed secrets to Russian spy rings, some of which operated across American borders.

Such events and his own hostility toward communism prompted President Truman to order a federal employee security program. "Loyalty review boards" soon began investigating everyone working for the government and set the tone for the era of McCarthyism that would follow. More than three million men and women came under scrutiny during the next five years. After Truman's directive to dismiss those alleged "bad security risks," some 2,000 resigned, although only 212 had been fired by 1951. The security program under Truman was thorough, even harsh on occasion, and so effective that the new Republican administration of 1953 could find no Communist-tainted employees remaining on the job.

The few security risks uncovered by the loyalty boards aroused little anxiety. But during the same years, several well-publicized investigations and court cases stirred Americans to anguished concern over communism. In 1948, for example, the administration indicted eleven leaders of the Communist party under the Smith Act of 1940, charging that they had violated its prohibition against teaching "the violent overthrow of the United States government." When these "Red cadres," as they called themselves, engaged in harassing tactics during their long trial, turning it into a political forum, public distrust of Communists solidified into hatred. Convicted, the Communists lost their appeal to the Supreme Court (*Dennis* v. *United States*, 1951) in a 6-2 decision. Chief Justice Fred Vinson argued for the majority that even conspiring to advocate or teach revolution (as distinct from conspiring to perform actual revolutionary acts) constituted a "clear and present danger" in the contemporary world and was thus punishable. Dissenting Justice Hugo Black mourned the disregard for liberties guaranteed by the First Amendment and hoped for their reaffirmation in calmer times.

Alger Hiss and the Rosenbergs.   Government legal maneuvers soon yielded to popular hysteria. In 1948 Whittaker Chambers, a former editor for *Time* and a confessed former Soviet agent, testified before the House Un-American Activities Committee that Alger Hiss, president of the Carnegie Endowment for International Peace, was a former Communist. Chambers had made such accusations earlier, but this time Hiss sued him for slander. During the trial, Chambers dramatically led investigators to a hollowed-out pumpkin on his Maryland farm that contained microfilms of classified documents he purportedly received from Hiss in the late 1930s. Because the statute of limitations prevented indictment for espionage, the government charged Hiss with perjury. Before a jury, Hiss would not explain why the keys of a typewriter identified as his own matched the typing characteristics of Chambers' documents. One trial resulted in a hung jury, but a second, which lasted from November 1949 to January 1950, convicted Hiss and sent him to jail for five years.

The defendant's background and breeding varnished the Hiss case with a significance beyond the alleged act of spying. Handsome, ambitious, liberal, the very model of the bright young intellectual the New Deal had brought to Washington, Hiss had held a variety of posts under the Democrats before advancing to a high-ranking position in the State Department. At his trials, distinguished national figures like Supreme Court Justice Felix Frankfurter and Governor Adlai E. Stevenson of Illinois testified in his behalf. On the other side, several ambitious Republicans, including Congressman Richard M. Nixon, pursued Hiss as a dangerous man who was subverting the American way. His conviction seemed a blow against the New Deal and all liberal Democrats, and the implication lingered that Republicans could better protect the nation against communism.

Only a few weeks after the sentencing of Hiss, far more spectacular espionage cases shocked the nation anew. The British government announced that Klaus Fuchs, a German-born physicist, had passed specific information on the atomic bomb to the Soviet Union. Following Fuchs' trial, American authorities arrested and tried his confederate Harry Gold, who was sentenced to prison for thirty years. And only three months later, in March 1951, Julius and Ethel Rosenberg stood before a court to be sentenced to death for atomic espionage. Because of the severity of the sentence, the Rosenberg case attracted international interest after the trial ended. During the course of their appeals, the Rosenbergs encouraged an outpouring of sympathy by writing about their relationship as husband and wife and their devotion to their children. Many in Europe believed them innocent; most Americans thought them guilty, but some regretted the death sentence. Nevertheless, in June 1953, the couple was executed in Sing Sing prison, the first Americans executed specifically for spying during peacetime.

The furor over Klaus Fuchs and the Rosenbergs confirmed what many in the United States had suspected in 1949—that Soviet spies in the West had delivered to the Kremlin the "secret" of the atomic bomb. Its possession by America's most bitter rival destroyed whatever tenuous security Americans had felt in the postwar world. Startling changes in foreign governments further undercut the nation's confidences. Czechoslovakia in 1948 had succumbed to a Communist coup, a striking defeat for democracy. Mao Tse-tung proclaimed the People's Republic of China in late 1949, forcing America's clients, the Nationalist Chinese under Chiang Kai-shek, to flee to the island of Formosa. What could have caused this succession of calamaties? To many, only massive espionage explained the slippage of American power.

A number of responsible politicians agreed that either traitors had sapped American strength or "Communist dupes" in government had unwittingly diminished America's influence. Senator Robert Taft, for instance, charged that State Department subversives had "surrendered to every demand of Russia . . . and promoted the Communist cause in China." But not all who found political use for the security issue acted out of conviction. One man manipulated the Communists-in-government issue more successfully than anyone else, making his name synonymous with the tactics of the bold lie and innuendo—Senator Joseph R. McCarthy of Wisconsin.

McCarthyism. Joseph R. McCarthy launched his political career in 1939 as a circuit judge in Wisconsin. Eight years later, riding the Republican tide of 1946 and stressing a largely fabricated war record, he won a Senate seat. He used the Communist issue against his opponent on occasion, although no more than many other Republicans. During the late forties, the only qualities that made the new Senator exceptional were his rudeness, driving ambition, and hunger for publicity. With no respectable legislative record to fall back on, McCarthy needed an issue to improve his chances for reelection. At a dinner in a Washington restaurant in early 1950, McCarthy laid his problem before a few friends, one of whom, a priest, casually mentioned communism as a possibility. McCarthy seized on the idea. A few weeks later, he addressed the Women's Republican Club of Wheeling, West Virginia: "Reds," he charged, "infested the State Department." He claimed to have in his hand a list of 205 subversives still working and "shaping" departmental policy. McCarthyism had begun.

Millions of Americans, prepared by five years of domestic and international security shocks, waited expectantly for further revelations. Their representatives in Congress boiled with hatred for the Communists by 1950. Late that year, the lawmakers passed the McCarran Internal Security Act, which required Communist party members to register with the Attorney General, prohibited employment of Communists in defense industries, set up internment procedures during national emergencies, and revoked passports of "known subversives." The Department of Defense, the Attorney General, and the CIA opposed the bill. Truman vetoed it, arguing that in a free country men should not be punished for their opinions. But the security-conscious Congress overrode the veto, reinforced in its action by another sudden cataclysmic event. In June 1950, Communist North Korea launched a full-scale invasion of America's stepchild, South Korea.

With his brashness and skill in publicizing himself, McCarthy caught the surge of response that followed and became the most visible spokesman for the millions worried about "internal subversion." Washington correspondents could depend on McCarthy to say something shocking on a slack day, thereby giving their papers a headline and the Senator his notoriety. He accused important people of disloyalty so freely and so vehemently that many ordinary citizens assumed there must be truth in his charges. To root out these uncommonly cunning "fellow-travelers" obviously required not reasoned argument but bold assault such as McCarthy displayed. Few had the judicial temperament or the inclination to discover the guilt or innocence of those attacked. Moreover, McCarthy found new targets so quickly that no one could keep up with his victims' denials and explanations.

McCarthy's resentment of easterners, intellectuals, and patricians was shared by his supporters. Volleys of invective showed his style, his antipathies. The Senator called Far Eastern expert Owen Lattimore of Johns Hopkins University "the top Russian espionage agent" in America. Respected State Department professionals John Carter Vincent and John S. Service drew McCarthy's wrath primarily because they had honestly reported on the corruption of Nationalist forces during the Chinese civil war. A subcommittee of the Senate Foreign Relations Committee, chaired by conservative Democrat Millard F. Tydings of Maryland, investigated McCarthy's early charges of Communists in the State Department and concluded they had "absolutely no basis in fact." But the Wisconsin Senator continued to trumpet his lies. McCarthy even took on General George C. Marshall, one of the nation's most respected leaders. He denounced the former army chief and recent Secretary of Defense and Secretary of State as part of a "conspiracy so immense and an infamy so black as to dwarf any previous venture in the history of man."

McCarthy's reputation ultimately depended on more than his barrage of assertions and his mastery of the press. Within months of his Wheeling speech, McCarthy possessed the aura of a man

---

Senator Joseph McCarthy cross-examines Army Secretary Robert Stevens during the Senate Investigations Subcommittee televised hearings on subversion at Fort Monmouth, New Jersey.

Wide World Photos.

who could swing votes. In the 1950 election, for example, McCarthy went after Senator Tydings, using scandalous charges to discredit the veteran legislator. When Tydings lost his campaign, many politicians attributed his downfall to McCarthy. Another strong foe of McCarthy's, Senator William Benton, was defeated in Connecticut two years later. While opponents trembled, many Republicans rushed to take advantage of McCarthy's presumed voter appeal. The party named Richard Nixon as its 1952 vicepresidential candidate largely on the basis of his anti-Communist credentials. When Eisenhower prepared a strong statement supporting his former boss and patron, George Marshall, against McCarthy's slander, Republican strategists prevailed on their candidate not to risk alienating those voters presumably convinced by the Senator's demogoguery. The defense of Marshall remained unspoken.

This ability to intimidate other politicians suggests more power than McCarthy actually possessed. Detailed studies of the campaigns in which he took a hand show no clear pattern of influence. But politicians, confused by shifting voter preferences, had to be wary of his possible impact. McCarthy claimed strong loyalty from working-class people and from his fellow ethnics, the Irish Catholics. Other minorities also supported the Senator. Germans often favored him, perhaps eager to demonstrate their patriotism after the recent war. With their hatred for the Communists who controlled their homeland, the Poles liked McCarthy. Despite these ethnic and religious considerations, by far the greatest enthusiasm for the Senator came from traditionally conservative and Republican areas. McCarthy's popularity depended partly on the general resurgence of his party after twenty years out of power, but mostly on his easy explanation of troubling world events. In the spring of 1954, a Gallup poll reported that the majority of Americans said they supported Senator McCarthy. For many, this meant asking if they opposed communism, since citizens associated him almost exclusively with that issue.

The coming of a trusted military figure to the White House and the ending of the Korean conflict in 1953 threatened to undo the whole basis of McCarthy's appeal. Americans began to relax their tense fears of world calamity. McCarthy plowed ahead with an investigation of the United States Information Service in 1953, but when he attacked Secretary of the Army Robert Stevens early the next year, his following began to dwindle. Televised hearings about subversion at Fort Monmouth transfixed the nation, but most Americans began to realize that McCarthy himself was a brutal, evasive, unlikeable bully. His downfall came at the gentle, deft hands of the army's special defense counsel, Joseph N. Welch. McCarthy accused Fred Fisher, one of Welch's assistants, of being "a member of an organization that is the legal bulwark of the Communist party." Outraged by this gratuitous and needlessly distorted charge, Welch pounced, "Have you no sense of decency, sir, at long last? Have you left no sense of decency?" Stunned Senators, reporters, cameramen then applauded wildly. McCarthy's credibility and his air of political omnipotence disintegrated amid the clamor. In December his colleagues in the Senate passed a resolution "condemning" him. Stripped of his audience and his prestige, McCarthy remained in Congress until his death in 1957.

For many years, thousands of ordinary Americans had come forth in the name of McCarthyism to punish their neighbors for their ideas or their associations. There was the plight of the Hollywood Ten, film writers, directors, and actors blacklisted for refusing to testify about their past affiliations before a congressional committee. The frantic attempts to cleanse harmless workers with liberal pasts from government and private bureaucracies, the censoring of books and more subtle intimidation of liberal and radical authors, and the purging of school boards reminded some of the totalitarian spectre recently laid to rest by the Second World War. But McCarthyism spawned no fascist movement. The Senator himself lacked the talents and vision necessary for a charismatic leader; he rarely planned beyond his next outrageous tirade. The loyalty of McCarthy's followers rooted itself in the frustration that affected all Americans in the early 1950s. When anti-Communist fears faded as the world settled down, the man simply passed from view.

Corruption and Crime

America's vaunted sense of its own honesty, its special morality, became subject to question in the early 1950s. Stories of corruption filtered into the American consciousness. A Senate investigating committee denounced "five percenters," men who sold their influence with high government officials to shady operators anxious for quick profits. Truman's long-time friend and White House adviser General Harry Vaughan, for example, apparently helped a cosmetics company outflank wartime bureaucracies. Its grateful executives later gave him a deep-freezer worth some $500. The wife of a Washington lawyer sported a $10,000 mink coat after her husband, Merl Young, expedited a huge loan through the Reconstruction Finance Corporation. Nor were men around government the only culprits. College athletes in New York, Ohio, and Kentucky took bribes, not to throw games but to rig scores for bookies. The judge told three players from the City College of New York that such "commercialism"—itself an instructive euphemism—"contaminated everything in sports." The United States Military Academy dismissed ninety cadets, including nine of the eleven members of its varsity football team, for cheating on examinations. For the average citizen, nothing seemed quite right anymore.

Many Americans took solace in the fact that a few, scattered incidents did not add up to a social corruption, and some sympathized with those caught in difficult situations. Then the networks began televising Senator Estes Kefauver's committee hearings into organized crime in New York City. The investigating committee cross-examined Frank Costello, reputedly a major figure in the underworld. He testified, willingly enough, that after a race track gave him $60,000, bookies no longer worked publicly at the track, thus saving its state license from revocation. Soon everyone in America was watching television. Virginia Hauser, wearing a mink stole and huge black hat, told the Senators about trips to Mexico, apparently to pass money among mobsters. The fellows down there, she explained, "bought me everything I want." A former mayor of New York, William O'Dwyer, told the committee: "There are things that you have to do politically if you want to get cooperation." Later witnesses were more specific: local government ignored crime syndicates in return for reelection, bribes, or lucrative business deals. Apparently dishonesty was becoming endemic, even organized, as it spread into more and more areas of national life.

The scandals, the war in Korea, apprehensions over internal security, and men like Joseph McCarthy who exploited the Communist issue gave a sour note to the end of the Truman era. Before the Watergate affair plunged President Nixon's popularity to an all-time low in 1974, Truman, toward the end of his administration, had the dubious distinction of being the most unpopular American president in the history of public opinion polling: only 31 percent of the people approved his handling of the nation's business. He has, however, received higher marks from historians and in more recent public opinion for his foreign and domestic policies, both of which set directions for the next generation of leaders. Truman's sympathy with an embryonic civil rights movement, his hopes for a better standard of living for America's citizens, and, above all, his determined effort to continue New Deal reform—redirecting private greed toward public responsibility—have prompted general praise. He revolutionized American foreign policy by turning the nation away from knee-jerk isolation to an intimate guidance of overseas economic affairs and a trenchant defense of national interests. Recent critics charge Truman with shortsightedness in dealing with the Soviet Union and even accuse him of starting the Cold War and launching the country on an imperialist expansion that culminated two decades later in Southeast Asia. But such carping overstates the case; it attributes to Truman more power, more freedom of action, and more prescience than he possessed.

Americans have also admired Truman for his spunk and personality. By the time of his death in 1973, he was one of the most beloved men in the country. A book of his pithy sayings and opinions, *Truman Off the Record*, became a bestseller. His trenchant honesty and old-fashioned morality reminded readers of the forthrightness, the sense of concern, that had characterized his presidency.

◄ 2 ►

EISENHOWER
AND THE QUIET
AMERICANS

THE 1950s contrasted vividly with the postwar forties. Inflation, corruption, Cold War traumas, all drifted into memory. The federal government demanded less of its citizens. The new era rejected both crusaders and extremists. People pursued immediate pleasures, or just more money, instead of Communists or social justice. American intellectuals spoke of consensus, of the lack of basic conflict in the nation's history and society. Only the Supreme Court, like some huge, slow-moving glacier, cut into the terrain of America's folk prejudices. Yet the country did not quite stagnate, for the fifties were a time of consolidation, of confirmation.

The Election of 1952

Both parties needed a fresh presidential candidate in 1952. The Democrats were in trouble. War-weariness and a general malaise had sapped the nation's spirit. Only an immensely popular candidate could avert the defeat that comes when one party has held office too long. Democrats dreamed of nominating the popular war hero Dwight D. Eisenhower. But Eisenhower rebuffed Truman's discreet inquiries; apparently "Ike" was a Republican, though no one knew his political philosophy.

Liberal Republicans roused themselves quickly, for their party seemed about to succumb to its right wing. General Douglas MacArthur had returned from Korea, disgraced by his insubordination to President Truman over war strategy there yet buoyed by the display of popular gratitude for his years of service. The former general launched a heavy-handed campaign for the nomination. But his reactionary speeches which spoke of "ordering the national life," soon discouraged popular enthusiasm for him, and conservatives began to hope that Senator Robert Taft of Ohio might succeed in his decade-long quest for the nomination. However, Taft, a man of high integrity, aimed to dismantle Roosevelt's "disspiriting" reforms. Few wanted that, not even most Republicans.

Eisenhower allowed a group of eastern internationalist Republicans, led by Governor Thomas E. Dewey of New York and Senator Henry Cabot Lodge, Jr., of Massachusetts, to draft him for the presidency. He defeated Taft in the early New Hampshire primary, and later in New Jersey, Massachusetts, and Oregon—in spite of the fact that he did not personally campaign in any of these states. The Republicans in convention nominated this easygoing and politically promising candidate on the first ballot. Dewey successfully recommended California Senator Richard M. Nixon for the vice-presidency, since his pursuit of Alger Hiss in congressional hearings had won him national fame. The Democrats, who had hoped to profit either from a divided Republican party or from an ideologically misplaced candidate, visibly girded themselves for defeat. Hoping that the magic of the New Deal coalition might still triumph, they nominated Governor Adlai Stevenson of Illinois, an intellectual and a reformer.

The monotony of the 1952 campaign was punctuated only by Stevenson's cultivated, witty speeches. Yet his cleverness persuaded many voters that he did not take seriously the charges against the Truman administration, even though he spoke repeatedly of "the mess in Washington." Republican election machinery worked efficiently, buoyed by the prospect of success while careful to avoid the consequences that overconfidence had bred in 1948. Eisenhower clinched the election with his pledge, "I shall go to Korea," convincing most citizens that the nation's greatest soldier somehow could end the war there.

There was a scandal about Richard Nixon's "slush fund" —money apparently provided by California businessmen for "personal expenses"—but the nominee countered the charges with an emotion-laden speech on television. His wife had "a respectable Republican cloth coat," he said; and although the newspapers would even have the Nixons give back their family dog, Checkers, "Regardless of what they say about it, we're going to keep it," the Senator's voice quivered. Soon dubbed the "Checkers speech," Nixon's performance had sidestepped the charges, but many voters seemed to appreciate his apparent humility.

The election results shocked no one. Eisenhower won 55 percent of the popular vote and even carried the southern states of Virginia, Florida, and Texas. The electoral count was even more lopsided, 442 to 89. Stevenson did not carry a single state in the Midwest, Far West, or East. Eisenhower's landslide victory provided presidential coattails long enough to return a Republican-dominated Senate and House for only the second time in twenty-two years. Yet many in America still wondered what the new President would do with his mandate. The campaign had not charted a new future but only rejected the past.

Eisenhower

Dwight D. Eisenhower, born in 1890 in the American frontier town of Denison, Texas, grew up in the modest surroundings of Abilene, Kansas. He secured entrance to West Point and later distinguished himself academically at Command and General Staff School in Fort Leavenworth, Kansas. As a soldier, Eisenhower did not affect the blunt arrogance and disdain for civilian direction that often goes with the military temperament. His famous military and strategic skill was perhaps best demonstrated during the Second World War in his conduct of the North African invasion in 1942, and later as Supreme Commander of Allied Forces in Europe. After the war Eisenhower served as Army Chief of Staff and then for two and one-half years as president of Columbia University. Late in 1950 President Truman appointed him military commander of the North Atlantic Treaty Organization (NATO).

His experience as a leader of coalitions taught him to diffuse conflict, and during his administration, he sought to ease the stri-

Photo by Burt Glinn. © *1968 Magnum Photos.*

Dwight D. Eisenhower, thirty-fourth President of the United States.

dency of political conflict—a goal he largely achieved. "Eisenhower never offered himself as an activist," notes the journalist Richard Rovere. "He never pledged any sort of basic reform. His style was well known to those who engineered his nomination and to those who elected and reelected him." Eisenhower believed that reform in American life must properly come from private business and individual initiative, not from the inefficient prod of government. When the government had to act, Congress should legislate, and the President administer its directives. Only in the defense of law or a Supreme Court decision could the chief executive act forcefully.

Such a limited view of the presidency produced a general political quiescence, especially since Congress returned to Democratic control in the 1954 election; this stalemate continued throughout the decade. Yet Eisenhower maneuvered skillfully, soon earning a reputation for political sagacity, praise for his ability to ameliorate conflict—and enormous electoral victories.

The Business of Administration

The new administration's most serious domestic problem was war-induced inflation. Eisenhower tried to balance the budget, reduce federal spending, and stabilize the dollar, all guidewords in the lexicon of conservative economics. The President surrounded himself with leaders from business and industry. They were committed to encouraging growth and reducing the powerful role of the government in the economy. The Secretary of Defense, Charles Wilson, once remarked that "what was good for the country was good for General Motors, and vice versa." The new administration hoped to end the "creeping socialism" of such government projects as the Tennessee Valley Authority. Republicans pared social welfare spending and turned over many federally sponsored projects to private industry. As a result, the 1950s were marred by substantial increases in unemployment and serious recessions in 1953-54, 1957-58, and again in 1959-60.

The President granted business tax concessions to boost industrial growth. But the continual cycle of recession during the eight years of Eisenhower's presidency indicated the stubbornness of a new kind of pressure against prices. Rather than deriving from shortages, inflation during the 1950s emanated from the "cost-push" of large unions and corporations able to raise wages and prices without providing a corresponding increase in productivity. Since Eisenhower refused to involve the government in the control of this process, prices advanced steadily, about 13 percent between 1953 and 1960. But since this increase averaged only 2 percent annually, most citizens did not complain. Avoiding chronic unemployment seemed more important.

The President and his cabinet of millionaires (and, at first, one plumber as Secretary of Labor) agreed that government should facilitate economic expansion, not direct it. They reoriented the business of government, especially to upgrade what economists call the nation's "infra-structure"—those prerequisites for industrial growth, like roads and schools, that private enterprise cannot profitably or efficiently provide. Succeeding where his three predecessors had failed, Eisenhower secured congressional approval for America's participation in a huge construction project, the St. Lawrence Seaway. By 1959, seven mammoth locks allowed seagoing vessels to travel into all five Great Lakes from the Atlantic Ocean; auxiliary projects brought much-needed electrical power to the area. Eisenhower also advocated large expenditures for a road-building program to gird the country with four-lane, limited access roads, soon familiar as interstate highways. Congress agreed in 1956. The proposed 41,000-mile network was to be financed by "user taxes" on gasoline and licenses for commercial vehicles. Always anxious to ensure fiscal responsibility and avoid waste, the President insisted on pay-as-you-go provisions in most public works projects, including his multibillion-dollar program for flood control along the Columbia and Colorado rivers.

Although the Republicans made no sustained effort to dismantle New Deal and Fair Deal programs, they were uncertain as to what to do about government subsidies for social benefits and the question of "public utilities." The owners of private power companies, as well as many conservatives, had long wanted to escape "yardstick" regulations for power rates by returning all utilities to private ownership. Without government power rates, it would be less apparent when private companies earned excess profits. Congress never approved such schemes—the prospect for monopoly was too obvious. But in 1953 a private utility attempted a more subtle challenge of the public utilities.

Congressional liberals saw the scheme as a plot to undermine public power companies. The controversy arose when the Atomic Energy Commission needed great amounts of electricity for its plant in Paducah, Kentucky, and the TVA volunteered to build a new generating station. Two men, Edgar Dixon and Eugene Yates, then offered to sell electricity from their private plants for the TVA to transmit to the Atomic Energy Commission. This maneuver would have limited the size of the TVA while creating a new market for private energy. Under the leadership of Senator Estes Kefauver, Congress rejected the plan, especially after an investigating committee uncovered major irregularities and conflicts of interest in the terms of the proposed contract. Although many thought the Dixon-Yates issue was overblown, the fact remains that Congress had thwarted the only postwar challenge to the principle that government-owned companies could best regulate private utilities by competing with them in the market place.

Despite this episode, some Roosevelt-Truman social policies were extended. In 1953 Eisenhower reorganized their far-flung, often overlapping welfare programs into a single cabinet-level agency, the Department of Health, Education, and Welfare (HEW). Even though it seldom received its full budgetary requests from the cost-conscious administration, HEW dramatically institutionalized the government's responsibility for providing its citizens with at least a minimum standard of living. Unfortunately, the early HEW administrators were overly cautious; Oveta Culp Hobby, for example, characterized giving free polio shots to children as "socialized medicine by the back door" and denied funds for it. Nonetheless, Eisenhower himself supported federal participation in, though not administration of, national health insurance, and he approved over $4 billion for hospitals and public health programs. The White House and Congress collaborated to increase social security benefits and expand its coverage to include nearly two-thirds of the work force by 1960, some 58 million people.

Republicans even extended the government's support of education. Skyrocketing birth rates after 1947 created an unprecedented need for schools by the mid-1950s, so Eisenhower proposed extensive federal aid for buildings and salary supplements. But conservative Republicans, concerned about the costs and implications of such grants, together with southern Congressmen who feared that federal money might force integration, successfully blocked such aid throughout the 1950s. Only in 1958, a year after the Soviet Union had demonstrated its technological superiority by launching the Sputnik space satellite, did Congress pass the National Defense Education Act (NDEA), which financed low-interest loans to college students and underwrote technical facilities such as laboratories. If not a startling departure, NDEA did reflect Eisenhower's concern for providing minimal standards—a "sense of fair play," as he called it—for America's citizens.

Labor and the New America

These moderate social improvements satisfied a large part of a public moving into an unfamiliar age of homogeneity and affluence. There was little pressure for more radical experiments in social engineering. One reason for inertia was the lack of any focus through which to channel discontent into political activity. The poor, as Michael Harrington later reflected, were "invisible" then. The main impetus for social change in the 1930s, the labor movement, had adopted a far more conservative stance. Unions had "housecleaned" during the Truman years, purging radicals and shifting priorities. By the early fifties the desperate struggle to organize new workers and achieve recognition in collective bargaining had dissipated.

With fresh growth no longer at issue, long standing conflicts between industrial and craft unionism eased. Moreover, both the Congress of Industrial Organization (CIO) and the American Federation of Labor (AFL) embraced the idea of "business unionism" —stability in labor-management relations. Since the fading antagonisms between these two organizations no longer justified the most visible split in labor solidarity, George Meany of the AFL headed a reunited AFL-CIO, with Walter Reuther of the CIO as second in command. Workers settled back to enjoy the fruits of their economic clout, satisfied now to receive larger paychecks rather than intent on redistributing income or reordering America's social structure.

A new issue preoccupied union leadership during the fifties: corruption. The Senate Select Committee on Improper Activities in the Labor or Management Field, chaired by Senator James L. McClellan of Arkansas, aggressively investigated financial abuses and racketeering in labor unions. With Robert F. Kennedy acting as chief counsel, the committee centered its investigation on the Teamsters Union, eventually forcing its president, Dave Beck, to resign. James R. Hoffa took over the union, attacking his opponent with the slogan "Haggerty for integrity, Hoffa for President." Subsequently tried and acquitted for bribery, Hoffa was finally jailed for jury tampering. In an effort to refurbish its image, the AFL-CIO expelled the Teamsters, as well as the suspect laundry workers and the bakery workers unions, thereby reducing its membership by over one and a half million.

The McClellan hearings resulted in legislation stringently regulating union procedures. The Landrum-Griffin Act of 1959 continued the principle of Taft-Hartley: government's right to supervise big labor for the general good. All unions were required to file complete audits with the Secretary of Labor. In addition, the law curtailed some strike activities by restricting picketing and certain secondary boycotts and protected local unions from predatory international trusteeships.

Government scrutiny, together with the pecuniary self-interest of most workers, reduced the number and intensity of strikes, although a 116-day work stoppage paralyzed the steel industry during 1959. Labor concentrated on obtaining long-term contracts that provided cost-of-living increases and fringe benefits such as pensions and health insurance. Unions did not organize new workers as aggressively as before; the burgeoning white-collar field and most women and blacks still remained outside the movement. The lack of growth in organized labor was not noticed at first. The unions were able to maintain the same share of the industrial labor force they had achieved in the 1940s, because the size of that work force did not change much. Increases were held down by introducing automation in production techniques and by the disturbing fact that manufacturing itself declined in relative importance to service-related employment; by 1960 manufacturing accounted for only slightly more than half the total work force. The full impact of this diminishing work force was not felt by organized labor until the next decade.

Industrial workers made moderate gains during the Eisenhower years, as their leaders worked within a framework set by government and management. Casting off its role as critic and antagonist of business, organized labor moved toward respectability.

The Black Revolt

Black Americans were the one group to succeed in breaking through the political and social tranquility of the 1950s. Blacks refused to resign themselves to a system that frequently abandoned them to poverty and illiteracy; instead, they formed the vanguard in a struggle for equal opportunity. Most Americans came to recognize either the justice of equal rights or its inevitability, although some preferred to preserve comfortable conventions or rationalized the security of the status quo. The impulse toward first-class citizenship for the nation's outcasts broke many delicate social mechanisms. The civil rights movement succeeded in evoking generalities about human dignity, but it played itself out against the ugly prejudice of many white Americans.

Pressure for change emanated from different sources. Truman's efforts to end discrimination had revealed early the limits of political action: the Dixiecrat rebellion ruptured the Democratic party in 1948, especially after liberals, led by Hubert Humphrey, forced an integrationist platform on the Democratic national convention. But the outbreak of the Cold War forced the nation to reaffirm its commitment to individual liberty. Home-grown racism ill-fitted protestations about "the land of the free." Efforts to win over newly independent countries in Africa and Asia produced outraged charges of hypocrisy when their diplomats suffered discrimination or public humiliation in America. A restaurant owner in Dover, Delaware, for example, calmly explained to the finance minister of Ghana that "we don't serve coloreds."

Though propitious circumstances may have encouraged advances, the blacks themselves undertook a determined commitment to reorder American folkways. During the Second World War, blacks had worked in northern industries and fought in overseas battles. Both experiences opened new alternatives and new desires. The white world of middle-class affluence, beamed into ghettos by television, became a cruel joke to a people hounded by prejudice and poverty. Integrationists, particularly the National Association for the Advancement of Colored People (NAACP), wanted to eliminate the caste system through legal means. More disgruntled voices argued that whites would never abandon the fears that fueled their prejudice, and urged separatism or revolution. All black leaders agreed that direct measures would ensure changes in their daily lives more certainly than acquiescence in federal benefactions. When genuine advances sparked fresh expectations, the legal maneuvers of the fifties gave way to the militant offensive of the sixties.

Brown v. *Board of Education*. The main goal of moderate black leaders was to end the legal system of segregation. The NAACP assumed early leadership in the battle. This biracial group focused its efforts on two of the most insidious prejudices inflicted on blacks: exclusion from the political process and segregation in inferior schools. In 1896 the Supreme Court had declared in *Plessy* v. *Ferguson* that southern laws which set up apartheid educational systems did not violate black civil rights if the separate schools provided equal education. But school boards in the South in 1950 spent only half as much money for each black pupil as for each white. The NAACP's Legal Defense Fund moved to end this disparity; if successful, either black education would improve or financial stringency in the southern states would force integration. Thus, by a clever use of the *Plessy* doctrine itself, lawyers extracted orders from the Supreme Court that the University of Texas must admit Herman Sweatt, a black, into its white Law School, since the only alternative, a ramshackle black school, was hardly equal. (*Sweatt* v. *Painter*, 1950). When the University of Oklahoma admitted G.W. McLaurin but forced him to sit in segregated classrooms and cafeterias, the Court concluded that such practices deprived him of "equal protection of the laws" (*McLaurin* v. *Oklahoma State Regents*, 1950).

Recognizing the implications of these decisions, the NAACP brought to the Supreme Court bench a number of cases that questioned the legality of segregation itself. The justices heard arguments for more than two years. Thurgood Marshall, counsel for the plaintiffs, emphasized the social and psychological damage suffered by black school children under a system that proclaimed their inferiority. Defense lawyers relied principally on nineteenth-century precedents and disputed federal court jurisdiction in the matter.

The contest between ideals and narrow prejudice never stood in doubt. Segregation embarrassed most citizens, including many in the South. Attorney General Herbert Brownell specifically asked the Court to overturn the separate-but-equal doctrine, and many groups petitioned the judges with supportive evidence. On May 17, 1954, Chief Justice Earl Warren announced the Court's decision in a representative case, *Brown* v. *Board of Education of Topeka, Kansas*. Rejecting the *Plessy* doctrine, the justices unanimously concluded that "in the field of public education, the doctrine of separate but equal has no place. Separate educational facilities are inherently unequal."

At first, racial integration promised to be rapid and wide-ranging. President Eisenhower moved forthrightly to end discrimination in schools in federally controlled areas like Washington, D.C. and military bases. But he hesitated to use presidential power elsewhere. Prejudice lay deep in personal opinions and long-respected social patterns. The *Brown* decision affronted many white southerners, not only because they opposed integration but also because the Court had expanded the scope of federal power. Although tactics proved neither monolithic nor uniform, local reaction was clear: a course of obstruction was to be pursued with almost hysterical intensity. The legislature of North Carolina provided money for private schools should desegregation be enforced. The governor of Texas called out the Rangers to preserve separate school systems in Mansfield. Random violence against blacks broke out, especially in rural areas. Throughout the deep South, and even in Virginia, extremists organized committees to prevent racial mixing. The most active groups, led by White Citizen Councils, usually avoided terrorism, but their barrage of propaganda solidified white opinion. Intimidation and economic reprisals against both black and white dissenters soon silenced moderates. In this atmosphere, southern legislatures passed hundreds of new restrictive laws, and school board lawyers conjured up imaginative—and often imaginary—reasons to delay integration.

Unwittingly, the federal government encouraged southern defiance. Worried about constitutional niceties, Eisenhower did not comment publicly on the Court's action. Privately he called people who wanted to force integration "just plain nuts" and wondered whether social conventions could be legislated. The Supreme Court itself modified the *Brown* decision when it substituted "all deliberate speed" for immediate compliance. Then in 1956, one hundred Congressmen issued the so-called Southern Manifesto, which in effect legitimized their constitutents' obstructing tactics.

Only a few renegades from among the southern leadership, including Lyndon B. Johnson, refused to sign.

Little Rock. Backed by such actions as the Southern Manifesto, white citizens in the South resorted to outright, massive resistance. In the fall of 1957, Governor Orval E. Faubus ordered the Arkansas national guard to prevent enrollment of nine black students in Little Rock's Central High School. Despite his earlier silence on the *Brown* decision, President Eisenhower acted vigorously to uphold the supremacy of the federal government. He federalized tne Arkansas national guard and sent nearly one thousand army paratroopers to help lead the black teen-agers through a hostile crowd, past sullen state troopers, and then to protect them in school corridors.

Faubus openly encouraged defiance, perhaps to bolster his own failing political appeal. Little Rock citizens conspired to prevent any black students from returning to Central High in the fall of 1958. Concerned by the potentially dangerous situation, a local federal district judge granted the school board a thirty-month delay, but the Supreme Court set aside his ruling. "Law and order," the justices agreed, "are not here to be preserved by depriving the Negro children of their constitutional rights." In the face of Eisenhower's determination to secure compliance with Court orders, the state government closed all four Little Rock high schools. Large-scale resistance in Virginia came to a similar dead end as whole counties boarded up their public schools.

During the last years of the 1950s, federal and state courts finally clarified the ambiguous orders that had created racist loopholes. Absolute segregation now seemed doomed, yet tokenism could itself be a bar to equal opportunity. Throughout the South *de facto* discrimination—the result of housing patterns, the availability of teachers, and pupil assignments based on "psychological factors"—sustained the substance, if not the principle, of separation. Six years after the *Brown* case, fewer than one percent of black children attended integrated schools in the South; rigid apartheid continued untouched in Mississippi, Alabama, and South Carolina.

Civil Rights Acts, 1957 and 1960. In still another area, the right to vote, promises from the Supreme Court turned sour when exposed

Photo by Blair Pittman. Black Star.

Martin Luther King, Jr.

to prejudice. In 1944 the justices had outlawed southern ordinances that disfranchised blacks by barring them from participation in Democratic primaries and thereby depriving them of meaningful political pressure in the one-party region *(Smith* v. *Allwright)*. But such victories proved ephemeral when forms of economic retaliation and corrupt registrars still kept blacks from the polls. In Congress a coalition of northern conservatives and southern commiteee chairmen blocked bills to ensure minority voting rights. In 1957 Senate Majority Leader Lyndon B. Johnson, finally maneuvered a moderate bill through a reluctant House and a Senate filibuster. More western than southern and something of a maverick, Johnson used the threat of harsher legislation in the future to secure the first civil rights act since 1875. The act authorized the Department of Justice to sue in federal courts on behalf of blacks denied the right to vote. A Commission on Civil Rights would investigate complaints and recommend further action, but it would not have subpoena powers.

Although the act was only a beginning, the government had at least abandoned its "hands-off" policy on local voting. In 1960 another Civil Rights Act quashed some abuses: if registrars resigned to avoid prosecution, the Justice Department could proceed against the state; federal courts could force local obedience through contempt citations; and economic reprisals against blacks who voted became a federal crime.

The Montgomery bus boycott and "sit-ins."   Many blacks refused to wait years for grudging handouts from white society. Aroused by accelerated judicial attacks on segregated housing, transportation, and recreation facilities, blacks in the urban South directly challenged Jim Crow laws. These local efforts usually adopted the pacifist strategies of Martin Luther King, Jr. In 1955 King, an eloquent and charismatic Baptist minister in Montgomery, Alabama, had galvanized the city's fifty thousand blacks into a boycott against the municipal bus system, which restricted blacks to an area in the rear of the bus. The protesters joined car pools or walked many miles rather than use public transit. Despite harassment from white citizens and police, black morale shot upward. After a year of declining revenues, the bus company neared bankruptcy; then a federal court action, only perfunctorily challenged by transit officials, ended segregated seating on the buses.

The Montgomery boycott triggered a widespread effort to remove racial restrictions in other areas of daily life. The protest movement at first modeled itself on the tactics of massive nonviolence, used against British colonialism in India by Mahatma Gandhi a decade before. King, throughout his life, tirelessly advocated this technique for discrediting segregation ordinances and embarrassing those who practiced them. He genuinely believed that, faced with the justice of such protest and the mixture of forbearance and determination displayed by demonstrators, segregationists would eventually accept integration. "Love those who hate us," he counseled.

The movement grew at the beginning of the 1960s when black college students, sometimes with white sympathizers, deliberately broke Jim Crow ordinances; they did not reply to abuse from outraged white citizens nor did they resist police arrest. The first "sit-in" protest took place in Greensboro, North Carolina, on February 1, 1960. Four black students requested service at a Woolworth lunch counter; when the manager refused, the students did not leave. National news photographers captured the unhappy scene of whites tormenting the calm demonstrators with curses and threats. A brilliant technique, the sit-in dramatized the injustice of discrimination and humiliated southerners anxious to modernize their part of the country.

Sit-ins spread rapidly, mostly the result of spontaneous action, though sometimes organized by national groups like the Congress of Racial Equality (CORE). Many chain stores desegregated their dining areas within a year. A plethora of "wade-ins," "kneel-ins," and "stand-ins" gradually changed the pattern of daily life in the border South. These changes, small as they were, suddenly suggested that a revolution in race relations was imminent, which would surely be the least expected and the most important legacy of the Eisenhower years.

The Second Term

Progress in civil rights was not matched in other areas of national life, where Eisenhower's predictable leadership perpetuated the traditional and the unexciting. It was the Supreme Court that moved forthrightly against abuses or neglect, providing a sense of movement for the late fifties.

Appointed for life, the justices ignored discontent with their controversial decisions, like the *Brown* case, which challenged a wide range of political customs and defended individual liberties. *Baker* v. *Carr* (1962) was the first and most important of a series of rulings designed to rectify the overrepresentation of rural areas in state legislatures by guaranteeing "one man, one vote." Concerned about government usurpation of civil rights, the Court set aside vaguely worded "antisubversive" laws, forced policemen and prosecutors to regard more scrupulously the rights of accused criminals, and even allowed advocacy of "the abstract principle" of communism, though not violent action in its behalf. Yet the Warren Court, named after Chief Justice Earl Warren of California, sometimes belied its activist, liberal image. By 1960 the judges had nearly granted states the right to censor "obscene" movies, upheld laws directed against unions, and backed off from immediate integration. Nonetheless, in the context of Eisenhower's tranquil America, the Court stood—with the civil rights movement—as an impetus for change.

For the most part, American society suffered few shocks. Presidential politics in 1956 repeated the contest four years earlier, except that Eisenhower won by an even larger margin—over nine million votes. His second term brought with it renewed problems of recession. High interest rates, together with a reduction in the amount of government spending, had cut both new investment and demand. Unemployment jumped to 6.8 percent by early 1958; local depression was particularly severe in southern California, where electronics and aircraft industries closed down, many permanently.

Curiously, the general cost of living rose slightly, as did the GNP, up $24 billion. Perhaps an illusion of basic strength induced the Eisenhower administration not to move vigorously to counter the economic slowdown. Secretary of the Treasury George Humphrey would not hazard budgetary imbalance with a tax cut to stimulate consumer demand. However, Republicans did spend $4 billion on interstate highways and eased home mortgage requirements, while the Federal Reserve System forced down interest rates. The recession bottomed out in September 1958, when unemployment reached 4.7 million people. Thereafter, the opportunity for inexpensive plant expansion, together with increased defense expenditures, ended the dreary slide. Oddly enough, American businessmen did not criticize Eisenhower for his static approach to economics. "Administered prices"—assured profits on a predictable volume of sales—seemed less risky than the competitive uncertainty of rapid expansion. Although the American people worried about the nation's slow growth rate, about 3 percent a year compared to the Soviet Union's 7 percent, American corporations contented themselves with the security of current profits, ignoring long-range consequences.

Partly because of the sluggish economy, voters acted perversely during the late fifties. Despite Eisenhower's landslide triumph, Congress became steadily more Democratic, and the 1958 elections returned a number of freshmen, liberal Senators. Fears of Russian technological gains, the recession, and especially labor's worry that burgeoning state "right-to-work" laws might destroy their unions prompted Democratic victories; Democrats captured almost two-thirds of Congress and many traditionally Republican governorships. While this stimulus for change was being felt elsewhere, the federal government remained mired in what one commentator described as "masterly inactivity." Conservatives in Congress from both parties did not push a cautious White House, so that little innovative legislation was enacted; there were only routine increases in social security benefits and limited federal aid to schools. Government became the lowest common denominator of agreement, not a force for change.

Washington was again troubled by corruption. Two of Eisenhower's appointees to the Federal Communications Commission, John Doerfer and Richard Mack, resigned after newspaper reporters discovered that they had taken barely disguised bribes from television networks and local stations. More serious, Sherman Adams, the President's closest aide, accepted a vicuna coat and a $2,400 rug from Bernard Goldfine, after having allegedly influenced the Securities and Exchange Commission not to prosecute the businessman for violating the Wool Labeling Act. Adams, whom many called "Mr. Assistant President," admitted to "errors of judgement" in accepting the gifts, but Eisenhower defended his friend, insisting "I need him." As in 1953, when he banned testimony from White House officials before McCarthy's subcommittee, the President again asserted that "executive privilege" protected his advisers, apparently even from investigation of wrongdoing. Republican politicians, worried about public reaction, and

Eisenhower's own sense that officials must be "clean as a hound's tooth" finally forced Adams to resign; but the initial lack of sensibility in the administration disturbed many commentators, who took an uneasy view of highly placed bureaucrats outside the political process and safe from scrutiny.

If many Americans somehow expected politicians to be shady, even the most jaded of them were shocked by unfolding scandals in broadcasting. Disc jockeys candidly told startled listeners about "payola," bribes from record companies to promote certain songs into hits. Quiz shows coached their contestants: "Twenty-One" even directed Charles Van Doren to grimace and hesitate in order to "heighten tension" for an unsuspecting audience. Van Doren, a college professor, won a fortune and soon came to symbolize urbane intellectualism. NBC hired him for its "Today" show, but in late 1959 a disgruntled "loser," Herbert Stempel, ended the charade by telling a grand jury about the program's rigged play. In November Van Doren himself told a congressional investigating committee, "I would give almost anything I have to reverse the course of my life in the last three years." He went on to explain that his profitable storehouse of information came from hurried, secret sessions with the show's producer the night before, not from years of study. In short, Van Doren said he was a cheat. A sense of corruption and declining values flooded America's consciousness once again. Disillusionment ran less deep than during Truman's last years, perhaps because no war and no bumpy ecomomy amplified the disappointments. But the sour taste remained.

Eisenhower as President

The nation's pleasure in its placid age of Eisenhower—"the bland leading the bland" was one assessment—gave way to a sense of urgency about the problems that the country had left unsolved. The decade of the sixties would begin with general expectations of change, new directions, "getting the country moving again," as John F. Kennedy repeatedly promised in 1960. Yet Eisenhower had responded to a national need for rest, and his presidency easily fitted his conception of executive leadership. Not since the 1920s had America witnessed such restraint, such reticence from the White House. Though quick to defend the prerogatives of his office, Eisenhower did far less than his immediate successors to aggrandize its power. He wore the presidency well; the office neither dominated the man nor distorted his sense of proportion. He believed that Congress should preside over change, and that the chief executive should administer the government. Since the 1930s the state had intervened more and more in individual lives and in the national economy. Less expensive, less demanding government seemed more attractive to the President.

◀ 3 ▶

THE
COLD WAR

THE HORRORS and dislocations of the Second World War all but destroyed any sense of predictability in world affairs. Stability in Europe and the Far East had collapsed, and the claims of legitimacy that had supported white empires in Asia and Africa had ceased, never to return. The defeat of the Axis also brought massive shifts in the international balance of power. These events precipitated an intense struggle for influence between two victor nations, the United States and the Soviet Union. Even the form of this struggle was unprecedented. Since neither the Soviet Union nor the United States could contemplate all-out atomic war, their competition became indirect, forcing much of the world into the emerging pattern of bipolarity.

More than just national interests divided the two major powers. Conflicting ideas locked their two systems into certain hostility: private property and production for profit versus state ownership and production for social use. In addition, Russia's subordination of the individual to communal needs repelled those dedicated to personal liberty and suspicious of bureaucratic power. Ideology took on increasing importance when it appeared that the ideological unity of Western civilization had been fractured. War had so weakened Europe's liberal capitalism that Russia's strange mixture of professed humanitarian concern and ruthless dictatorship seemed likely to attract disillusioned people everywhere. The United States and the Soviet Union each came to believe that the safety, even the existence, of its domestic culture required that its institutions be exported to the rest of the world. A complicated struggle over abstractions and very real national interests ensued that diplomacy could not resolve. Frightened nations stumbled through an Alice-in-Wonderland world of neither peace nor war; it was the dilemma of Cold War.

Conflicting Visions of the Postwar World

The Cold War was not inevitable. Indeed, during the war years, President Franklin D. Roosevelt nurtured a far different vision of the postwar world. He thought self-determination throughout eastern Europe and the colonial empires, together with global institutions and an effective system of collective security, would contain disruptive change and eradicate war. His administration wanted to set up a United States dominated network of international trade, rooted in stable currencies, low tariffs, and equal access to markets and raw materials. Economic integration would not only restore overseas demand for American goods but also ensure world peace and prosperity. Realizing that such generous peace required unity among the big powers, Roosevelt spoke often of the "Four Policemen"—Britain, the Soviet Union, China, and the United States. But while the fighting continued, military necessity and rapid victory concerned the President more than hypothetical postwar arrangements. Perhaps he speculated that an immensely powerful victor—backing its diplomacy with atomic weapons, industrial power, and the lure of reconstruction loans—could dictate its yearnings. Whatever the reason, America had no specific plans for the postwar world, only a grand objective.

Unfortunately, Britain and the Soviet Union had far different hopes built on fears of the past and economic needs for the future. Churchill grandly announced that he had not become Prime Minister "to preside over the dissolution of His Majesty's Empire." England must dominate western Europe or at least enforce Franco-German amity to check the growth of an alien Russian ideology and thwart an expansive American capitalism. A rigid system of preferential tariffs and import quotas would bind the British Commonwealth, the Middle East, and industrial Europe into an economic unity. Russian dreams were less grandiose. Stalin demanded security for his country, especially against Germany. Friendly (that is, subservient) governments in eastern Europe and weak states on Russia's other frontiers would soothe Soviet anxieties. Satisfaction of their need for capital and raw materials to rebuild a nation devastated by war would protect what most Russians considered their central goal, a Communist state free from external menace. Russia's quest for security and Britain's imperial ambitions clashed with Roosevelt's vision of self-determination and free trade.

Wartime diplomacy had not resolved these cross-purposes; it had only delayed their inevitable appearance. The Grand Alliance against Hitler was simply a marriage of military convenience, and negotiations during the war usually produced more dissent than cooperation. Stalin wanted his allies to open a western front at once, presumably to lessen pressure against his country on the eastern front and to make eastern Europe more vulnerable to Soviet armies. Churchill favored an invasion through southern Europe, the "soft underbelly," less as a means to defeat Hitler than as a way to set up pro-British regimes in Italy and the Balkans in order to protect the life-line of the empire through the Mediterrean. The United States, the only allied nation fighting a war on two fronts, did not want to invade western Europe until certain of success. Some Americans, including Senator Harry Truman, and most Englishmen speculated that Soviet and Nazi armies might destroy each other on the plains of eastern Europe. Why, then, rush to Stalin's aid when by doing nothing the Western allies might pick up all the pieces?

Conference Diplomacy

Pursuing their own interests and their own particular visions of the postwar world, the three nations never reached acceptable compromises on military teamwork or the political future of Europe. Instead a glow of rhetoric covered over many disagreements and ambiguities.

Roosevelt first set forth American ideals in the Atlantic Charter, an assortment of principles pledging a future of self-determination, freedom, and individual dignity. Stalin and Churchill endorsed it, albeit conditionally, in 1941. Then, at a conference in Casablanca in early 1943, the United States and Britain called for Germany's "unconditional surrender," perhaps to forestall a separate German-Russian pact, and sketched out a familiar world of peace and prosperity under Anglo-American tutelage. When Stalin, Churchill, and Roosevelt met at Teheran during November-December 1943, the Western powers promised to invade France; in return, Russia would send troops to the Far Eastern front, but only after Hitler's final defeat. Both sides wanted their armies present when the Nazi empire collapsed.

At the same time, Churchill pursued a more traditional sphere-of-influence diplomacy with Stalin. During meetings at Moscow in late 1944, the two men divided the spoils of eastern Europe: Russia would dominate Bulgaria, Rumania, and Hungary, while Britain would have an almost exclusive role in Greece. The two would "share preponderance" in Yugoslavia. Churchill had, in a sense, eased Britain's difficulties with the Soviet Union, but the result was only to confirm, perhaps even sharpen, differences between the two major powers themselves.

By February 1945, with final victory certain, the three powers could no longer ignore the future or awkwardly compromise it at the expense of an absent party. Stalin, Churchill, and Roosevelt met again, this time at Yalta, a Black Sea resort. Diplomacy functioned smoothly, perhaps because it did not attempt to undo reality. In Poland, completely occupied by the Soviet army, the Western allies accepted a formula for a pro-Soviet provisional government. Roosevelt could only hope that Stalin's promise of "free, democratic elections" would change the situation. The three leaders compromised on a curious plan for Germany: each power would dominate a part of the country, but a four-nation authority would deal collectively with its future. To satisfy Soviet and, to a lesser extent, French reconstruction needs, Germany would pay reparations. A Declaration on Liberated Europe promised self-determination for the rest of occupied Europe, although it ignored the delicate question of who would oversee the interim period. Russia would regain its influence in Manchuria, Outer Mongolia, and certain off-shore islands lost to the Japanese in 1905. In return, Stalin renewed his pledge to enter the Pacific war as well as to negotiate an alliance of friendship with Chiang Kai-shek's pro-American regime in China.

To exterminate the fascist impulse toward war, the three powers insisted upon not only destroying German and Japanese military potential but also reorganizing those societies. Small-scale governments must replace old ruling cliques, particularly the landed military aristocracy and giant industrial combines. Individual mobility would eliminate the ridigities of class; pluralism would supplant dictatorship. In addition to this unprecedented occupation policy, Roosevelt demanded that his allies approve a collective security arrangement, a United Nations to institutionalize a stable international peace.

But the Yalta agreement soon shredded apart. Personal misconceptions, clashes of national interest, and enormous disparities in power soon crumbled the common ground necessary for a lasting peace. Roosevelt too easily assumed that he could encourage Soviet mellowing and ease Stalin's worry about capitalist encirclement. The President wanted to preside over a grand reconciliation of world tensions. Yet Stalin feared America's weapons and Churchill distrusted the purpose of America's economic power more than either trusted Roosevelt's good intentions. The Prime Minister, apparently unaware that the second world war in thirty years had permanently weakened England and destroyed the legitimacy of its empire, pursued irrelevant dreams. Stalin knew only that he must protect Russian frontiers. Realizing he could not long support huge armies, given the devastation of his country, the Soviet dictator set about subjugating eastern Europe. Roosevelt never entirely abandoned his dreams for a cooperative peace. The formal organization of the United Nations in mid-1945 and Washington's synchronized economic policies, schemes for international control of atomic energy, and continued efforts to adjust disagreements by diplomacy testified to his larger vision. Nevertheless, the two sides moved further apart. The shape of Germany's future and the use of atomic power especially eroded hopes for a concert of powers directing international affairs.

Roosevelt's death on April 12, 1945, accelerated the drift away from collaboration. The new President acted decisively, even brusquely. Truman believed that a display of vigor would establish his position and demonstrate his competence. Certainly, events demanded rapid decisions. For instance, although the three major powers had vowed at Yalta jointly to assist the peoples of Europe in solving their economic and political problems "by democratic means," national military commanders, pressed by a rapidly moving fighting front, ignored both democracy and the requirement of multilateral assent in the occupation of the liberated countries. The United States organized a capitalist, pro-West regime in Italy; Stalin set up friendly governments in Hungary, Rumania, and Bulgaria. The Polish occupation was not negotiable, at least for the Russians. Given its strategic, economic, and psychological importance, Germany was not amenable to a simple partition. Only immediate, detailed talks could prevent chaos within the Grand Alliance and dangerous disputes over the liberated countries of continental Europe.

During July 1945 Truman traveled to Potsdam, a small city outside Berlin, to meet with Stalin, Churchill, and later Clement Attlee, who, during the conference, replaced Churchill as Prime Minister. Public opinion at home constrained Truman to bid for eastern Europe's independence, despite the fact that the Soviet Union, clearly intent on dominating the area, showed no willingness to negotiate. Americans naively thought Russian armies no match for atomic bombs, thus binding Truman into the paradox of having to deal with ballooning public expectations yet shrinking maneuverability. The declaration that emerged from the Potsdam Conference satisfied Truman's need for action, but it was otherwise inconclusive and became a source of tension. It called for a peace conference to deal with Germany, while a council for foreign ministers was to prepare four-power treaties with the rest of the belligerents: Italy, Austria, Hungary, Bulgaria, Rumania, and Finland. Poland's borders were shifted westward, giving its government much of prewar Germany in return for large sessions to Russia in the east. Stalin again vowed to enter the war in the Far East as soon as possible.

Despite his earlier assurances to Roosevelt about Polish self-determination, Stalin proceeded to install a client regime in Warsaw. The Western politicians avoided ultimatums, fearful that an adamant stand might result in Russia's boycott of the UN. Attlee and Truman realized, given Poland's hatred of all things Russian, that the Soviets would never allow that country independence, although both men still hoped for free elections. In any case, the presence of the Red Army there precluded direct action. The inevitable outcome in Poland—a Communist-led, pro-Soviet government—shocked world opinion and angered Truman.

Churchill, Truman, and Stalin at the Potsdam Conference, July 25, 1945.

The Potsdam Conference inaugurated a chain of diplomatic dead-locks over central Europe. Aside from an easy agreement to "de-Nazify" their former enemy, the trio had left German occupation policy uncharted. Military authorities would oversee "local mat-ters," but a Four-Power Control Council jointly would supervise "national questions." In practice, elementary relief measures for a distraught population, demands for military supplies, and the maintenance of order forced local administrators to make wide-ranging decisions.

Each of the occupying powers quickly set up institutions in its slice of the German pie that would complement its own future needs. Socialist Britain nationalized major industries in northeast Germany, while Americans sought to restore private enterprise in the south. France and Russia worked to dismantle German industrial power and extracted reparations to reconstruct their own devastated regions. The Russian military commander, Georgi Konstantinovich Zhukov, set up a puppet regime that stripped the eastern zone of its movable wealth; French diplomats maneuvered to "internationalize" the Saar and the Ruhr, Germany's manufacturing centers. Their sense of self-righteous revenge clashed with Anglo-American hopes for a revival of liberal democracy based on a prosperous economy. The Potsdam Conference glossed over these disagreements, which the clash of national power, not the compromises of diplomacy, would resolve.

The End of the Grand Alliance

Differences over Germany, or any other postwar problems for that matter, became merely a rhetorical framework for the central dilemma: future relations among the members of the Grand Alliance. The noisy Russian-American confrontation obscured a quieter, but just as portentous, struggle between Britain and the United States as the center of world capitalism shifted from London to New York. Americans broke down England's protected trading area and opened the "free world" to their corporations, investments, and self-serving trade agreements. Wall Street came to dominate international finance, and negotiations during late 1945 for a huge loan to Britain clearly reflected this. Unable to pay for food, fuel, and raw materials, London had to accept a short-term policy, with conditions that eventually caused Britain to lose markets to United States industry. Only Britain's relative weakness compelled Prime Minister Attlee to acquiesce in such one-sided terms.

While America's assertive capitalism endangered relations with England, its prescription for a postwar political settlement aggravated differences with Russia. Truman was uncertain whether to accommodate Stalin with concessions or to move toward hard bargaining. He found that many of his advisers wanted to substitute economic power and a rather ostentatious atomic threat for diplomacy. But the President wavered. For one thing, the bureaucrats had not discovered how to use the bomb as a bargaining tool; if Soviet armies invaded western Europe, America could hardly destroy Paris and Rome. For another, the Senate's narrow approval of the British loan indicated the domestic limits to foreign economic aid. Other considerations increased Truman's reluctance: Roosevelt's hopes for the United Nations and the prospects for mutual disarmaments and joint control of atomic energy, all depended on collaboration with the Soviets.

This hesitancy over "the Russian question" nearly scuttled the first meeting of the Council of Foreign Ministers held in London in September 1945. But when the group convened again at the year's end in Moscow, Secretary of State James F. Byrnes negotiated a sensible compromise with his counterpart, Vyacheslav Molotov, on the worrisome problem of liberated Europe. Although formal multilateral occupation would continue, in practice the powers worked out spheres of influence based on military control, giving the West a free hand in Italy and Japan, and the Soviet Union primary interest in Hungary, Bulgaria, Rumania, and Poland. Such *quid pro quo* diplomacy might resolve other issues as well. An American loan to Russia, for example, could relieve Stalin's need for German reparations, thereby lifting a burden from Germany and advancing Washington's hopes for a prosperous, democratic central Europe.

Yet such diplomacy had little chance. Stalin's efforts to protect his borders—or to extend his empire, depending on the point of view—prompted a major shift in American foreign policy away from accommodation. A growing realization that the Soviets had been given open access to eastern Europe alarmed Western opinion. Then, during the early months of 1946, Stalin began a slow takeover in oil-rich northern Iran. Using a combination of diplomatic browbeating, internal subversion, and Russian troops, he seemed near success. But Iran appealed to the United Nations and received prompt diplomatic support from Britain and the United States, themselves dependent on Middle Eastern oil. When Truman sent part of the Sixth Fleet to Istanbul as an unmistakable warning, Stalin withdrew his battalions from Iran. Most American experts believed that the Russians were testing the weak line in the West's strategic position, England's deteriorating power in Asia. The incident convinced President Truman that Stalin would "back down" if firmly resisted. Winston Churchill, in a speech in Fulton, Missouri, on March 5, 1946, had outlined the possibilities of resistance to Russia. After conjuring up fears that an "Iron Curtain" of Soviet imperialism had fallen across half of Europe, the former Prime Minister suggested an Anglo-American alliance to check the expansion of the Russian state and Communist ideology. The idea surely intrigued the listening Truman: rather then feud over economic policies and the future of colonial empires, the United States and Great Britain should focus on this greater danger.

Ruminations from American intellectuals and from others unhappy with the President's foreign leadership reinforced this view. George Kennan, a career diplomat with extensive experience in Moscow, analyzed the relationship between Communist philosophy and Stalin's diplomacy in several influential memorandums to the State Department. He argued that Russian foreign policy responded not to world events but rather to Marxist paranoia and Stalin's need to justify his own autocracy. Washington bureaucrats too easily inferred from this analysis that concessions to the Soviets were necessarily futile. Truman himself reached the doubtful conclusion that America's former ally had an inevitable need to expand and that negotiation was therefore useless. Domestic politics encouraged a hard line. "Appeasement" brought Republican criticism and public dissatisfaction; America's monopoly of the atom bomb created a sense of omnipotence and allowed the President to reconsider Roosevelt's hopes for collaboration. A hard line would help restore bipartisan foreign policy and forward plans to use American financial power to reform the world economy, a goal that cost-conscious Republicans and isolationists vigorously questioned. Truman moved from accommodation with the Soviet Union to alliance with western Europe, dovetailing economics, politics, and ideology.

If the Americans exaggerated hypothetical fears, the Russians also distorted reality. Specific events only magnified their readiness to assume the worst. Negotiations on the future control of atomic energy, for example, only muddied the already murky waters. Secretary of War Henry Stimson wanted to deal directly with the Soviet Union and, to show our good faith, stop further production of atom bombs. Truman again hesitated. Although convinced that such a generous approach would probably gain Stalin's trust, the President also knew that most military officers, some influential Senators, and a growing segment of the public worried that he might give away the very weapon they believed made America's power unchallengable. Yet scientists knew that any "secrets" would soon become known anyway. Truman finally hit on what he hoped would be a practical compromise: the United Nations would negotiate and police a system of international atomic control, but until then, the United States maintain its monopoly. Most diplomats, however, predicted ....spection and an American trusteeship would provoke a Russian veto. A special Board of Consultants to the State Department outlined a much bolder approach. Led by its chairman, the physicist J. Robert Oppenheimer, these businessmen and professors proposed an independent, worldwide authority to own and operate all atomic plants and mines and to conduct future research. Truman turned the perplexing question over to Bernard Baruch, a stock market speculator who dabbled in government affairs, and whose influence with Congress was much touted. Yet even this professional manipulator could not surmount the many difficulties that disarmament proposals brought.

The scheme that America finally carried to the United Nations early in 1946, the so-called Baruch Plan, embraced a number of bureaucractic compromises. All nations, except the United States, must stop research and construction on atomic weaponry. An international agency would control all forms of radioactive energy and have wide inspection powers. The UN Security Council was to run the new agency by majority vote; no nation could unilaterally veto its decision.

The Russians countered with a much different plan. Worried about exposing its war-weakened position, the Soviet Union rejected outright any inspection system and instead suggested that each country first simply destroy all its atomic weapons. Then talks for worldwide control might begin. Fully aware that America dominated the Security Council, Stalin insisted upon his unrestricted veto powers. Although discussions continued for more than a year, the diplomats found no common ground: no plan could give the United States enough immediate information or Russia enough security. Most Americans felt that their doomsday weapons should induce concessions from the Soviet Union, not from America. This stalemate did not create the Cold War, but it did increase the mutual hostility.

Conflicting interests also plagued efforts to abate East-West tensions over central Europe. Some superficial success came out of the Foreign Ministers Conference held in the spring of 1947 to rationalize the victors' economic controls over eastern and western Europe, but difficulties in Germany remained insoluble. Unlike in the other parts of Europe, no single nation predominated there militarily—all power faded into a vast zone of gray. The Russians and the French wanted extensive reparations, which would produce a weak, impoverished nation. London and Washington believed that German domestic prosperity would ensure both liberal democracy and European recovery. A strong, probably anti-Soviet Germany that might again isolate Russia from European affairs could never suit Stalin, just as the West could not accept a weak, neutral Germany under Soviet tutelage. The Foreign Ministers Conference came to a ragged end in mid-summer when Molotov again demanded heavy reparations from all of Germany. In response, Britain and America began plans for the economic merger of their two zones. A strong "Bizonia" would counter Russian power, thwart French plans for an internationalized Ruhr, ease the burden of Britain's occupation—and formalize the division of Germany.

The Truman Doctrine and the Marshall Plan

East-West tension, rooted in Europe's future, slowly developed into a global American effort to contain Russia and to ensure a prosperous capitalist world. The crisis that finally destroyed wartime hopes and justified this new strategy began in February 1947, when the British told Truman that they must withdraw their troops, some forty thousand men, from Greece and end their economic aid to the pro-West regime within thirty days. Financial necessity had prompted the maneuver, but Attlee had another motive as well: to draw the United States into European affairs.

The Truman administration almost immediately accepted the challenge, despite its awareness of the corruption and unpopularity of the conservative Greek government. The State Department began vigorously insisting that American experts administer all aid, reorganize the domestic economy, reform the bureaucracy, and support a military effort against Communist-led guerrillas. Most Congressmen, however, remained frankly skeptical about a hazardous, costly intervention that benefited England more than the United States and came at a time when domestic inflation, not problems abroad, preoccupied the American people. During a meeting at the White House to drum up legislative support for Greek intervention, Truman's new Secretary of State, the cryptic, much respected General George C. Marshall, emphasized that "the choice is between acting with energy or losing by default." Dean Acheson, an Under Secretary of State, predicted that a Communist victory in the

Mediterranean would undermine pro-West governments in Italy and France as well as encourage the Chinese Communists. This early version of the "domino theory" did not itself convince doubting Senators, but, as Chief of Staff Admiral William D. Leahy later recalled, everyone present realized its usefulness in gaining public support.

On March 12, 1947, Truman asked Congress for $400 million for economic and military assistance to Greece and to support Turkish diplomatic resistance to recent Soviet attempts to win control over the waterway connecting the Black Sea and the Mediterranean. The President cast his appeal in global terms: the United States was engaged in a fundamental struggle to halt Russian expansion. Warming to his theme, Truman divided the world into two ways of life: the individual freedoms, civil liberties, and representative governments characteristic of the West confronted Communist oppression, terror, and police states. "I believe," Truman continued, "that it must be the policy of the United States to support free peoples who are resisting attempted subjugation by armed minorities or by outside pressures." To allay fears that he contemplated perpetual military actions, the President explained that such support "should be primarily through economic and financial aid, which is essential to economic stability and orderly political processes." The rousing address swept away congressional obstacles to his program, quickly dubbed the Truman Doctrine.

The new policy, which would set the United States on the road to policing the world for the next quarter century, was puffed up with assumptions of American righteousness and omnipotence. The United States policy became much more than a passive defense of Western prerogatives against Stalin's experimental probes. As disagreement over the German question settled into frustrated stalemate in 1947, the United States responded with several direct challenges to the Soviet Union. Britain and the United States accelerated plans for common monetary and financial reforms to stabilize Bizonia's economy. At the same time, local military commanders cooperated with German industrialists to increase the level of production. These vigorous measures by themselves would have scared the skittish Russians. Then the Americans launched a massive rescue operation throughout western Europe that created a determined capitalist bloc, ultimately dependent on the United States. This policy, known as the Marshall Plan, finally fractured

Soviet-American relations and molded Washington's attitudes toward Europe for nearly two decades.

Its economy stagnant, its peoples nervous, western Europe during the early months of 1947 was disheartened. Violence had already erupted in Italy and northern France. With high unemployment, scarce food and raw materials, rampant inflation, and wrecked factories, reconstruction could not begin without vast amounts of money. Labor unrest and heavy commitments to a fading empire had a particularly disastrous effect on England. Truman brooded that "the British have decided to go bankrupt and if they do that, it will end our prosperity and probably all the world's too. Then Uncle Joe Stalin can have his way." Within the administration, officials reacted to the prospect of Europe's social and economic disintegration in markedly different ways. Anxious to modify the President's jingoism, George Kennan suggested that the United States coordinate a plan for the entire continent, for which the Europeans themselves would formulate the details. Recovery then could dull the allure of radical solutions, and a joint project might help repair relations with the Soviet Union. In an article he signed only as "X" in *Foreign Affairs*, Kennan also explored the doctrine of "containment," maintaining free world security and economic strength so as to force the Russians toward compromise. But men like William Clayton, an assistant Secretary of State, sought more immediate parochial advantage of the situation. In return for aid, he wanted Europeans to reduce tariffs, end trade discrimination, and remove currency restrictions—in short, to open up their economy to American investment and raw materials, especially farm products, and, once recovery was underway, to its industrial goods as well. Since private capital would not risk investing the initial flow of dollars, the United States government should "prime the pump" and ensure America's economic welfare.

Combining both altruistic and self-serving motives, George C. Marshall offered a plan for American aid to restore "normal economic health in the world" in a commencement address at Harvard University on June 5, 1947. Confident that economic recovery would dissolve political differences, the Secretary of State wanted a plan that would ensure the existence of "free institutions." Just three weeks later, the British, French, and Russian foreign ministers met in Paris. Molotov viewed the Marshall Plan cautiously. Worried by the inclusion of Germany in Marshall's offer, almost panicked at the prospect of American intrusion into eastern Europe, and determined to maintain Communist prestige, the Russians refused to submit to capitalist hegemony over Europe. Moscow also refused to allow its satellites to participate in the plan.

Despite these major abstentions, the nations of western Europe, except Germany and Spain, quickly approved preliminary plans for regional tariff and monetary systems. On July 12, 1947, they formally created the Organization for European Economic Cooperation (OEEC), which forwarded to Washington a broadly conceived program for aid. The political implications of these events revolutionized international affairs. German unity was postponed, its western zones slowly integrated into Washington's bloc. France also was now firmly tied to the West, having given up its dreams of reviving the alliance with Russia to dominate Europe or of becoming a focal link between Soviet and Anglo-America. But most important, sixteen nations had committed themselves to America's vision of the future.

The Debate over Internationalism

Truman's headlong internationalism in the spring of 1947 provoked controversy at home. His policy disturbed conservative politicans such as Senator Taft, who approved aggressive policies in Asia but not in Europe. "The United States," he maintained, "should set an example of living so well at home that all other nations will wonder, envy and decide to emulate us." Cold War, at least for Taft, meant an ideological contest, not threats of a military clash with the Soviet Union. Worldwide involvements, he thought, would do more to destroy America's domestic freedoms than to spread democracy. Pacifists like Senator Claude Pepper of Florida thought Truman's actions needlessly provocative.

Walter Lippmann, an influential journalist, added yet another note to the rising criticism. The President had launched "a crusade for democracy, not a limited defense of America's security." The Secretary of Commerce, Henry Wallace, denounced Truman for "building up a preponderance of force to intimidate the rest of mankind." During a speech in New York City on September 12, 1946, Wallace outlined an early version of detente, saying "I am . . . neither anti-Russian nor pro-Russian." He thought the two powers should avoid challenging each other, perhaps by dividing the world into spheres of influence. But Byrnes, already mounting a "get-tough" policy in Europe, forced Wallace out of the cabinet, although not out of public attention. Wallace persisted in public pronouncements favoring a pullback from spreading commitments.

Although the prescriptions of liberal and right-wing critics differed, Truman's opponents were united in expressing a public hesitation about radical departures from the securities of past isolation. No one knew how to deal with the strange new world of postwar dislocations: the extremes of preventive war or a "fortress America" retreat from alien problems might at least end uncertainty.

The debate over internationalism might well have become interminable had not two events intervened. Republican Arthur Vandenburg, the internationalist chairman of the Senate Foreign Relations Committee, who shared Truman's desire for a bipartisan foreign policy, patiently guided the European Recovery Act (the Marshall Plan) through Congress. Meanwhile, East-West tensions flared up again, causing domestic debate gradually to fade into consensus. During the summer of 1947, America and Britain continued to isolate their increasingly prosperous zones in Germany. Convinced that they would never receive reparations from Bizonia, the Soviets called yet another conference of Foreign Ministers. But neither side budged in its conception of a unified Germany: for the Russians, a socialist economy and, at the least, neutralist politics were requisite; for the West, only a strong, capitalist nation would do. By December 1947, the diplomats sullenly agreed to disagree.

The hostile feelings left by the conference gathered in intensity. The Russians knew well the ultimate purpose of the Marshall Plan—to revive European capitalism—and they recognized the barely disguised diplomatic soundings that were to result in a North Atlantic military defense alliance. To Stalin each act was part of a conscious, articulated plan to weaken Russia and attack its Communist system. In protest, the Soviets obstructed meetings of the Four-Power Control Commission for Germany. And when the West only accelerated moves to integrate their zones into an anti-Soviet combination, Stalin decided on a more aggressive response in central Europe.

Taking advantage of a ministerial crisis in Czechoslovakia, itself the result of Communist agitation, Soviet agents and local sympathizers fomented a general strike on February 24, 1948. Stalin massed the Red Army on the border. Rather than test the loyalty of Czech troops, and aware of his country's military weakness, President Eduard Beneš acquiesced in the formation of a Communist-dominated cabinet. It soon abolished other political parties, nationalized most industries, and followed Moscow's lead in foreign policy. Czech industry partially compensated the Russians for lost German reparations; and Czechoslovakia's absorption into the Soviet sphere protected Russia's last vulnerable frontier. But the speed and cynicism of the takeover shocked and angered the West.

The Berlin Blockade

On March 20, 1948, the Russians walked out of the Four-Power Control Commission. Ten days later Stalin announced that all persons and trains moving in or out of the Western-occupied sectors of Berlin, located some 110 miles within the Soviet zone, would be subject to "inspection"—ostensibly to halt black-market operations. Neither side pressed the issue then, largely because of events taking place in Italy and Yugoslavia. The United States, maneuvering to influence the April elections for the Italian parliament, was fearful that any crisis over Berlin would jeopardize efforts to win votes for moderates. In Yugoslavia, the Communist leader, Marshal Josip Tito, had set about industrializing his country rather than allow it to become only a source of raw materials and a market for the Soviets. Stalin wanted to replace the obstreperous Tito, but the Yugoslavs rallied around their popular war hero. If the rift stayed Stalin's hand in Berlin, it also made him more determined not to yield further.

The West more than matched Stalin's resolve. Ernest Bevin, the British Foreign Minister, envisioned a regional military pact directed against the Soviet Union. The Truman administration garnered support for the project on June 11, when the Senate overwhelmingly approved a resolution in favor of collective self-defense measures. Only nine days before, the London Conference on German Affairs, which had excluded the Soviet Union, had submitted its final report. The western zones in Germany were to receive economic aid and limited self-government; an international agency would control the distribution of steel and coal from the Ruhr, although Germans would retain ownership. Clearly, the Atlantic powers had decided to incorporate Germany economically, politically, and militarily into their anti-Soviet combination.

Berlin became the focus of Stalin's effort to destroy this prospectus for Western unity. At the least, he hoped to absorb the city into his European empire. On June 24, 1948, several days after the report of the London Conference, the Russians halted most ground traffic between Berlin and the West. Postwar agreements concerning access to the city had assumed a unified Germany, which no longer existed; in any case, no document forbade the Russian action or guaranteed Western rights of access. Temporarily uncertain how to proceed, Britain and America went ahead with plans to introduce a new currency, the so-called westmark, into their zones. This maneuver further split Germany, and the Russians banned the use of the new paper money in Berlin. As Communist-led riots broke out all over the city on June 23, the Soviets blockaded movement by railroad, highway, and canal. Another Czech-type coup seemed imminent.

Truman responded energetically to the crisis and to its larger implications. Determined to stay in Berlin, the President decided to supply the city's essential needs by air. The Russians could not counter this tactic as easily as an attempt to send land convoys to Berlin, and war was therefore less likely to result. Truman also rather ostentatiously dispatched to Europe sixty B-29s, the only American bombers capable of carrying atomic weapons. Britain cooperated fully with Truman's ripostes and contributed much to their ultimate success.

Attempts at compromise failed. Certain that the people of Berlin would succumb to the blockade, Stalin calculated that the Anglo-Americans would eventually have to accept a Communist city. For almost a year, the grim test of strength continued between Russians and Berliners, between Stalin and Truman. Then, in May 1949, the Soviets abruptly yielded. Soviet policy had only increased pro-Western sentiment in Germany and prompted a collective resistance to all things Russian. Moreover, the incident convinced most Americans that Stalin would not resort to war unless directly threatened. Moscow agreed to lift the blockade in return for another Foreign Ministers conference to discuss German problems. The episode had been a disastrous setback for Stalin.

The Atlantic powers had moved quickly in the meantime to organize a West German state. A Parliamentary Council, under the presidency of Konrad Adenauer, first met in September 1948. After six months of deliberation, the representative body submitted a federal constitution for the three western zones. In May 1949, the military governors approved this Basic Law, which in effect granted internal self-government. An Occupation Statute reserved ultimate tripartite control over the Ruhr, foreign trade, reparations, foreign policy, and disarmament. The Russians could never accept such an arrangement, and the Conference of Foreign Ministers, Stalin's only gain from the Berlin crisis, angrily broke up over the issue.

It was more than a revitalized Germany that menaced the Soviets. During these same months, the major west European powers had concluded a far-reaching military alliance with the United States and Canada—the North Atlantic Treaty Organization (NATO). Sent to the American Senate in April 1949, and two months later ratified 83 to 13, the new pact pledged its members to collective security and set up a unified, permanent command structure. Each of the nations of the North Atlantic agreed that "an armed attack against one . . . shall be considered an attack against all." The United States was to supply nearly $1.3 billion in military assistance to Europe during 1950, the beginning of an annual flood of defense dollars. This dramatic departure from American isolation emphasized Truman's determination to contain communism; at the same time, the vast appropriations would ensure a steady market for American industry.

The NATO pact was not a perfect instrument. Although pleased with America's commitment to mutual defense, most Europeans, including Ernest Bevin, were aware that the United States would necessarily preside over the Atlantic community. Moreover, the NATO alliance, like other tactics in the Cold War, could not ensure peace or Western security. Moscow quickly organized a rival, though much less powerful bloc called the Warsaw Pact. But the Russians played their trump card in September 1949; they exploded an atomic bomb. The line painfully drawn across Europe during five years of postwar uncertainty had hardened into an Iron Curtain of mutual terror. For more than a decade, Russia and the United States would stand athwart their hegemonic spheres in Europe. But just as the balance of power set in Europe, it collapsed in Asia.

The Transformation of China

From the time of the fall of the Manchu dynasty in 1911, China suffered decades of turmoil. A southern warlord, Chiang Kai-shek, and his party, the Kuomintang, consolidated their control over most of the nation by the late 1920s. Then the fourteen-year Sino-Japanese war began in 1931. But peace did not come in 1945. Instead, a civil war broke out between revolutionary Communists, led by Mao Tse-tung, and Chiang's corrupt, tentatively pro-Western regime.

Preoccupied by European events, Truman avoided a fundamental commitment to Chiang. He was convinced that historical forces, not American military power, would decide the issue. In any case, Washington was never happy with Chiang's ruthless dictatorship. His feudal land policies alienated peasants, and he profiteered at the expense of the city dwellers. Primarily to conciliate domestic public opinion favorable to Chiang, Truman sent several billions of dollars in military aid to Nanking—far less than the Kuomintang's needs. Meanwhile, the United States began to seek a compromise solution. In November 1945, Truman sent George Marshall, the former Army Chief of Staff, to arrange a truce between Chiang and Mao, possibly even a coalition government. By January 10, 1946, Marshall had achieved a cease-fire, perhaps because Mao knew that Stalin could not aid him. But Chiang broke the armistice two months later when he sent his troops into north China and Manchuria. Despite some initial successes, he could not hold the countryside, where the Communists "swam like fishes in the peasant sea." The Kuomintang regime slowly rotted away, its armies at last in mutiny against their self-serving leaders. The Chinese people realized that peace and stability were more likely under Mao than Chiang. On a more mundane level, Mao's People's Army slowly reconquered Manchuria during 1948 and then overran its enemy's stronghold in south China. Mao Tse-tung became President of a Communist China on October 1, 1949. Chiang fled to the island of Formosa.

The upheaval in China was the most spectacular change, but the postwar years also transformed the rest of Asia. Japan had encouraged nationalist movements throughout its briefly held empire. The question of how to treat these anticolonial regimes at first perplexed the United States, divided between its own revolutionary heritage and its commitment to imperial European powers. In Indonesia, Washington supported indigenous attempts to throw off clumsy Dutch efforts to reimpose harsh rule. But where similar nativist movements in the Philippines and Indochina became linked with radical, "pro-Communist" leaders, the United States opposed them. Sometimes strategic necessity intervened; for example, the Soviet Union and America partitioned a helpless Korea. In Japan itself, Washington held virtually unopposed control and embarked on a massive reform of Japanese culture. As with Germany, the Truman administration wanted a strong Japan for two reasons: to balance an impending Communist success in Asia, and to contribute to a prosperous, American-dominated capitalism.

But the ideal of stable nations based on liberal governments and private enterprise was impossible to achieve in such alien cultures. By 1950 the Japanese economy had stagnated; Mao had signed a treaty of friendship and aid with the Soviet Union; French efforts to retrieve its Indochina empire neared collapse. Motivated by Senator Joseph McCarthy's demogogic assertions that internal "subversives" were to blame for recent "defeats" in China and eastern Europe, bureaucrats made the Truman Doctrine global: the United States would contain Moscow's monolithic Communist conspiracy against the free world wherever it surfaced. The National Security Council formulated the new strategic doctrine in its famous report, NSC 68. NSC 68 moved beyond the pursuit of traditional national interest to potentially unlimited commitments rooted in an unquestioning self-righteousness. The security of the free world now became synonymous with America's security. Although the State Department estimated $35 billion yearly for such defense and European rearmament, no one expected Congress to appropriate even half of so large an amount. Then, on June 25, 1950, the North Korean army broke across the 38th parallel, which divided the country.

The Korean War

Like most other events in the Cold War, the Korean War was mired in ironic misconceptions. The ruler of South Korea, Syngman Rhee, a petty dictator who terrorized his opponents, could not divert the leftist assembly from its plan to reunify Korea around a coalition government. Northern Communists under Kim-il-Sung perhaps believed that the South would welcome them as liberators; in any event, no one expected their invasion to provoke an American intervention. Stalin did not forbid the planned attack, perhaps because the new Secretary of State, Dean Acheson, had said on January 12, 1950, that America's "defense perimeter" ran through Alaska,

Japan, and the Philippines, a line that clearly excluded the Korean peninsula. Such calculations set off a chain of events that transformed a local dilemma into an international crisis.

The global ideology of NSC 68 guided Truman's vigorous reaction to the North Korean aggression, which he termed "the opening round of World War III." Two days after the invasion began, Truman told several friends that "Korea is the Greece of the Far East." As the President spun a huge globe around and around, he explained, "If we are tough enough now, if we stand up to them [the Communists] like we did in Greece three years ago, they won't take any next steps. But if we just stand by, they'll move into Iran and they'll take over the whole Middle East. There's no telling what they'll do, if we don't put up a fight now."

By his decision to intervene militarily in Korea, the President broadened the powers of his office. Truman seldom consulted Congress about Korean policy, except to inform it of actions already taken. Only on June 27, for example, literally hours before the United Nations adopted an American-sponsored resolution calling on its members to render "all necessary aid" to Rhee's forces, did he confer with a few congressional leaders. Despite years of large-scale conflict, Truman never asked for a declaration of war. Capitol Hill had little inclination to interfere and no stamina to challenge Truman's independence. Its only weapon—"the power of the purse"—provided, ironically enough, too much power. The legislature could hardly suspend appropriations in the middle of a war or risk the safety of American soldiers just to reestablish the delicacy of Constitutional balance.

The administration moved rapidly. The Soviets were momentarily absent from the Security Council, so the Americans were able to avoid certain veto of their resolution. The sweeping phrases of the American resolution committed the UN in advance to whatever countermeasures the President chose. At first Truman hoped that American money, equipment, and air power alone would repel the invaders, but the rapid advance of Kim-il-Sung's troops ruined such hopes. (Some evidence indicates that General Douglas MacArthur and President Rhee calculated that a precipitous, but orderly, retreat might scare Washington into committing ground forces.) On June 30, Truman sent American soldiers stationed in Japan to Korea and promised more, but he still aimed at a limited war. "Their purpose," the President declared, "will be to restore peace and

. . . the border." Throughout this mobilization, Truman insisted that a holding action would prevent further takeovers; he even informed Stalin of his desire to contain, not destroy, communism in the Far East. Whatever the Soviet dictator thought of this peculiar message, Truman's own actions soon belied his sincerity. The White House announced large-scale military aid to France in Indochina, to Chiang in Formosa, and to moderates in the Philippines. Congress, declining to speculate about Truman's motives, rapidly approved these massive defense expenditures.

Within three months, Washington sought not only to repel the North Korean invaders, but to conquer their country as well. First, Truman moved to secure his European flank against Russia. On September 10 he asked that Britain and France acquiesce in the creation of ten German divisions. To calm their vociferous protests, Truman promised four more American divisions for Europe and appointed General Dwight Eisenhower as supreme commander of these integrated NATO forces. Then the President turned to the ground war in Korea. Sung's troops had conquered all of the peninsula except the area around the southern port of Pusan. American optimism revived, however, when General MacArthur made an amphibious landing at Inchon, behind North Korean lines, on September 15; within two weeks his troops recaptured the capital, Seoul, and surrounded most of the enemy forces, now trapped at Pusan. During the next month, a pliant United Nations authorized an advance beyond the 38th parallel and even expanded the powers of the General Assembly to circumvent a Soviet veto in the Security Council.

Truman worried about a wider war with either Russia or China. He was unwilling to risk a major commitment in Asia before America and Europe completed their rearmament. So the President ordered American troops and planes not to cross the Yalu River —North Korea's border with China. He reiterated this stipulation during a meeting with MacArthur on Wake Island on October 15 and also criticized the headstrong general's recent public statements advocating war to restore a pro-Western Chinese government. Mao Tse-tung warned that he "would not sit back with folded hands" if United States soldiers headed for the border. On October 25 some of MacArthur's advance divisions reached the Yalu River at the Chosin Reservoir; Chinese troops struck hard, and after one of the bloodiest battles of the war, the Americans fell back. So did

Mao's armies, apparently indicating that China wanted to negotiate.

But Washington was not ready. Although Russia, Britain, and France had invited the Chinese to discuss the Korean crisis, as well as the future of Formosa, at the United Nations, MacArthur launched a second, much larger drive toward the Yalu River on the very day talks were to begin. He miscalculated when he divided his troops into two widely separated columns, for the Chinese once again moved south, this time 300,000 strong, right between the two American armies. In less than two weeks, the Chinese forced MacArthur's troops back into three isolated bridgeheads and occupied most of Korea. Everyone responded differently to the disaster. MacArthur wanted to launch an atomic war against China; on November 30, Truman hinted at a press conference that he had not ruled out the possibility. At this point, Clement Attlee flew to Washington. The British Prime Minister told the President that only peace in Asia, not war, would serve Western interests. Acheson countered that the United States "could not be isolationist in the Pacific and interventionist in Europe." The ironies of Cold War had apparently trapped the administration.

If he could not rescue "enslaved" nations, Truman could at least draw the line. On December 15 the President decreed a state of emergency, thus rallying public support for American rearmament. MacArthur resumed the offensive in January 1951; by spring, the military front had stabilized roughly around the 38th parallel. Truman wanted to settle on this basis, but his ambitious general sabotaged talks for a cease-fire and issued a near ultimatum for China to leave Korea.

The President, already angry with his proconsul's announcements about "unleashing Chiang," now resolved to oust MacArthur. The problem shifted to a war of wills between the President and his commanding general. As if anticipating Truman's intent, MacArthur sent a letter that was read on April 5 by the Speaker, Joe Martin, in the House of Representatives. With an eye toward the Republican presidential nomination, MacArthur called for a new foreign policy, centered not in Europe but in Asia, "where the Communist conspirators have elected to make their play for global conquest." He warned that "there is no substitute for victory." Truman could not ignore such insubordination, and six days later he relieved MacArthur of his command. During the public controversy that followed, no one questioned the President's right to fire any

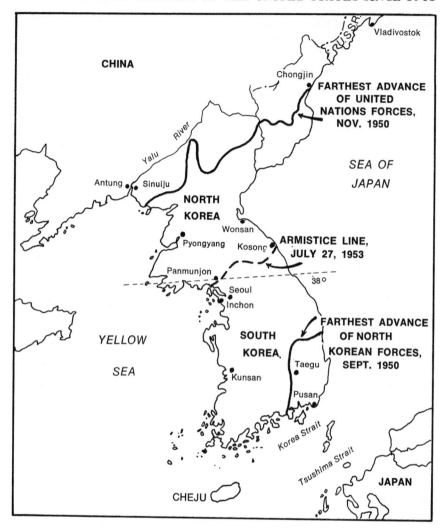

THE KOREAN WAR, 1950-1953

general. Military experts testified at a special congressional hearing, and most of the American people soon accepted the professional opinion that, as MacArthur's superior, Joint Chiefs of Staff Chairman Omar Bradley, put it, war with China would be "the wrong war at the wrong time in the wrong place with the wrong enemy."

Meanwhile, the Korean War had stalled both on the ground and at the conference table. In the early summer of 1951, Stalin offered an armistice in the field without mentioning the withdrawal of American troops and the future of Formosa, issues that had wrecked past compromises. At first Truman rejected the proposal, perhaps to maintain the momentum of Western rearmament or, more simply, to preserve his bargaining power, but pressures from the United Nations and NATO allies forced him to participate in peace talks. Negotiations began on July 10, 1951, at the village of Panmunjon, without a cease-fire. Military diplomats quickly deadlocked on two fundamental issues, the location of the future dividing line between north and south, and the return of North Korean prisoners of war.

The intractable POW problem—both regimes hesitated about returning thousands of military recruits to its enemy—would elude solution for two years. On the ground, a war of attrition developed, each side carefully limiting its thrusts to maintain an "acceptable" level of casualties while avoiding decisive engagements that would create immense problems in Asia. Three years of such "limited" war killed 54,246 Americans and wounded another 103,284. Since the problems that sustained the Korean War lay outside it, the conflict dragged on until events elsewhere made it irrelevant.

Harry S. Truman and American Foreign Policy

Even though Korea had apparently marked off the limits of American action, the administration moved to protect the "free world" that remained. A stalemate at war justified global containment, backed by massive military power, to all the American public, to Congress, and to the European allies. Ironically, the possession of atomic weapons forced rearmament into conventional channels. On November 1, 1952, at Eniwetok Atoll in the Pacific, the United States triggered its first thermonuclear weapon, the hydrogen bomb. Unlike the race to split the atom, the competition to fuse atoms was short-lived: Russia tested its first H-bomb on August 1953. Although a true nuclear standoff would not come until each power had devised methods to deliver waves of atomic bombs against the other—the arms race of the 1950s and 1960s— possession of "ultimate" weapons still made total war between superpowers unthinkable. Truman, and later Presidents Kennedy and Johnson, believed that conventional armies and limited wars could pursue goals that did not directly threaten the Soviet Union or its principal national interests. As a result, Truman immediately doubled American forces to three million men, sent abroad hundreds of thousands of soldiers, and spent billions for conventional armaments. The United States would not only stymie Russia but also end global instability.

Truman was anxious not to carry this burden alone. But he realized that England and France were many years away from the ability to both maintain colonial empires and contain communism. America turned to its former enemies, Germany and Japan. Discussions for a peace treaty with Japan had dragged on since 1948, largely because Moscow insisted on Tokyo's neutrality. After the Korean War broke out, however, the United States simply ignored Russian protests, and on September 8, 1951, concluded a treaty with Japan. The arrangement limited Japanese rearmament but abandoned efforts to restructure Japanese society. That same day, Prime Minister Yoshida and Secretary of State Acheson signed a mutual security pact that granted bases for American troops.

In Europe, Germany's integration into a defense system under American control ended continental attempts at economic, and perhaps military, federation. Usually backed by Britain, Washington incorporated German soldiers directly into the NATO alliance, blocking France's alternate design for Europe to be a "third force" in world affairs. Not that the French abandoned their hopes: the Schuman Plan created a common European authority for coal and steel production and distribution, thus taking the capacity for war away from individual nations; the Pleven Plan envisioned a European army, mutually financed and staffed. Washington regarded such regional schemes as a threat to an integrated world economy and the joint struggle against communism.

Truman's successors modified his foreign policy only in detail. An impregnable Western alliance and a strong international capitalism would contain communism throughout the world. Massive military spending put America, Europe, and Japan on the road to prosperity. As the only source of reconstruction dollars and military security, America reached the peak of its hegemony during the early 1950s.

The Truman years restored a balance of power in Europe and Asia, but the achievement came at great cost: vast armaments and permanent tension. As their hostilities polarized the world, neither the Americans nor the Russians could respond effectively to changing circumstances. Only revolutions in Asia and the emergence of a powerful Europe would alter the scenario that Truman and Stalin had created during eight years of countermaneuvers. The superpowers gradually learned over a period of two decades that the legacy of Cold War did not serve their national interests in an atomic, postcolonial world. By the time the United States modified its proselytizing ideology, it had lost its economic and military supremacy in both western Europe and Asia.

Western historians have long argued about the origins and perpetuation of the Cold War, especially America's response to the novel opportunities of the Truman years. Marxist writers, and their cousins on the New Left, postulate America's needs for overseas markets as the driving force in its foreign policy. Capitalism's outward thrust not only undermined postwar collaboration with the Soviet Union but also replaced Europe's older imperialism in the third world with a new form of exploitation. Those who defend the President's actions in rejecting any compromise point out that Stalin's extreme suspicions of the West would have thwarted any productive cooperation and that, in any case, the totalitarian version of communism as practiced in the Soviet Union threatened America's commitment to individual freedom.

Very recent scholarship emphasizes the domestic political constraints—Republican critics, the hard-line atmosphere, McCarthyism—that severely limited the range of Truman's options and criticizes the assertions of inevitability among New Left writers. According to these latest views, an honest belief in American ideals, together with a careful calculation of the nation's strategic, political, and economic interests—not the overriding force of a single motive—explains the actions of America's policymakers. Mistrust, domestic pressures, and a traditional search for national advantage on both sides shaped the postwar world.

The Great Thaw

The new Republican regime cauterized Truman's trenchant globalism and escaped the morass of limited war. World problems and leaders in 1953 had changed from those of 1945. An influx of American dollars carefully guided western Europe toward prosperity and Japan into an American-dominated world capitalism, while nuclear capability locked the superpowers into a standoff. New arenas for influence beckoned. Throughout Asia and Africa, nativist movements threw off a stifling European colonialism and turned toward the problems of nation-building and economic modernization. The bipolar world of the 1950s shifted from chilling conflicts to fairly peaceful competition in the nonwhite world.

Dwight Eisenhower's landslide presidential victories in 1952 and 1956 provided him with a reservoir of public and congressional good will that Truman had lacked. Once McCarthy's hysterical anticommunism had died amid its own excesses, the former general began his self-appointed search for peace. Eisenhower eloquently recalled the terrors of war in his memoir, *Crusade in Europe:* "It was literally possible to walk for hundreds of yards at a time, stepping on nothing but dead and decaying flesh." Both Eisenhower and his somber, but able, Secretary of State, John Foster Dulles, believed that the deterrent power of nuclear weapons would prevent war and aid in their relations with the Soviet Union. Yet the more militant Dulles spoke often of "massive retaliation." If provoked into war, the United States must respond instantly with all available forces. Convinced that bargaining required an extreme initial position, Dulles soon became famous for his willingness, at least rhetorically, to risk war to contain communism. He argued that, if America were to broadcast its planned response to given situations, the Soviets could not miscalculate; in this way, he thought the United States might have prevented war in Korea.

Dulles's strategy, dubbed "brinkmanship," produced "more bang for the buck," in the colorful words of economy-minded Charles Wilson, the Secretary of Defense, and countered any possible criticism from McCarthy or other right-wing Senators. But the nuclear approach, however easygoing on the federal budget, generally restricted Washington either to doing nothing or to threatening catastrophe. Eisenhower himself probably never considered total war an option. His summit meetings, disarmament proposals, defensive alliances, and support for the United Nations, were all designed to avoid confrontation.

The new tenor of Washington's foreign policy coincided with dramatic changes in the Soviet Union. Stalin died on March 5, 1953. Perhaps sobered by Truman's determined containment politics and the reviving strength of "decadent capitalism," Stalin's nominal successor, Georgi Malenkov; Foreign Minister Molotov; Defense Minister Nikolai A. Bulganin; and First Secretary of the Communist party Nikita S. Khrushchev sought détente. But a struggle for power soon erupted among the four men over domestic policy and control of the Soviet state, introducing new uncertainties into Russian foreign policy. Khrushchev came out on top largely because of timely support from Marshal Zhukov, a war hero who controlled the Red Army. Curiously, the three-year dispute actually stabilized international relations. These policy differences fertilized pluralist sentiments long suppressed by Stalin's colorless totalitarianism. So far did the so-called thaw go that Khrushchev later repudiated part of Marxist orthodoxy in defending peaceful coexistence and economic competition with the capitalist powers. Old habits and problems did not disappear, but given new opportunities and new faces, the world seemed headed toward a more peaceful future.

The most dramatic break the Eisenhower administration made with the past concerned Korea. A tour of the embattled country after the 1952 election convinced the new President that the United States must end the stalemated conflict by diplomacy. Yet the resolution of delicately balanced issues required six months of tedious negotiations, peppered with threats and more battles. After Eisenhower vaguely mentioned "retaliation," perhaps with Chiang Kai-shek's aid, the Communists resumed armistice talks in April 1953, but negotiations soon broke down again over the POW issue. Dulles then warned China, through India, that the United States might use atomic weapons to secure peace quickly. Within two weeks, the two sides agreed to split the country at the 38th parallel; neutral powers would handle prisoner repatriation. Worried about his future control over South Korea, Rhee aborted the settlement by releasing twenty-seven thousand Communist POWs in the South rather than repatriating them to the North. The Chinese replied with a major attack that demonstrated the weakness of South Korean troops. The United States, angry at Rhee's treachery, pressured him into accepting the inevitable, and on July 27, 1953, an armistice agreement—not a peace treaty—ended the fighting that had killed more than two million people, mostly Korean civilians. Dulles's militancy balanced Eisenhower's good sense about the limits of American power.

This balance, combined with a growing, almost bipartisan demand for government economy, produced the Republican prescription for containment—the "New Look." Eisenhower replaced Truman's manpower rearmament with an arsenal of nuclear bombs. Even if the Soviet Union struck first, the Kremlin could not prevent the destruction of its own country. This predicament would presumably deter Russian leaders from war. So the American strategic principle became sufficiency rather than superiority. Army generals also wanted to train elite ground troops capable of a "flexible response" in the event of insurgent movements and limited wars. But Eisenhower, unlike his successor, John F. Kennedy, rejected this strategy. American money, not combat divisions, would fight brushfire conflicts. Local soldiers would do the fighting. After all, it cost $3,500 a year to maintain an American soldier, but only $485 for a Pakistani.

Although such a formula could fill in the gap between Dulles's all-or-nothing brinkmanship, it required many regional allies. In a fit of "pactomania," the Secretary of State set about signing military conventions with nations along Sino-Soviet borders. The Southeast Asia Treaty Organization (SEATO) linked Australia, the Philippines, Thailand, and Pakistan with the United States, Britain, and France in collective self-defense. The United States also underwrote Britain's Central Treaty Organization (CENTO) with Turkey, Iraq, Iran, and Pakistan. The presence of Britain and Turkey linked CENTO with NATO; Pakistan connected SEATO with CENTO. Finally, the United States signed bilateral defense pacts with Formosa, South Korea, and Japan.

If the American eagle had shown its lightning bolts, it also extended an olive branch. The Eisenhower-Dulles foreign policy, like that of the Democrats, always focused on European stability and the dilemma of coexistence with the Soviet Union. Unlike Truman, Eisenhower pursued these goals imaginatively. In perhaps the most significant departure from the techniques of former years, Eisenhower sought direct meetings with Soviet leaders to compromise disputes and to avoid war. In the afterglow of the Korean settlement, Winston Churchill, once again Prime Minister, proposed a summit meeting to resolve outstanding European problems. Four nations met at Geneva in mid-July 1955. Bulganin and Khrushchev representing the Soviet Union, the new British Prime Minister Anthony Eden, Premier Edgar Faure of France, and Eisenhower discussed three principal topics: German unification, disarmament, and increased communication between East and West. Although considered the least important at the time, only the third objective was realized. Since 1955 a sustained trickle of people, ideas, and goods has breached the barriers between the almost quarantined blocs.

When the foreign ministers of the four countries met again in the fall of 1955 to work out concrete proposals for uniting Germany and reducing armaments, they failed to make any progress. The West's NATO and the East's Warsaw Pact had already divided the continent. Not just the Soviet Union but every nation in Europe feared a revival of German militarism. Within Germany, many people in the Rhineland and Bavaria questioned whether the prosperous western zones should have to bail out the depressed east. And so Germany remained divided. The greater failure, however, concerned disarmament. During the July summit at Geneva, Eisenhower had outlined his famous "open skies" proposal for mutual aerial surveillance and an exchange of military blueprints. Now the Russians politely rejected the scheme, preventing a test of congressional sentiment on "spy flights" over the United States. Despite this setback, both sides moved away from the Cold War rhetoric of accusation and threat. The Russians apparently accepted the President's protestations of America's peaceful intent; everyone understood that nuclear war would be, in Eisenhower's words, "race suicide." The summit launched the "spirit of Geneva": fundamental tensions remained, but peace—defined as the absence of war—seemed possible.

Alliances in Decay

Throughout 1956 and 1957 caution dominated American foreign policy as abrupt changes bewildered the administration. Both Communist and Western blocs suffered convulsions during the summer and fall of 1956. First, the Soviet empire in eastern Europe nearly collapsed. Some fifteen thousand impoverished Polish factory workers revolted in Poznana on June 28. Clearly caught off guard, Kremlin leaders hesitated while the Poles demanded that Wladyslaw Gomulka take over the government. A national Communist who opposed "hasty" collectivization and Moscow's self-serving economic policies, Gomulka forced Moscow to accept a revisionist politburo in Poland under his leadership.

Gomulka's success triggered the much more devastating Hungarian rebellion a few months later. On October 23, a demonstration for reforms similar to Poland's attracted a huge mob of workers, soldiers, and students who demanded the restoration of Imre Nagy, a former Communist minister. Like Gomulka, Nagy opposed Soviet overlordship; he set up a new government on the Polish model. But the protests turned into armed rebellion against the Russians. Encouraged by signs of support from the West, the revolutionaries opted for complete independence, not just reforms. Moscow offered a remarkable and often overlooked compromise solution—Hungarian membership in a "commonwealth of socialist countries" —but Nagy and his cabinet could no longer control events. When the Hungarians persisted in demanding political freedom, Moscow resorted to military force. Fearing a piecemeal breakdown of the Warsaw bloc, the Russians brutally suppressed the fledgling uprising, moving hundreds of tanks and thousands of troops into the defenseless country. Soviet soldiers with fixed bayonets patrolled the streets of Budapest, while elsewhere in the city tanks leveled buildings occupied by Hungarian "freedom fighters." To escape arrest or to protest the colorless, subservient regime that took over from Nagy, nearly a quarter million Hungarians went into exile, mostly to the United States and England.

Anxious to avoid atomic confrontation, the West tacitly recognized Soviet hegemony in eastern Europe and never considered intervention. In any case, the Western nations were all too occupied elsewhere. In early November 1956, England, France, and Israel attacked Egypt, ostensibly to reopen the Suez Canal, which Egyptian President Gamal Abdel Nasser had nationalized in July. But the Canal issue was only a pretext. The Israeli part in the operation had all the trappings of preventive war. Since its founding in 1948 as a national home for Jews, Israel's relations with its Arab neighbors had remained poor. Arabs resented the "interlopers" who, they claimed, mistreated native Palestinians. Israeli leaders, accustomed to American diplomatic support and financial succor, too readily relied on their tactical military superiority. The French Premier Guy Mollet hoped to revive the Fourth Republic, already moribund after disasters in Vietnam and Algeria. British diplomats, although desirous of American approval, misread Eisenhower's mild warning (the President did not want to antagonize the Jewish vote during his presidential campaign). London pushed on, determined to topple the Arab leader whose action against British interests in the Suez created a dangerous precedent.

Given Russia's preoccupation in Hungary, only Washington could scuttle the tripartite invasion. Anxious to avoid identifying itself with either European colonialism or Israeli extremism and determined to abate, not exacerbate, Arab-Israeli antagonism, America swiftly condemned the attack. Eisenhower even threatened to bankrupt the British pound unless Eden withdrew his forces. Beset on all sides, especially after the entire Arab world had broken off diplomatic relations, the Prime Minister and a reluctant Mollet accepted a Canadian-American proposal for a United Nations peacekeeping force in the Sinai peninsula. If this solved a diplomatic riddle for the West, Egypt did not forget that troops remained only on its soil, not on Israel's.

The next tremor occurred outside of politics. On October 4, 1957, the first earth satellite, Sputnik, beeped the beginning of the space age and seemed to tip the tactical balance in favor of the Soviet Union. Economies in the Defense Department and an exaggerated reliance on manned bombers by the air force had limited America's missile development program. The new earth satellite had little strategic significance, despite its propaganda value. Although Russia had developed intercontinental ballistic missiles (ICBMs) ahead of the United States, America's military technology, its huge fleets of conventional bombers, submarines, and aircraft carriers, bolstered by the world's mightiest gross national product, far surpassed the Soviet's war-making potential. Yet the sequence of changes in the fourteen months from the Polish strikes to the Soviet space coup radically altered the postwar world. Bipolar blocs, once uniformly impregnable, now threatened to dissolve; Cold War now afflicted the third world; and Soviet rocket engineers symbolically opened a foreboding era of doomsday techniques.

These crises revived Eisenhower's determination to "wage peace," continuing a drive already evidenced by his Atoms for Peace proposal in 1953 and the Geneva Summit of 1955. Events overseas facilitated such plans. Khrushchev's colleagues had rebuked him severely for the disastrous propaganda effect of Soviet intervention in Hungary, particularly among the new nations in Asia and Africa. But with the decisive help of the army, Khrushchev skillfully solidified his control over the Soviet state by 1958. While Russia's rapid economic development, coinciding with evidence of cross-purposes within the Western alliance, may have tempted Khrushchev, to a more aggressive policy, memories of Poland and Hungary and the devastation of modern war held him back. It was a curious balance that developed almost by chance, creating a minute-by-minute policy. Until the bellicose John Kennedy invented the "missile gap," the two superpowers moved, if not to reconciliation, at least away from nuclear suicide.

The Eisenhower Touch in Foreign Affairs

Despite his careful reaction to potentially explosive situations, Eisenhower never made a virtue of weakness. With his support, Secretary Dulles strengthened collective security in Europe by granting Germany a nonnuclear role in NATO. Then in 1957 the President proclaimed the Eisenhower Doctrine for the Middle East: if requested, economic support and American troops would be given to governments threatened by Communist subversion or territorial attack. The new policy resulted from the rapid erosion of the West's position throughout the strategic oil producing area. Nasser's obsession to unify the region politically, together with general Arab confidence that oil reserves would fend off reprisals and gain concessions, accelerated the region's trend toward nationalism.

Meanwhile, a confused, intricate civil war erupted in Lebanon among the mosaic of minorities, Christians and Arabs, pro-Nasser and anti-Nasser politicians, sophisticates in Beirut and natives of the hill country. Shortly after an Iraqi coup, the pro-Western President of Lebanon asked the United States for military support to end the domestic turmoil. Spurred by a vague sense that the United States must do something, Eisenhower invoked the new doctrine on July 15, 1958, and dispatched thirty-five hundred marines, a force that eventually grew to fourteen thousand. The three-month intervention—brief, bloodless, and well executed—deserved commendation for its technical skill. But the larger purpose of the landing failed; western hopes for an alternative to Nasser in the Middle East collapsed around Arab fears of renewed imperialism and the Arabs' reluctance to combine with outside powers against one another.

The Republican administration, like its predecessor, equated indifference to Western values with procommunism. But the breakup of Europe's empires had promoted political and economic revolution, as nationalists sought to destroy the remnants of colonialism, particularly its class structure. Accompanying this struggle was the need to restore economic vitality. Throughout Africa and much of Asia, imperial emphasis on extractive wealth and protected colonial

Photo by Sergio Larrain. © *1963 Magnum Photos.*

Soviet Premier Nikita Khrushchev addressing the United Nations General
Assembly.

markets had inhibited native manufactures and weakened agriculture. American policy seemed ill prepared to understand—no less to deal with—this emerging third world struggling with national revolution and the problems of modernization.

Similar dramas played themselves out in the western hemisphere. On January 1, 1959, a revolutionary leader, Fidel Castro, overthrew the heavy-handed Cuban dictator Fulgencio Batista. At first the Eisenhower administration welcomed the change; only six days after Batista fled the island, Washington recognized his bearded, thirty-two-year-old successor. After declaring 1959 the Year of Revolution, Castro took widespread, violent reprisals against his enemies in Cuba and even spread discontent among American minorities. Cuba's relations with the United States fell apart during 1960, the Year of Agrarian Reform. Castro nationalized American property worth $1 billion and publicly consorted with Khrushchev at the 1960 United Nations General Assembly meeting. Eisenhower tried to discipline Castro by cutting Cuba's economic lifeline, the all-important sugar quotas, and then by severing its political connections with the Organization of American States. Castro's subsequent turn to the Communist bloc surprised no one except the American public. Eisenhower had already authorized a possible attack on Cuba, which ultimately materialized as the Bay of Pigs fiasco under Kennedy.

Events in Europe also conspired against Eisenhower's hope for a stable world. With Russia and the United States both developing ICBMs, the weapons race became stalemated. The superpowers could destroy each other many times over, but neither had any defense other than its opponent's fear of retaliation. Another crisis in Germany demonstrated that the expensive nuclear deadlock forced mutual coexistence. When Russia sealed off East Berlin in the late summer of 1958 to thwart black market currency operations by West Berliners and to halt an embarrassing emigration from East Germany, Eisenhower deftly handled the showdown, potentially the most serious of the decade. His firm, well-modulated stand quickly diminished tension. As if to ratify a common resolve to avoid nuclear war, Khrushchev visited the United States in September 1959 and met cordially with Eisenhower at Camp David, Maryland. Observers spoke of the "spirit of Camp David" as a dissipation of mistrust. The Eisenhower peace offensive was to culminate in another summit conference at Geneva, planned for May 16, 1960.

But on May 1, far inside the Soviet Union, Russian artillery shot down an American reconnaissance plane, a U-2 piloted by Francis Gary Powers. Angered by foolish White House denials of the incident, and anxious to placate his opponents inside the Soviet Union, Khrushchev refused to attend the meeting.

Although a disillusioned Eisenhower frankly admitted to John Kennedy in 1961 that foreign affairs were "in a mess," he referred only to immediate problems. The Republicans had modified Truman's globalism in several ways. Although devoted to containment and initially spouting the tough line of brinkmanship and massive retaliation, the President and his staunch Secretary of State had pursued foreign policy less brashly, less provocatively. They had fashioned a sophisticated and, for the most part, successful relationship with the Soviet Union, a task made easier by its new leaders' acceptance of détente. Republican concern over the federal budget and Eisenhower's sensitivity to the limitations of technological force had resulted in a military stalemate. The atom bomb produced a balance of power that decades of war and diplomacy had not achieved. Eisenhower's greatest legacy was eight years of peace and a livable coexistence with the Soviet Union.

◄ 4 ►

POSTWAR AMERICAN SOCIETY: THE CONTINUITIES

BOTH PEOPLE and institutions changed during the postwar era. Even though America had left its familiar moorings and was headed out to open, often uncharted seas, uncertainty about the future turned into confident expectations of perpetual material advance. At the same time a curious restlessness enveloped most citizens, buffeted by bewildering growth, confronted with a plethora of choices, organized into categories of statistical abstractions—homeowners, do-it-yourselfers, Sunday football viewers, users of fluoridated toothpaste, and the like. This uprooted world required of its inhabitants steady adaptation. Many sought solace in the predictable comforts of conformity, either that of social behavior exerted by groups or that of the consumer ethic inculcated hourly, almost ritually, by television. Unfortunately, America's institutions did not adapt as rapidly as its people. Eventually rebels or those just vaguely ill-at-ease with the emerging society challenged the uprooting affluence of the postwar years. The cacophony increased, and soon modern America seemed like a gaudy merry-go-round—a brassy machine chasing its own tail.

The first fifteen years of the postwar epoch set patterns of continuity that gave American society some sense of predictability. Affluence and technology conferred on postwar America an unaccustomed style of democratic luxury: growth and migration created new suburbs; mass education and religion grappled with the needs of an often mysterious future; mass culture alternated between conformity and the desire to shock. Eventually, Americans grew dissatisfied with a predictable culture; some, like adolescents and the beats, reacted against it as early as the 1950s.

Population Boom

Growth characterized much of postwar American life. The nation even expanded in geographic size: the admission of Alaska and Hawaii as states in 1959 added nearly 600,000 square miles, boosting the United States to more than 3,600,000 square miles. But above all, Americans increased their numbers at an extraordinary rate between the end of the Second World War and the mid-1970s. The approximately 140,000,000 Americans of 1945 added 12,000,000 to their number within five years. A remarkable growth of 18.5 percent during the fifties—the highest for any decade since the First World War—brought the count to over 179,000,000 in 1960. Ten years later, the census reported more than 203,000,000 citizens.

In the absence of large-scale immigration, severely restricted since the 1920s, this population explosion rested on a "baby boom." The general fertility rate—annual births per 1,000 females aged 15 to 44—rose from 80 in 1940 to 106 by 1950, peaking at 123 in 1957. Since then, the figure has declined sharply; it fell to 97 in 1965, and after 1967 it remained in the eighties.

No explanation for the baby boom is definitive. The most plausible one points to the advantageous job market for young people. Previously in American history, surges of immigration brought foreigners to fill any demand for labor created by economic cycles. Alternately, pools of native workers might be recruited from unemployed groups or from depressed areas such as agriculture. During the late 1940s, a combination of fresh job opportunities, negligible immigration, and insufficient workers to keep pace with the labor market provided excellent employment possibilities. Earnings in lower income occupations, where younger people tended to be concentrated, rose quite rapidly; when workers were scarce, advancement came more readily. Other sources of income, particularly veterans' benefits, also helped out young families. With much better than average prospects for steady employment and a decent income, people married earlier and had babies sooner. This human explosion fueled the economy and filled the schools.

Within the ever more populous nation, Americans moved about freely, establishing several important patterns of migration. One old trend continued: the stream of farm folk, particularly the young, still flowed out of the countryside to swell the cities. This flight from the land reflected the remarkably improved productivity of farm labor. More and more machinery tilled and harvested even larger fields; new chemicals more effectively killed weeds and insects; special feeds made livestock meatier and more profitable. Output per man-hour rose over 95 percent from 1947 to 1960. As a result, during the 1950s alone, the number of farm workers dropped nearly 25 percent, from 9.9 million to 7.4 million. By the mid-1970s barely one-tenth of the population earned its living through farming. Although the actual number of people living in rural areas remained stable at about 54 million, their proportion of the total population fell from 36 to 26.5 percent.

Most of America's mobile citizens heeded Horace Greeley's advice, and the nation's center of population moved westward. It had taken some sixty years, from the 1880s to the 1940s, for this statistical point to cross Indiana. Yet from 1950 to 1970 it raced across Illinois until census officials pinpointed it "5.3 miles east southeast of the Mascoutah City Hall in St. Clair County, Illinois," not far from St. Louis, Missouri. Washington and Oregon experienced great growth in the 1940s; their burgeoning aircraft industries attracted the jobless toward America's last frontier. Warm and dry climates in Arizona and Nevada had long beckoned a trickle of emigrants, but it was the postwar generation that carved out cities like Phoenix, irrigated vast tracts with the waters of a tamed Colorado River, and mined the region's mineral wealth.

Most of all, people went to California. The state became a great magnet, pulling over 2.6 million citizens from other states in the forties, 3.1 million in the fifties, and 1.9 million in the sixties. By 1970 nearly one American in ten lived in the Golden State. As California's population swept past the 20-million mark in 1970, the state, fifth in population in 1940, moved to first. The near-tropical weather of southern California entranced those long accustomed to

POPULATION OF THE UNITED STATES, 1970

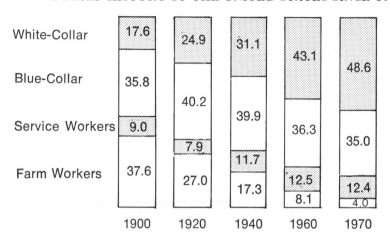

SHIFTS IN OCCUPATION, 1900-1970
(in percent of total)

the rigorous extremes of the Plains. Diversity within the state also sustained growth: the urban sprawl of Los Angeles, the sophistication of San Francisco, mountains and deserts, exotic vegetable farms and vineyards all attracted new people. Advances in technology created jobs for them in defense industries, electronic plants, and "aerospace." Prosperity fed on itself. Construction of all kinds raced forward as the Californians built houses, highways, schools, and shopping centers.

Of the more populous states, only Florida even approached California's enormous growth through migration. Between 1940 and 1970, Florida absorbed nearly 3.5 million roving Americans. Like California, Florida offered a warm climate and miles of seashore. Yet while California drew people of all ages, Florida appealed particularly to older citizens seeking comfortable retirement. The presence of the grandparent generation produced the highest median age in the nation—32.3 years—as compared with a national average of 28.1.

Blacks shared some migration patterns with whites, especially the rush to California, but they also developed clear directions of their own. Continuing a prewar trend, many migrated to northern cities—pushed by the stronger racism of their native South and pulled by presumably greater job opportunities in the industrial

North. By 1970, nearly 4.5 million blacks had abandoned the old Confederate South. Most left rural areas, contributing to the mass movement away from farms: in 1950, 38 percent of America's racial minorities lived a rural life: by 1970, only 19 percent remained in the countryside. California, New York, Illinois, and Michigan were the lodestones that drew the hopeful migrants. Between 1960 and 1970, for instance, the proportion of blacks in the population of virtually every important city in these four states increased significantly: New York City climbed from 14 percent black in 1960 to 21 percent by 1970; Los Angeles, from 13.5 to 18 percent; Chicago, from 23 to 32 percent; Detroit, from 29 to 44 percent.

Perhaps the most significant movement of people was a pervasive one that affected all areas of the country. The postwar generation accelerated a trend cut short by depression: white residents flowed out of urban centers, turning country fields into suburbs. By 1950, when this boom was only five years old, already one-seventh of the white population, or about twenty million people, lived on the urban fringe, along with more than one million nonwhites, 6 percent. Ten years later the suburbs held more than fifty-four million people, almost one-third of all white citizens and one-eighth of all non-whites. Technology and postwar affluence created the mass transportation systems—primarily, the privately owned automobile traveling on public highways—that the suburbs required.

In their move to the suburbs, Americans were simply following the available supply of housing. The "housing development," spurred by the availability of high government mortgages for G.I.s, became the hallmark of the suburbs beginning in the late 1940s. Building corporations virtually duplicated houses, one next to the other, enabling them to cut costs per unit and finish homes rapidly. Spurred on by the housing shortage after the war, one of the better known firms, Levitt and Sons, built and sold more than 17,500 new homes in Levittown, Long Island, within five and one-half years. The price of a Levitt house included landscaping, kitchen appliances, and legal fees; mass production techniques kept prices well below those for custom-built homes. But the early housing developments were unimaginative, and even residents occasionally became lost among identical houses on identical streets. Developers therefore attempted to improve later projects. Levitt curved streets to break monotony and cut traffic speed. The same floor plan fitted into four different exterior shells; these were painted in seven dif-

New York's Levittown was typical of the suburban housing developments that proliferated in the 1950s.

ferent colors, so that, at least in theory, only one out of twenty-eight houses would be identical to the twenty-ninth. Some developers even built community swimming pools and playgounds, which they then turned over to local governments.

Critics carped that suburbanites lived in a sterile atmosphere. No real community could exist, they argued, without centers of local activity and involvement integrated with housing—stores, churches, and schools. Others attacked the conformity of the tract houses; one popular song poked fun at "little boxes made of ticky-tacky" and charged that the houses and their inhabitants "all look just the same." Despite aesthetic or organizational failures, efficient construction enabled thousands of Americans to buy their own homes.

Urban Decay, Suburban Sprawl

A combination of blacks moving into central cities and whites moving to the suburbs created new difficulties for urban governments. As more affluent city residents bought houses in outlying communities and commuted to work, the city lost both their civic spirit and their tax dollars. The migrants who replaced them in the city had less tax money to offer and more need of municipal services. Industrial plants and offices often located in suburban areas as well, depriving the city of property and corporate tax income. One urban planner, Victor Gruen, commented that "we turned our cities into doughnuts, with all the dough around the center and nothing in the middle."

The rising costs of providing traditional services placed further burdens on the narrowing tax base of the city. Policemen, firemen, garbage collectors—the whole range of city employees—demanded higher salaries to maintain and improve their buying power in the face of chronic inflation. Meanwhile, their work week rapidly diminished; policemen put in as many as seventy-six hours per week in 1945, but the standard soon fell to forty hours or less. With more pay for fewer hours, police budgets nearly doubled in the fifteen years after the Second World War. Fringe benefits like more vacation time and improved disability coverage added to soaring costs.

The performance of public service employees did not always convince taxpayers of the wisdom of such wage hikes. While workers throughout America gained similar wage boosts, in industry—where man-hour output rose over 35 percent between 1947 and 1960 —increased productivity more than compensated for additional wage costs. Public service employees, on the other hand, usually could not significantly improve their productivity. Rising crime rates and poor performance brought particular criticism to police departments. According to FBI reports, serious crimes rose 98 percent from 1950 to 1960; some of the increase could be attributed to improved record-keeping, but the figures still deserved serious attention. At the same time, scattered cities uncovered police corruption—the "shakedown" of merchants for gifts, the acceptance of bribes to ignore individual infractions, the receipt of regular payments to condone ongoing illegal activities, and occasionally the involvement of police officers in specific crimes. Commuters brought the cities a further woe—their automobiles. Settlement no longer followed the routes of public transportation, but spread at will around the city. The family car provided door-to-door service: access to work, stores, and most recreation areas lay as close as a set of car keys. The only major city to have developed primarily since the advent of the automotive age, Los Angeles, sprawls across the landscape without any "downtown" business district. A giant web of freeways joins a series of industrial and residential enclaves, speeding traffic but contributing to the cloud of smog that frequently envelops the area. One resident has fittingly described the town as "a collection of suburbs in search of a city."

As the nation's suburbs grew, so too did the number of vehicles on the road. The count of registered automobiles doubled between 1940 and 1955 and doubled again by 1975. Anyone trapped in a line of barely moving cars at rush hour can readily understand the resulting "auto-sclerosis," a hardening of urban arteries. To permit free traffic flow and provide convenient parking, more and more highways and garages were built in the cities. The acres claimed by these projects robbed municipal governments of still more taxes. In Cleveland a three-mile section of superhighway removed an estimated $20 million of assessed property from city tax lists. Los Angeles paid the greatest homage to the automobile and probably lost the most land; by the early sixties, as much as two-thirds of that city's downtown area had been swallowed by highways, garages, and parking lots. The interstate system constructed in the 1950s and 1960s occupied at its completion more land than the state of Rhode Island. Although these sacrifices seemed shocking, many businessmen argued that areas not readily accessible by car simply could not prosper. The city of the postwar era found it difficult to live either with the automobile or without it.

But what of mass transit? Could not subways, buses, and trains ease the problem of intrametropolitan travel? Here too the automobile and the suburbs had wounded urban centers. The dramatic increase in use of cars in the 1940s and 1950s forced scores of transit systems in towns and cities throughout the country out of business by the early 1960s, while others needed even larger subsidies to remain operative. In addition, the rush to suburbia scattered people too widely and sparsely for effective and economical service. Much discussion about public transportation and a few experiments emerged in response to a growing realization of the automobile's baneful effects, but problems still outnumbered solutions well into the 1970s.

Facing such a broad spectrum of needs, ranging from transportation to city services to emerging problems of pollution, many urban planners outlined a battery of corrective programs. Yet in most metropolitan areas the fragmentation of governmental jurisdiction limited the effectiveness of such efforts before they had even begun. Because suburbanites wanted to manage their local politics, incorporated towns and villages on the edge of large cities sprang up. Local residents occasionally imposed ethnic or economic restrictions on newcomers. Budding tycoons incorporated industrial areas as suburbs in order to avoid higher municipal taxes. All these practices were justified with the traditional American argument that government could best remain responsive to the people if the community were small.

Chaos often resulted. Los Angeles County by the 1960s contained over 70 cities, and more than 600 taxing bodies. There were 950 local governments in the Chicago metropolitan area, the figure for New York reached 1,100, including some 550 cities, towns, and villages. Houses burned while frantic telephone operators searched for the fire department with proper jurisdiction. Speeders were pursued by a whole string of police cars as they careened across multiple town lines. In many cities, the same street changed its name several times as it passed through various jurisdictions in the metropolitan area; sometimes different roads with identical names in neighboring towns confused mailmen or visiting friends. Some cities, like Tucson, Arizona, and Las Vegas, Nevada, annexed their surrounding territory, but because of weaker tax bases and legal constraints, older, industrialized towns did not follow their example.

The real tragedy of fragmented authority lay in its debilitating effect on urban reform. Metropolitan-wide planning required a tax base that would support needed projects. Efforts in this direction met strong forces defending small government units, particularly in regard to issues involving schools, such as desegregation or community control. Happy in their enclaves, suburbanities ignored city problems. The idea of a small community attracted large numbers of Americans, whatever its social cost.

Mass Education

Every institution was put to the test of meeting the needs of a restless, affluent America. The educational systems were particularly vulnerable to the pressures shaping postwar society. Economic fluctuations or a city's troubles with its tax base were reflected in the construction and operational budgets of schools. Local, national, and international political issues—jurisdictional disputes, racial integration, and world status—injected deep emotion into discussions of school organization and curriculum. Research in educational techniques led to new classroom methods and drastically revised courses. As a result, American schools passed through a period of intense debate, change, and experimentation after 1945.

The pressure for change emerged quickly. Responding to new economic opportunities, teachers left their traditionally low-paying vocation in large numbers. School construction, almost at a standstill during the war, became urgent as the first wave of "baby boom" children reached the lower grades. School enrollment in grades one through eight, which had risen by less than a million in the 1940s, climbed by nearly ten million in the next decade until more than thirty million students attended the primary grades in 1960. America's rivalry with the Soviet Union stirred concern over the quality and content of the country's education in comparison with that in Communist countries.

The quality of public education. The new, ill-defined kind of education needed for a complicated economy created large areas of uncertainty for school boards and parents. Teachers and school administrators had taken up the gospel of "progressive education" in the mid-1920s. Inspired primarily by the writings of John Dewey, this approach insisted that schools weigh the needs and capabilities of individual children, emphasizing the student rather than the subject. Courses were designed to give experience with "life situations." Developing skill in manual crafts, artistic self-expression, and social adjustment became a legitimate goal for the schools. Early in the twentieth century, progressive education had opposed rote learning and rigid educational forms; by the 1940s, however, it had itself become conventional. The original concepts little served the postwar era, but no innovative thinking had updated their appeal.

In the late forties and early fifties, criticism and outright assault on progressive forms exhibited a broad range of sophistication and motivation. The central arguments remained much the same, regardless of the source. Antiprogressives maintained that the schools failed to teach academic fundamentals like reading or arithmetic, and that instructors no longer inculcated the salutary lessons of religion. Instead, they attempted to teach social adjustment, which, according to these critics, properly should be handled in the home. Charges of moral neglect peaked when the Supreme Court banned prayer in the public schools in 1963. Then too, appeals for lower taxes focused on trimming school programs to emphasize only "essentials."

Progressive teachers and administrators countered that a calculated, far-reaching "plot" threatened "good education." In some cases, critics did link up with conservative political movements or fundamentalist religion, but sincere critics presented insights uncompromised by the grinding of larger axes. Arthur Bestor, a historian and educator, defined the ultimate purpose of education as "the deliberate cultivation of the ability to think." In this view, schools should teach traditional disciplines in undiluted form to foster intelligence and preserve cultural standards. Bestor wanted to remove both school control and teacher training from "professional educators" in order to reassert the primacy of academic learning over technique. Clearly, a basic reconsideration of American educational philosophy was underway.

The launching of Sputnik in October of 1957 stimulated what one scholar has called "a bitter orgy of pedagogical soul-searching." Most Americans had simply assumed that the United States led the world in science, as well as in most other forms of knowledge. The Russians' feat prompted a fevered search for an explanation or excuse. Many vented their dismay by blaming the country's "soft" schools with their "frills." Whatever support for progressive education had remained soon disintegrated. A greater emphasis on academic achievement, particularly in the sciences, became the dominant characteristic of the new education.

By 1970, school expenditures as a precentage of GNP had risen to 7.2 percent, doubling in twenty years. Well-equipped language facilities and science laboratories, closed-circuit television systems and educational networks attempted to reach more students in new ways. Many of the developments of the 1960s probably would have come eventually to expanding school systems, but the shock of Sputnik had boosted concern over education and laid the basis for community support of exceptional schools.

Teacher qualifications. Improvements in the formal qualifications of teachers paralleled these changes in the schools. In 1948 almost 60 percent of American teachers did not hold a college degree. By the late 1960s over 90 percent had earned a bachelor's degree and about 25 percent boasted an advanced degree. Most states required the bachelor's degree for all teachers, and many demanded graduate work within a specified time limit. State education departments sought—with only partial success—to have teachers trained predominantly in the subjects they taught rather than in educational methods.

Salaries kept pace with presumed quality improvements. The 1948 salary average for public school teachers of about $2,500 ballooned to $6,500 or more by the late 1960s. Like public service employees, teachers unionized and fought for more than salary increases. Working conditions became a thorny problem involving issues of paperwork, hall or cafeteria duty, and disciplinary authority. Like policemen, firemen, and garbage collectors, teachers discovered the strike and used it with mixed success. But the greatest threat to continued improvements in qualifications and salaries seemed to be the receding wave of children as school enrollments in the seventies began to level off or decline. Fewer children meant fewer jobs. The tight financial conditions of the Nixon years forced school districts to hire only the minimum number of teachers, and in some cases, to use those less qualified because they came cheaper. With large numbers of college graduates prepared to teach a diminishing school-age population, the early 1970s saw a surplus of trained teachers for perhaps the first time in American history.

Community control of schools. Struggles for control of the schools often provoked sharp political skirmishes. The relative affluence of many suburbs, and the above-average education of most who lived there, created the basis for schools of high quality. But along with suburbanization came a certain homogeneity. Children in a particular school often came from similar economic backgrounds and from broadly similar religious or ethnic groups. School boards joined local governments in protecting this homogeneity in the classroom as well as in the community. Resistance to desegregation outside the South may well have been fueled by a desire to maintain uniformity as much as by simple racism. Few considered the benefits of a diverse student population—the social learning resulting from contact with people in some way different. Within large cities, struggles to decentralize school administration usually were motivated by a sense of conscious community. Minorities wanted to select their own teachers and create courses that would build pride or cohesiveness in their group.

Curriculum control fights revealed that the issues of the struggle over progressive education lived on after the fifties. Proponents of sex education, for instance, sounded much like progressives in emphasizing the school's responsibility to teach social behavior and adjustment when such lessons were not taught elsewhere. Their opponents, like critics of progressive education, wanted to limit the schools strictly to academic subjects, arguing that discussion of sex belonged only in the home. All these problems involving control over schools and curriculum promised to persist.

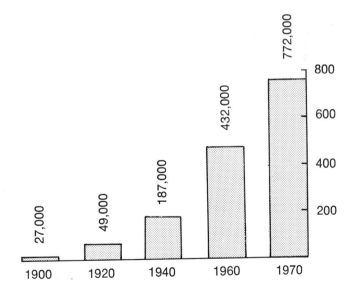

COLLEGE GRADUATES, 1900-1970
(in thousands)

Higher education. Higher education enrollments grew even more rapidly than those of the public schools in the postwar era. In 1940, 1.5 million students attended college; with a transfusion from the G.I. bill, the figure rose to over 2.6 million by 1950 and crept upward to 3.4 million by 1960. Then in the 1960s the "boom" babies reached college age. This potential public for enrollment, the need for highly trained personnel, and the financing available after the Sputnik challenge encouraged the rapid expansion of colleges and universities in the 1960s; enrollment more than doubled in that decade, reaching more than 7 million by 1970. The National Defense Education Act of 1958 provided an extensive program of loans and fellowships to aid both undergraduates and graduate students. The growth and proliferation of state, community, and junior colleges allowed many students who could not attend universities to obtain at least two years of college work, usually close to their homes.

By the late 1960s a new question had arisen: faced with possible shortages of high-paying jobs for college graduates, were perhaps too many people obtaining degrees? Some advocated alternate routes to satisfying occupational goals. But enrollments pushed upward, at least until the mid-1970s.

Religion: Ecumenical and Activist

An affluent society, awash with new products and reveling in its material splendors, would seem an inhospitable climate for a religious revival. Yet churches flourished in the new age, its very motion and uncertainty creating a need for stability. Such religious leaders as Norman Vincent Peale, the popular Protestant minister who preached about "the power of positive thinking"; Bishop Fulton J. Sheen, broadcasting to a large television audience; and Rabbi Joshua Loth Liebman, author of a best-selling tract entitled *Peace of Soul* became national figures. Hollywood stars paraded their religious beliefs and church attendance as they once had their love affairs or their divorces. Congress added the phrase "under God" to the Pledge of Allegiance. Cementing the prosperity of religion, church membership rose impressively in the forties and fifties: 65 million members in 1940 accounted for just under half of the population; by 1960 two-thirds of the population, over 125 million people, belonged to a church. Nineteen out of twenty Americans identified themselves—when asked—as Protestants, Catholics, or Jews.

In the midst of this increased joining and giving, a majority declared that their religion had little effect on their political or economic ideas. More than half of a largely volunteer force distributing Bibles across the land proved unable to name even one book of the New Testament. Four out of five people claimed to believe Jesus was divine, yet when asked to pick history's most important event, they demoted Christ's crucifixion to fourteenth on a list easily topped by Columbus's discovery of America. Theologians lamented the seeming paradox of religious boom accompanied by spreading secularization.

A plausible explanation came from a sociologist, Will Herberg, who found the roots of religious identification in the ending of mass immigration. Having experienced more than three decades of blending since unrestricted immigration's end in 1924, Americans were no longer identifying themselves by ethnic background, but sought out the personal identification of religion. Most white Anglo-Saxon Protestants gradually accepted a limited ecumenicalism and a tentative equality of the three major faiths.

Outside the mainstream of liberal religion flowed a smaller, but no less active, current of fundamentalism: evangelicals of the old school interpreting the Bible literally and searching the political and social horizons for evidence of apocalypse. About thirty million American fundamentalists, many scattered in tiny sects, constituted the most rapidly growing religious group of the postwar years.

Yet this sizable minority attracted little attention except for the antics of a few of its more flamboyant leaders. One of the most successful fundamentalist preachers, Dr. Fred Schwartz, founded the Christian Anti-Communist Crusade in 1953 to spread the good word about fundamentalist Christianity and, more important, the bad word about communism. The crusade sponsored schools to educate patriots on the Red menace and held revivalistic rallies to unify the faithful. Schwartz himself demonstrated a capacity for restraint that separated him from some of the wilder elements on the far right, but his rallies attracted many whose behavior deserved the label "fanatic." As in other ultraconservative rallies, key phrases like "atheist creed bent on world domination" and "subjugation of the freedom-loving peoples of the world under the yoke of Godless, Communist totalitarianism" set off near hysterical applause. A special target of the religious anti-Communists, the Federal Council of Churches of Christ, came to symbolize all the evils of liberal religion. Carl McIntire, a deposed Presbyterian minister, founded the American Council of Christian Churches in 1941 to harass the Federal Council for its ecumenicism and support for social reform. This group even hinted that Catholic leaders were Communist conspirators.

No one elaborated the possibilities of fundamentalist anticommunism with more success than Reverend Billy James Hargis, founder and leader of the Christian Crusade based in Tulsa, Oklahoma. Aided by a public relations adviser, Hargis's annual budget climbed to a million dollars by the end of the fifties. His crusade transmitted over more than two hundred radio stations its message that "communism has infiltrated, subverted, perverted and sabotaged practically every phase of the American way." Believing communism a direct manifestation of the Devil, Hargis asked Americans to call on Jesus to defeat "Satanic Communism" with "Christian soldiers." Any criticism of anti-Communist excesses Hargis dismissed with, "It came from Moscow." A national convention of the Christian Crusade in 1963 attacked the Kennedy family, State Department officials, the NAACP, liberals, Communists, the United Nations, the Supreme Court, civil rights legislation, Dwight Eisenhower, and Harvard University, all standard targets of the far right. Yet the crusade lost ground in the sixties to rival organizations, especially the more secular, but equally right-wing, John Birch Society.

Mass Communications and Culture

Postwar America gave impressive support to its traditional institutions of culture: schools, churches, museums, and libraries, as well as the theaters, orchestras, and art galleries of its cities. But one new cultural medium clearly won its heart and—so advertisers believed—its pocketbook: television.

The impact of television. In the 1920s the mass use of radio and the automobile had revolutionized American notions of entertainment. After the Second World War television began a similar conquest that made the miraculous radio broadcasts of twenty years before seem old-fashioned. Although television had existed in crude form since at least the 1920s, in mid-1947 only ten stations were broadcasting in the United States, and manufacturers were producing only 7,000 sets per year. Then the industry exploded. At the end of 1948, there were 127 active stations. In one year, 1950, Americans purchased more than 7.3 million television sets. The percentage of homes with at least one set rose constantly: from 66 percent in 1955 to 96 percent fifteen years later. In 1971 consumers set a new record, purchasing 15 million sets in one year, nearly half of them color units.

Many wondered about the effect of the new medium on American life. The intellectual content of television programs was very low. Every Tuesday the nation watched Uncle Miltie (Milton Berle) cavort mindlessly in front of a live audience. When millions read newspaper headlines in 1955, "It's a Boy!" they knew that Lucille Ball—the lovable, wacky star of the country's first well-known situation comedy, "I Love Lucy"—had delivered. Television changed politics: its practitioners now seemed more worried about broadcast images than issues. Mass spectator sports, formerly restricted to the capacity of a stadium, began an expansion via the air waves that would engulf the nation. Some suggested that television would bring families together, repeating an argument heard in the early days of the automobile. But critics pointed out that with all attention riveted on the TV set, family members could sit in the same room for hours without speaking one word to each other.

For every comment extolling the educational possibilities of television, several decried the deadening effect of its undemanding drone. Leading academic figures feared that television would mold the population into a passive and unstable mass relying on a box of tubes for guidance. "Television," explained FCC chairman Newton Minow in the early 1960s, is "a vast wasteland."

Television's impact on politics impressed or alarmed many observers. When the 1948 Democratic Convention passed a civil rights plank, southern delegates stalked out of the gathering, placing their identification badges on a table near the door. Television cameras picked up the exodus and the growing mound of badges. Prominent journalists claimed this broadcast (transmitted only in the Northeast) kept Truman in the presidency by convincing Negroes in the East that "Mr. Truman had, indeed, stuck out his neck for them." In the summer of 1948, however, less than 500,000 people in the country owned television sets, and few of them were black. Truman, in fact, lost the major states that had received convention coverage. Despite this clear case of exaggeration, many scholars and politicians continued to believe in the power of television. Senator Joseph McCarthy's political decline in 1954 was widely

By 1950 television had become both a major industry and a national pastime.

___

attributed to his exposure on national television as a blustering, nasty bully. Senator Estes Kefauver, after conducting televised hearings on crime and labor racketeering, became a potential presidential candidate—perhaps because politicians assumed he had acquired a following. Critics looked at television as a persuader rather than as an entertainer, but that may be because they did not watch it themselves very much.

Decline of the movie industry.   Television's role as entertainer was not at all obscure to the motion picture industry. As families across the country clustered in their living rooms to watch quiz programs or variety shows, attendance declined at the local Bijou. Between 1954 and 1958 alone, twenty-five hundred movie theaters closed, about one out of every six in the country. Major Hollywood studios entered a period of prolonged shock. Some relied on lavish super-spectaculars, filmed in color and shown on wide screens. Biblical themes predominated (one critic carped, "There's more old-time religion in the movie house than in the pastor's house"), but the era ended in the early 1960s when budget overruns on *Cleopatra*, starring Elizabeth Taylor, forced Twentieth-Century Fox into receivership. Thereafter, the industry turned to topical movies appealing primarily to young people. Somewhat ironically, the first generation of television children provided the largest audience the theaters could attract. Hollywood also produced many "TV-movies"—quickly made, low budget dramas. Most American film-makers still pursued commercial success rather than artistic excellence, and this was perhaps one of the most unfortunate economic side effects of televison's popularity.

The book industry. Contrary to the predictions of some TV-haters, the production and sale of books did not wither but flourished. The value of all books sold in 1947 totaled $435 million and in 1958 passed the one-billion-dollar mark. The number of new books and new editions rose from just over eleven thousand in 1950 to fifteen thousand in 1960; despite the omnipresence of television, the number of books published annually surged ahead still further in the sixties. Bookshelves groaned under the weight of thirty-six thousand new titles in 1970 alone. Reasonably well-educated viewers could acquire information much faster through reading than through watching television news. And with a high school education becoming the norm, more and more literate Americans found enjoyment in reading.

An innovation in the publishing industry itself probably helped to boost the rising popularity of books. Paperbacks, long considered disreputable in the United States, began to appear in large numbers in 1939 when Pocket Books began to publish good fiction in inexpensive softcover editions. This and similar experiments prospered; in 1953 Doubleday inaugurated its Anchor Book series using higher quality materials. The success of these better-made softcover volumes sent all major publishers scurrying to produce paperbacks. By 1965 Americans bought nearly one million each day. The new books were not only cheap and easy to carry, but readily available in drugstores and airports. School and college teachers found a wider range of titles available and assigned them freely; students could purchase three or four paperbacks for the price of one hardbound book.

Not all these books were educational or literary gems. Most readers bought mediocre books—bestsellers about Hollywood or far-away places or advice on how to improve one's love life or health or popularity. One striking change in the reading public was the growing preference for nonfiction over fiction, suggesting an increased desire for practical information rather than escape—perhaps too readily available from television. The Reader's Digest Book Club reached a membership of 2.5 million in 1958, each member receiving a "condensed book" (actually several best-sellers in shortened form) four times per year. Each time an edition rolled off the presses, it automatically became one of the all-time best sellers in history. "Condensation" went far beyond abridgement to include changes in wording, in plot, in scenes, and even in the author's meaning or intent. Staff members carefully rewrote passages to homogenize the package.

Despite such pools of blandness, the publishing industry as a whole laid before the American people in the postwar decade the greatest variety of books any nation had yet seen. Some excellent books managed to make the best-seller lists, like Norman Mailer's *The Naked and the Dead* (1948) and James Jones' *From Here to Eternity* (1951), both novels about the Second World War. J. D. Salinger's sensitive portrait of a troubled adolescent, *The Catcher in the Rye* (1951), became required reading among the nation's college youth during the 1950s. Joseph Heller's hilarious *Catch-22* (1961) disturbed many who were worried about the bureaucratization of American life.

More trenchant criticism came primarily from playwrights. Eugene O'Neill probed man's self-destructive urges in two great works, *The Iceman Cometh* (1946) and *Long Day's Journey into Night* (1956), both commercial successes. Arthur Miller protested America's misguided values, especially its materialism, in plays like *Death of a Salesman* (1949). The country's greatest novelist, William Faulkner, continued studying the effect that past evils have on contemporary men in such books as *A Fable* (1954) and *The Mansion* (1960). In his acceptance speech for the Nobel Prize for Literature in 1955, he expressed the beleaguered, but still hopeful, attitude of several generations of American writers: "I believe that man will not merely endure. He will prevail."

Conformity and Diversity

In many ways, the success of Reader's Digest books mirrored the desire of many Americans to conform. In the 1950s especially, it appeared that Americans joined larger and larger units and displayed increasingly common patterns of thought and behavior. Suburbanites lived in identical homes in housing developments that imposed unity on the countryside. Class differences appeared to vanish as dress became more casual, as more and more people owned cars and houses, and as the line between popular and high culture fuzzed into a broad area of what one critic called "mid-cult." Responses to the Kinsey reports on sexual behavior suggested that Americans even worried about whether their conjugal habits conformed to those of their neighbors.

Observers feared that the rootless postwar American had become what William H. Whyte called "the organization man." The individual, Whyte claimed, now saw "belongingness as the ultimate need." The security of a niche, the comforts of affluence seemed to have beguiled a generation. The president of Yale University, A. Whitney Griswold, brutally told graduating seniors, "You share the prevailing mood of the hour, which in your case consists of bargains privately struck with fate—on fate's terms."

Television, in particular, wove the nation into a common cloth. It was not just that millions of people watched the same programs week after week. Television's influence was more pervasive, more subtle. Newscasters slowly imposed their carefully cultivated midwestern accents (though without twang and hard *r*'s) on the nation's speech patterns. Even Brooklyn accents and southern drawls could be modified by daily doses of "newspeak." Commercials reinforced the consumer ethic: Americans learned that they were supposed to buy things. Situation comedies and hackneyed dramas convinced millions that every problem, no matter how complicated or indeterminate, could be resolved in a maximum of sixty minutes. Life was becoming a series of episodes.

The physical world became more and more uniform. Chain stores replaced local shops. Franchised enterprises had the same trademark, even the same products. People could travel from the Atlantic to the Pacific coast buying the same brand of gasoline all the way. All over the country, the Golden Arches of McDonald's announced the fourteen "fast foods" served inside, including a perfectly round four-ounce hamburger, french fries, and chemically flavored milk shakes. And those who preferred slower food could go to Howard Johnson's restaurants. The automobile caused thousands of miles of highways to be paved over, which sprouted millions of stop lights. Drive-in banks, drive-in movies, drive-in grocery stores proliferated. The shopping center—stores ringed by huge parking lots—became "downtown" for the new suburbs. Modern architects built hundreds of nearly identical glass cubes, obeying Mies van der Rohe's dictum, "Form follows function." But apparently the function was to ensure the predictability of form.

This entire image of tidy organized America suffered dramatic eclipse in the 1960s as the nation uncovered the diversities that had always simmered beneath the bland surface of life in the fifties. The prominence of new styles and values startled observers who had been persuaded by their own visions of a conformist nation. People discovered, to their surprise, that the "silent generation" of young people had been quietly thinking and were ready to act mostly in a bewildering variety of new and venturesome ways.

The youth revolt seemed the great divide marking off the apathetic fifties from the dissident sixties. Yet such mechanical contrasts between the decades distort understanding of both eras. The revolt of the students became conscious and public in the 1960s, but its crucial prerequisite, the development of a separate subculture among young people, came directly from the center of middle-class life in the fifties: the home and the school. The element that upset parents about the increasingly separate adolescent world —rock-and-roll music and heavy petting, delinquency and teen-age rebels without a cause—were early hints that Americans were not really so much alike as the image of a conforming society would suggest.

Adolescents

The expansion of high schools after the Second World War, absorbing for the first time virtually all Americans of the appropriate age, created a separate adolescent culture. Continuing industrialization encouraged a teenage subculture. With the creation of more and more white-collar and bureaucratic jobs, and with most blue-collar workers tied to assembly lines, children seldom saw their parents at work; apprenticeship systems largely disappeared, and fewer sons followed their fathers' trade. Such changes helped to destroy the traditional, gradual introduction to an adult role. Instead of encouraging parents to teach their children adult activities, modern society required that the parents involve themselves in the children's world of Little League, Girl Scouts, or school clubs. High school students, certainly no longer children and just as clearly not yet adults, felt cut off in both directions. To teen-agers isolated from adult roles, peer values naturally became very important. And when the prosperity of the postwar era made even teen-agers comparatively affluent, adolescent tastes gained real commercial significance. Movie makers and music publishers aimed specifically at the teen market, thereby reinforcing its distinctiveness and separateness. The high schools became the incubators of a genuine subculture.

Adult perceptions of teen-agers rested on limited information. Parents had some first-hand exposure to the subculture, but they generally saw their children as part of the family, not as functioning members of adolescent society. Adults also learned about teen-agers through the mass media—newspapers, magazines, radio, television, and films. But these sources, as always, provided information on the unique or spectacular, not the mundane. In the 1950s, the media reinforced an intense concern with juvenile delinquency. Between 1948 and 1960 the number of juvenile crimes rose each year. Speculation on the causes of this surge pointed to unemployment rates—about three times as high among unskilled teen-agers as among adults—and to rising incidence of divorce, which weakened family ties. Special library collections were concerned exclusively with teen-age misbehavior; community groups—more than ninety in Los Angeles County alone—tackled the problem of juvenile delinquency. Certain newspaper and magazine stories painted high schools as hives of violence and teen-agers as masters of the switchblade. Adults had only to hear movie titles like *Rebel Without a Cause* to wonder whether Hollywood had glorified misfits. Leonard Bernstein based his hit musical *West Side Story* on recent sociological research, but the Oscar-winning film version convinced millions that street gangs like the Aces and the Jets typified a bored generation of hoodlums.

The media also promoted a new kind of music for the young. If adults did not hear rock-and-roll blaring from their own record players or radios, they read about it in magazines. Rock-and-roll derived primarily from two long-established strains of American music: "race" and "hillbilly"—politely renamed "rhythm and blues" and "country and western" by the record industry. These musical styles had existed before the Second World War on the fringes of American popular music. During the late 1940s changes in both the music and its availability brought these styles into increasing prominence. First, the record industry came into its own, producing cheap records in vast quantities so that recorded songs became the standard form of radio music. Second, rhythm and blues, along with country and western, sounded harder, louder, and more urbanized as blacks and southerners moved from country to city. Blues were played in crowded bars now, electric guitars pounding a beat that could penetrate urban noise. Popular music had already developed the cult of the singer; Frank Sinatra made girls swoon or scream in the forties much as Pat Boone and Elvis Presley did later.

In 1951 a disc jockey named Alan Freed, alerted by a record store owner to the popularity of rhythm and blues records outside the black ghetto, organized "Moondog's Rock-and-Roll Party" on station WJW in Cleveland. Rock-and-roll did not develop a life of its own, however, until 1954, when Freed joined a medium-sized New York station and drove both the new music and its new name to the top of radio ratings. A white band, Bill Haley and the Comets, was the first to label itself as a "rock-and-roll" group; their song "Shake Rattle and Roll" reached the "Top Ten" late in 1954. A new era began in May 1955 when Haley's hit "Rock Around the Clock" opened the highly successful movie, *The Blackboard Jungle*, thus linking rock-and-roll with wild and rebellious teen-agers. Adolescents made such films an instant success. In 1956 Bill Haley and the Comets produced a low-budget movie called *Rock Around the Clock*, which grossed a million dollars in that year alone. In England minor riots occurred as theaters showing the film turned into dance halls. The *Encyclopaedia Britannica* yearbook described the new music as "insistent savagery."

Adults worried about the racial and sexual overtones of the new music. When one of Alan Freed's dances brought together eighty thousand black and white teen-agers in a segregated city, most adults protested. The language of rock and dances like the jitterbug came mainly from blacks. Rock-and-roll songs often voiced sexually explicit lyrics. Radio stations banned dozens of songs with titles like "Drill, Daddy, Drill," "Work with Me, Annie," and "Baby, Let Me middle-class families did not predominate, their children stood out naturally by virtue of their educational, economic, and social advantages. But in the prosperous, uniform suburbs a child needed unusual qualities to achieve prominence. Parents tried to develop accomplished and sophisticated children through early dancing lessons, art and sports instruction, and the like. They provided a surfeit of material possessions and allowed their children to make decisions. When these youngsters reached adolescence, they in fact were more sophisticated and more self-reliant, but the result did not always please parents. Freedom released teen-agers from many family ties so that they could enter more completely the adolescent culture where peer values ruled. Adult social norms became increasingly difficult to enforce.

A further tendency contributed to adolescent independence. Within a stable community, a teen-ager might gain status among schoolmates because of family position, the 'right" friends, or leadership abilities. But none of these claims to prominence worked in the highly mobile suburbs, where many people stayed only two or three years. Families developed little status, and teen-agers often entered a new school with neither friends nor reputation. Under these circumstances, material signs of affluence assumed importance: those with snappy clothes and plentiful pocket money could lay claim to leadership. Parents invested heavily in their children's social success, and the teen-ager with money grew ever more ubiquitous. Then too, boys reached social popularity most easily through athletics while attractive girls found cheerleading nearly as effective. Even though parents claimed to want scholars in the family, teen-agers felt that athletic accomplishment made their parents most proud. Boys and girls both declared the brilliant student an undesirable dating partner, although good grades, not outstanding ones, were considered helpful for membership in the "leading crowd" and acceptance at a good college was considered important.

Membership in the best clique of a suburban high school, then, often required good grades, athletic or cheerleading ability, a winning personality, and active leadership all rolled into one. The student who attempted all this lived a life under pressure. If these youths, isolated from the adult world and increasingly involved with peer values, realized every goal set for them—social success and entrance into an outstanding college—the time might come during college years to release some of that pressure. Out of the adolescent culture of the fifties would grow the youth movements of the next decade.

Beats

Predictably, most observers considered college students and young people of the 1950s remarkably nonpolitical and conformist. Professors issued public warnings about the eagerness of the "silent generation" to enter corporate bureaucracies and settle down in the suburbs. Against this background, the cultivated uniqueness and social alienation of that era's rebels, the beats, stood out sharply. Living in scattered enclaves across the country, although drawn primarily to New York City's Greenwich Village area and to San Francisco, the beats came from extremes in educational and social background: graduates and drop-outs from Columbia University mingled in "pads" with exconvicts and Times Square hustlers. Conscious of the legendary disillusioned youth of the 1920s, many beats saw themselves as part of a new "lost generation."

Individual experiments with startling literary forms and roving life styles began in the late forties, but not until 1955 and the so-called San Francisco Renaissance did these personal questings seem united enough to be called a movement. Ever since the late twenties, Kenneth Rexroth, a Berkeley professor and veteran poet, had cultivated a radical innovative approach to both life and poetry that attracted students and made him the reigning sage among San Francisco's avant-garde writers. Then in 1951 two easterners started a magazine called *City Lights,* which quickly spawned yet another center for literary experimentation—the City Lights Bookstore. The tabloid folded in a few months, but the bookstore, under the management of the remaining partner, Lawrence Ferlinghetti, prospered on the sale of paperbacks and became a gathering place for beat poets in the North Beach area of San Francisco. Public readings provided an opportunity for mutual criticism among a small, but devoted, following. In 1956 Ferlinghetti, a poet of some skill himself, introduced beat authors to a wider audience by publishing a series of City Lights books.

A migrant to North Beach provided the inaugural poem for a conscious beat movement. Allen Ginsberg, recent nemesis of Columbia professors, possessed a unique talent for aggressive, irascible denunciation. In 1955 he composed in one weekend, while under the influence of a strange concoction of potent drugs, the brutal and now famous poem "Howl."

> I saw the best minds of my generation destroyed by madness, starving
>   hysterical naked,
> dragging themselves through the negro streets at dawn. . . .

> What sphinx of cement and aluminum bashed open their skulls and
>   ate up their brains and imagination.
> Moloch! Solitude! Filth! Ugliness! Ashcans and unobtainable dollars!
>   Children screaming under the stairways!

Performed rather than read in a gathering at the Six Gallery coffee house in North Beach, "Howl" climaxed a night of fresh and exciting poetry that made literary history. Ginsberg had produced a new kind of poem that came close to transmitting the energy and emotion he had felt while writing it. Ginsberg demonstrated—in addition to genuine poetic talent—two traits that would keep him among the leaders of cultural innovation throughout the next decade. "Howl" reflected a talent for staying ahead of the crowd, leading it in a direction in which it was inclined to go. Ginsberg's other gift was a sense of timing and publicity that, in combination with his organizational skills, supposedly led one temporarily disgruntled friend to call him "a Jewish businessman."

The single best-known prose work of the beats was Jack Kerouac's *On the Road*. Written in 1951, the manuscript kicked around from publisher to publisher for six years before The Viking Press finally accepted it under the prodding of another author, Malcolm Cowley. An immediate success among both critics and the public, *On the Road* introduced a large general audience to the "beat generation" and Kerouac became a talk-show celebrity. The book chronicled in cascading phrases the frantic, electric, high-velocity adventures of one Dean Moriarty—whose prototype in real life was Neal Cassady, the prototypical beat who himself did not write a word but inspired authors like Kerouac and Ginsberg. Kerouac believed intensely in a form of rapid, uncorrected writing that he dubbed "spontaneous prose." Much of *On the Road* was written on a roll of teletype paper because the author resented the time lost changing individual sheets of typing paper.

Jack Kerouac had been the first to label his generation "beat"—worn out, wearied beyond recovery, alienated from all the world's conventions—but his later life reminded everyone that the beats were individualistic, far from unified, and without any particular political ideology. In the ten years before his death in 1969, Kerouac became a vocal conservative in the tradition of his French Catholic heritage.

Others added distinctive ingredients to the beat potpourri. Poet Gary Snyder introduced the flavor of Far East mysticism that soon pervaded beat sensibility; Gregory Corso contributed a durable poetry combining prison-learned toughness with waiflike innocence. And a whole group of poets at the experimental Black Mountain College in North Carolina gave richness to the movement. In prose the beats only intensified a movement toward personal journalism and free prose already underway. But in poetry they instigated a revolution; the academic, formal poems of established 1950s poets gave way by the 1960s to a much freer, franker style of expression.

The movement of weary rejection begun by the beats gradually broadened and became more political. As more and more flocked to the banner of alienation in the early sixties, protest grew more generalized and took on the trappings of a mass movement with established orthodoxies, slick magazines, and celebrity leaders. The original beat hatred of organization was smothered beneath the surge. Literary magazines folded and exclusively personal writers dropped out of sight when they refused to serve politicized revolt. Yet early beats left a considerable legacy to the youth of the 1960s. They made beards a sign of alienation; they popularized among whites the use of drugs, particularly as an aid to artistic perception or creativity. Many beats accepted socially deviant groups like homosexuals, and respected "flipping out," or bouts of craziness. An emphasis on love as a basis for social relationships, a rejection of the nuclear family, experimentation with communal living, a concern with spiritual matters, and an interest in eastern religions—all these forms of experimental living that flourished in the 1960s could be attributed to the beats.

PART TWO

1960-1975

◀ 5 ▶
AMERICAN POLITICS 1960-1975

THE PATTERN of the first fifteen years following the war curiously repeated itself in the next fifteen years, especially in politics and economics. Aggressive, reforming Presidents were followed by more stabilizing, conservative chief executives. Years of economic prosperity and a "go-go" stock market merged into a quiet plateau of consolidated affluence. Another Asian war once more divided the country, reoriented its politics, and revolutionized its foreign affairs. Middle-class Americans continued to abandon the cities for the suburbs, and communications media brought more and more people into a common experience, a shared perception of their society.

Yet there were some departures. Violence punctuated the slow evolution in America's values, forcing a radical shift in the country's complacent self-assurance. The young and many minorities challenged old folkways, which suddenly seemed inane and unjust. New heroes directly challenged the rigid past, while their followers often sought shortcuts to change by stepping outside normal conventions of restraint. America's intervention in Vietnam's civil war, undertaken with seemingly honorable intentions, somehow transformed itself into a nasty, brutal, and long effort to impose an artificial democracy on an agrarian society. The cost became enormous —nearly fifty thousand Americans died, and the war's $150 billion price tag did much to undermine America's overseas financial strength. Yet no one seemed able to lead the nation out of its misguided mission. The interminable war discouraged Americans, diluting their natural optimism with large doses of self-doubt. Many wondered whether the foreign war and domestic turmoil of the sixties had permanently changed American society or just flagrantly underlined its abuses. Did the tumultuous years of the late sixties or the self-serving years of the early seventies forecast the mainstream of America's future?

The Election of 1960

The presidential campaign of 1960 indicated the consensus that the fifties had stamped on American society. Perhaps because the two major candidates, Senator John F. Kennedy of Massachusetts and Vice-President Richard M. Nixon, had faced obstacles to the nomination, both emerged as moderates, very close to agreement on most issues. Kennedy won leadership of the Democratic party after a long primary campaign that demonstrated to skeptics that his Catholicism did not automatically destroy his chances and impressed regulars with the technical polish of "the Kennedy machine" of money, youth, and enthusiasm. His victory in the primary in West Virginia, a heavily Protestant state, over Senator Hubert H. Humphrey of Minnesota, long-time friend of the area's labor unions, ended overt challenges, although some local politicians charged that Kennedy's immense spending had actually "bought the election." At the convention, supporters of Lyndon B. Johnson and Adlai E. Stevenson launched a cloakroom effort that nearly blocked Kennedy's nomination on the first ballot. Nixon, too, had his problems. The powerful governor of New York, Nelson Rockefeller, agreed to bow out of the race for the nomination only if the Vice-President agreed to sign the so-called Compact of Fifth Avenue, a document advocating a more vigorous defense posture and expansive economic tactics. Its content scared conservative Republicans, and the implied criticism stung President Eisenhower. Nixon won the nomination by acclamation, but he had learned the necessity for gingerly compromise.

John F. Kennedy and Richard M. Nixon as they appeared to millions of viewers during the second of their televised debates.

In the ensuing campaign the issues quietly slipped away. Nixon enjoyed an enormous early lead in the polls, reflecting the good effect of a campaign strategy that emphasized his greater "experience" and public exposure. But during September and October, the candidates debated four times on television. Both agreed on most issues, but Kennedy's charm and handsome demeanor contrasted with his opponent's dour earnestness and what appeared to be unshaven jowls, the result of an unflattering camera image. Nixon's strategy foundered altogether when President Eisenhower was asked at a press conference what decisions Nixon had helped him with? Angered by his Vice-President's aloofness, Eisenhower replied, "Give me a week and I might think of one." Then the Republicans blitzed the country with a telethon that probably alienated more voters than it convinced. Meanwhile, Kennedy had whistle-stopped—or more accurately jet-stopped—the nation, his staff carefully building up ever more enthusiastic rallies with flashy, hard-hitting TV "spots."

For the second time in the twentieth century, Americans had to stay up all night in order to identify their new President. Kennedy carried the East, and as he had calculated, his running-mate, Lyndon Johnson, returned much of the South to the Democratic coalition. Nixon swept the West. It was Illinois and Minnesota that pushed Kennedy's electoral count past the majority mark, eventually reaching 303 to Nixon's 219. Ballot counting continued for weeks in this election, which proved to be the closest in American history: less than 120,000 votes, or two-tenths of one percent, separated the contenders. The drama of the campaign's ending obscured its irresolution, its lack of focus. Kennedy had often spoken of "getting the country moving again"; now people would find out what he meant.

John F. Kennedy's New Frontier

Kennedy had no difficulty evoking a fresh vision for his countrymen in his eloquent acceptance speech to the Democratic convention on June 15. "We stand today on the edge of a new frontier," he told the delegates, "a frontier of unknown opportunities and paths—a frontier of unfulfilled hopes and threats." Nor did such rhetoric fail him during his inaugural address, one of the most stirring ever delivered. "The torch has been passed to a new generation of Americans—born in this century, tempered by war, disciplined by a hard and bitter peace, proud of our ancient heritage," he began. Although anxious to end the Cold War, Kennedy with remarkable bellicosity reminded listeners overseas that Americans would "pay any price, bear any burden" to protect the country's freedom. He concluded loftily: "And so, my fellow Americans: ask not what your country can do for you—ask what you can do for your country."

Such oratory reflected the style of a new President determined to get on with rescuing the nation from stagnation. Youth held the spotlight: Kennedy, forty-three years old, was the youngest man ever elected President; the First Lady, Jacqueline, was only thirty-one; and Attorney General Robert F. Kennedy, the President's brother, was thirty-five. The Kennedys exuded action, and all were admirers of careful, intelligent reform. The President himself com-

Pictorial Parade—Paris Match/EPA.

In May 1961, President and Mrs. Kennedy made a state visit to France. His wife's reception by the Parisians caused Kennedy to introduce himself to a French audience as "the man who accompanied Jacqueline Kennedy to Paris."

bined an articulate poise with a desire for power that bothered some. He revealed a sense of humor too often lacking in men of great power. Many observers thought that the new regime seemed more like Camelot—King Arthur's mythical kingdom of grace, beauty, and achievement—than a government. Yet the Kennedy style soon acquired substance, and for 1,000 days he and his advisers pursued a vigorous defense of America's influence overseas while grappling with obstacles to change at home.

The New Frontier quickly ran up against old traditions, especially those of a cantankerous Congress. Despite good-sized majorities in both houses, the Democrats did not control the legislature; power belonged instead to an informal, but influential, coalition of ideological conservatives from both parties. The seniority system had installed southerners in positions of great influence. Because the politics of the South remained the politics of race, these men traded votes with Republicans, thereby blocking both civil rights legislation and fiscal experiments. Most conservatives considered Kennedy more movie star than politician, an easy man to outmaneuver. Aware of the closeness of the election, the White House, for its part, had to move warily, not risking overt defeat. It concentrated on issues, like defense, for which it could expect cooperation from Congress. Overseas military aid programs and augmented military budgets passed with heavy margins. Predictably, Kennedy acted most confidently in foreign affairs, where restraints were far fewer. On most domestic issues, the Kennedy years became years of preparation, not achievement.

Civil rights.   Black activism had deeply affected the 1960 election. By that time, the black minority was far more powerful in urban areas of the North than in the rural South. In such states as New York, Michigan, and Illinois, city ghettos could decide traditionally close elections. Both major parties had courted the black vote, but a dramatic incident ensured most of it would go to the Democrats. On October 24 a judge sentenced Martin Luther King, Jr., to four months at hard labor for sitting-in at an Atlanta lunch counter. Kennedy immediately telephoned Mrs. King to offer his sympathy and express concern for her husband's safety; his brother Robert pleaded privately with the judge for King's release, which came the next day. The Republican candidate, Richard Nixon, ignored the episode. Although most blacks probably would have voted Democratic anyway, Kennedy's electoral popularity in black areas surpassed even Truman's, in some precincts reaching near unanimity. This lopsided support provided his margin of victory in Illinois, Michigan, and South Carolina. America's oldest minority anticipated a prominent place in the New Frontier, for the success of organized protest during the fifties had prompted "a revolution of rising expectations." Humiliations no longer need be endured. Now they could be ended.

But President Kennedy responded to these new black attitudes slowly. His brother did encourage voter registration drives in the South and voluntary reform in private business. And executive orders did finally end discrimination in areas of undisputed federal authority, particularly employment and housing. But the White House did not press Congress for a new civil rights act. Kennedy thought such a move would hamstring other parts of his legislative program to which he gave a higher priority. Without strong presidential succor, liberal Congressmen could never overcome their southern opponents. Kennedy appointed some blacks to high government positions; as circuit court judge he appointed Thurgood Marshall, whom President Johnson later made a justice on the Supreme Court, and as head of the Housing and Home Finance Agency, Robert Weaver, whom Johnson chose as the first black cabinet officer when the agency was given cabinet status in 1965. Kennedy also appointed George Weaver to be Assistant Secretary of State and Carl Rowan to be Deputy Assistant Secretary of State. Kennedy's program, however, like the NAACP's continuing legal battles, seemed more symbolic than real, more political than permanent.

Impatient blacks refused to compromise their expectations. More and more of them repudiated evolutionary prescriptions and took up direct action, even though such efforts often provoked white anger or officially sanctioned violence. An organization to contend with de facto segregation in northern cities, the Congress of Racial Equality (CORE), sent "Freedom Riders" into the South during the summer of 1961 to challenge discrimination on buses and trains. After mobs in Montgomery, Alabama, had set on the interracial teams and Mississippi police had arrested hundreds more, Attorney General Robert Kennedy ordered federal marshals to protect them. The Interstate Commerce Commission, prodded by the President, forced desegregation in interstate vehicles and terminals. Also during 1961, the newly organized Student Nonviolent Coordinating Committee (SNCC) initiated local community action that usually resulted in jail terms for its organizers but in a new sense of unity and hopefulness among young blacks.

Building on lessons learned during the Montgomery boycott, Martin Luther King, Jr., involved his Southern Christian Leadership Conference (SCLC) in a few massive projects, hoping to focus national attention on specific abuses. The NAACP, too, became more militant. When the University of Mississippi refused to enroll James

Meredith, a black air force veteran, the organization's state secretary, Medgar Evers, sought federal help. But Governor Ross Barnett defied a circuit court order, arguing that a state could reject any federal action it thought illegal. When Kennedy sent thirty thousand troops to Ole Miss to assure Meredith's admission and reassert federal supremacy, a mob ran amuck: in one night, two died and seventy were injured.

The struggle for racial equality raised the nation's conscience, especially during the twelve months from mid-1963 to mid-1964. During April of 1963, the SCLC launched massive demonstrations against unfair employment practices and segregated public facilities in Birmingham, Alabama. "If we are arrested every day, if we are exploited every day, if we are trampled over every day," King had once said, "don't ever let anyone pull you so low as to hate them. We must . . . have compassion and understanding for those who hate us." His formula of passive resistance worked. Despite large-scale arrests, the marches continued; on May 3, 1963, Birmingham city police, under orders from their chief, "Bull" Connor, attacked the crowd with dogs and high-pressure fire hoses. After some whites bombed SCLC headquarters and several of its leaders' homes, riots enveloped the black ghetto. These events, televised into living rooms in the North and West, sickened the rest of the nation, prompting sympathy protests at home and direct criticism abroad. The murder of Medgar Evers by white extremists, who shot him in the back while he was walking up his driveway, further intensified the nationwide clamor. Demonstrations held all over the country called for an end to southern barbarity, more job opportunities for minorities, and abolition of de facto segregation in housing and education.

Unable to ignore the rising protests, President Kennedy called on the country to face its "moral crisis" and submitted a strong bill to end segregation in public places. Then in August 1963, the March on Washington for Jobs and Freedom enlisted over 200,000 people in a giant demonstration for equality of opportunity. The acknowledged leader of black protest, Martin Luther King, Jr., stirred the crowd, and sensitive Americans everywhere, with an impassioned plea for a peaceful, integrated society. "I have been to the mountaintop," he said, "and I have a dream." All black organizations, the nation's major churches, and powerful labor unions galvanized civil rights into a cause with a broad political base. Despite this concerted effort, for months Congress debated inconclusively, arguing whether equal public accommodation would infringe private property rights and whether forcing compliance with integration laws by withdrawing federal funds from local agencies was constitutional.

President Kennedy's assassination in November produced a wellspring of emotion to memorialize him with passage of the civil rights bill, a sentiment his successor, Lyndon B. Johnson, used to good effect. Sure of his persuasiveness on Capitol Hill and certain of victory in the coming presidential election, Johnson, aided by Hubert Humphrey in the Senate, skillfully outfoxed opponents. In June 1964 he signed the most powerful civil rights act yet passed by Congress: discrimination in public places became a crime; federal agencies would protect the right to vote; the government would supervise employment practices; and, most important, the President could impound federal money from any agency—state and local governments as well as private businesses engaged in public contracts—that countenanced segregation.

New economics. When Kennedy entered office, the national economy had been stagnating for six months, signaling the onset of yet another "Eisenhower recession." In 1962 one of the worst stock market crashes in the twentieth century aggravated fears about the country's economic health, especially in Europe where America's increasingly adverse balance of trade provoked the first of a chronic series of speculations against the dollar. To stimulate domestic production and ease the nation's economic malaise, Kennedy used fiscal policy—government spending and the taxing power—rather than the more conservative monetary controls, which regulated the supply of currency in circulation. His advisers outlined a "new economics" of the multiplier effect: initial federal outlays would generate future private expenditures several times over. Spending on the space program, for example, would stimulate the growth of other space-related industries, which in turn would create jobs, thereby increasing consumer spending, and so forth. By mid-1962, however, increased business failures showed that economic recovery had slackened; even an 8 percent tax credit on capital spending and revised depreciation schedules could not revive it.

Eventually Kennedy, influenced by his economic advisers Paul Samuelson and Walter Heller, proposed in his 1963 State of the

Union message a $13.5 billion tax cut. Eisenhower had viewed tax cuts as a reward to industry for doing well or as a bribe to do better. But the reasoning behind this tax cut—the economic tenets of John Maynard Keynes—insisted that high taxes act as a drag on economic expansion and were required only in the midst of an "upturn" in the economy when overproduction or inflation threatened. Conservatives in Congress blocked any final action on a tax cut at the time. The liberating influences of more spendable income arrived only later when Johnson forced the "new economics" on the reluctant legislature in 1964.

By then recovery had already begun. Low federal interest rates in mid-1962 stimulated a boom in the housing industry, while accelerated expenditures on highway building, veterans' benefits, and other government procurement programs revived consumer demand. Anxious for a real rise in the standard of living, Kennedy moved forcibly to contain inflation, which he held to less than 1 percent annually. Journalists dubbed his major tactic "jawboning," for the President publicly opposed excessive price or wage increases when executives or labor union leaders ignored his private strictures. Kennedy could use the full force of government when his lobbying failed, as in the "steel crisis" of 1962.

The administration had pressured U.S. Steel and the United Steelworkers during March to sign a noninflationary contract that gave the workers only miniscule pay increases. But then, in what Kennedy thought a blatant disregard for the country's welfare, U.S. Steel president Roger M. Blough raised the price of raw steel by over $6 a ton. The President told a group of startled reporters that "a tiny handful of executives, whose pursuit of private power and profit exceeds their sense of public responsibility," show utter contempt for the interest of 185,000,000 Americans. The Defense Department announced that it would buy only cheaper steel, maybe even purchase supplies overseas; Treasury officials spoke of a tax investigation of U.S. Steel; the Attorney General began an antitrust suit. U.S. Steel and the six other companies that had followed its lead rolled back prices scarcely two days after their advance. The first great test of Kennedy's hopes for a noninflationary prosperity had been successful.

The greater vision. Kennedy entered office with ambitions to eradicate poverty and to raise America's eyes to the stars through the space program. Congress passed a significant amount of anti-poverty legislation, including aid to economically distressed areas, several housing bills, increases in the minimum wage and in social security benefits. A few antirecession public works packages became law, but the Senate scotched Kennedy's hopes for a $2 billion "standby-authority" for public works spending to counter future economic cycles.

Spending on the new space program made up for some defeats. In May 1961 the President told Congress, "This nation should commit itself to achieving the goal, before this decade is out, of landing a man on the moon and returning him safely to earth." Emboldened by the headiness of such an undertaking and spurred by Russian competition, the legislators regularly voted nearly $5 billion annually for the new National Aeronautics and Space Administration (NASA). The space program seemed pure Kennedy, somehow symbolizing the nation; a huge, arrogant enterprise, costing billions, organizing workers by the hundreds of thousands. For eight years taxpayers, bureaucrats, test pilots, technicians, and scientists struggled toward fulfilling the Apollo 11 mission, finally launched in July 1969. An almost incredulous world watched astronaut Neil Armstrong step onto the moon's surface, saying, "One small step for a man; a giant leap for mankind." The spectacular success summarized America's memories of Kennedy—his successes, not his failures.

Another legacy also reminded the nation of Kennedy's penchant for experimentation. During 1961 he created the Peace Corps, a new technique for winning friends abroad. Volunteers pledged eighteen months of service in backward regions throughout the world at nominal wages (about $75 per month). Usually young and always idealistic, "PCVs" taught hygiene in India, demonstrated fertilizer in South America, built schools in Africa. Small-scale, immediate, personal successes counted for more than the exotic confrontations of Cold War, according to Peace Corps Director R. Sargent Shriver. The new agency quickly earned a well-deserved reputation for seriousness and high purpose, although some countries, particularly in Africa, worried about the potential for an informal imperialism from these wholesome Americans who controlled the technology of development. In general, however, the humanitarian achievements of the Peace Corps enlisted thousands of self-sacrificing youths and refurbished the country's attitudes toward young people as well as

In a photograph taken by Neil A. Armstrong, Edwin E. Aldrin poses beside the Lunar Module of Apollo 11 at Tranquility Base, the Moon.

its image overseas. Above all, Kennedy had caught the temper of the American people, bringing out an idealism that, although it ultimately soured, was nonetheless genuine.

Perhaps even more than his confident innovation, the trauma of Kennedy's tragic assassination lifted him into the iconography of the nation's heroes. In order to assuage a feud between the liberal and conservative wings of the Democratic party in Texas, the President visited Dallas on November 22, 1963. As he rode through the streets there, a sniper shot and killed him. Three days of national mourning culminated when the Kennedys' small son bravely saluted the presidential coffin as he stood beside his young, widowed mother. Americans never forgot the picture, and most memorialized Kennedy with grandiose "might have beens."

The country's dreams somehow ebbed away during those last days of November. A new decade of disillusion and turmoil followed Kennedy's death, which undid many hopes of fulfilling "rising expectations." The old order seemed to respond more slowly to peoples' needs than to its own requirements for survival.

Lyndon B. Johnson's Great Society

The new President, Lyndon Baines Johnson, labored under handicaps he did not deserve: relentless comparisons with Kennedy's charisma and with the promise of the New Frontier. Yet Johnson accomplished more, largely because of his driving hopes and his legerdemain with Congress deriving from his tenure as Senate Majority Leader. Never a part of the Dixiecrat elite, Johnson battled for society's outcasts, not from a sense of duty, but from childhood memories of poverty and insecurity. No other white man did so much for the civil rights movement; no other wealthy man did so much for the poor. Johnson often recalled Franklin D. Roosevelt's words to him, "You will go far," and he energetically took up the unfinished legacy of the New Deal. A master politician, the new President became intrigued by his nearly limitless power and abilities. Johnson toyed with Washington politics as cat with mouse, but irony plagued his administration: foreign entanglements engulfed his humane vision for a Great Society.

Often invoking Kennedy's memory while reminding politicians of his anticipated reelection in 1964, Johnson moved rapidly in the twelve months following the assassination. Congress passed a civil rights act protecting minority voting rights. At the same time, he continued Kennedy's efforts at fiscal stimulants to ensure prosperity. Embracing Keynesian economics and banking on his own reputation for budgetary restraint, Johnson used, according to Eric Goldman, "every form of arm twisting known to political osteopathy" to achieve tax reduction. Accordingly, the $10 billion tax cut of 1964, which lowered the taxes of corporations and of wealthy individuals, seemed enormously successful. By year's end, employment had risen 1.5 million, the gross national product was up by $500 million, and government revenues from taxation had increased, despite lower rates.

The Tax Act of 1964 became only one of an unprecedented series of important budgetary laws enacted that year. A Higher

Education Facilities Act stimulated campus construction. Mass transit appropriations passed Congress easily. Most far-reaching of all, the Economic Opportunity Act—Johnson's "War on Poverty" —provided almost $1 billion for a three-thousand-member domestic peace corps known as VISTA (Volunteers in Service to America) to offer skills and basic education to twenty-five thousand young people; a Neighborhood Youth Corps, a work-study program for needy students; and Community Action programs.

The federal government had moved quickly and efficiently under Johnson to meet modern social problems and ease social injustices. The election of 1964 became a great mandate for the reforming President, especially since his opponent condemned "government interference in our daily lives." Then too, the campaign freed Johnson of charges that he was only an interloper in Camelot. The nominating convention became a ritual. No Democrat challenged this almost quintessential Democratic party leader. As his running mate, Johnson picked liberal Senator Hubert H. Humphrey, longtime civil rights advocate, friend of unions, and very much in the mold of New and Fair Deal politicians.

Republicans nominated Senator Barry Goldwater of Arizona, an appealing but doctrinaire man who opposed welfare payments, even social security, and the creeping socialism of public utilities; he vowed to end federal activities at the rate of 10 percent a year. Such wholesale challenges to American life frightened most citizens, now convinced that Johnson was the less "radical" of the two. Johnson trounced the Republican in the nation's largest landslide victory, earning 61.1 percent of the vote. Only five states in the Deep South went with Arizona for Goldwater.

Now secure in office, his power almost irresistible in Congress, Johnson rapidly forced through many more Great Society programs. The Public Works and Economic Development Act added $3 billion to further antipoverty efforts, and the Appalachian Regional Development Act filtered $1 billion to that distressed area. Congress also enacted Medicare (a program of health insurance for the aged), the $1 billion Elementary and Secondary Education Act, another Higher Education Act, a major housing program that granted rent supplements, and a Demonstration Cities program. Two new cabinet-level agencies, the Department of Transportation and the Department of Housing and Urban Development (HUD) focused on the new needs of America's expanding society.

But the War on Poverty succeeded only partially. Funds often proved insufficient; many programs eventually were forced to curtail their projects or discontinue operations altogether. Johnson tried to sustain both "guns and butter"—support of the war in Vietnam and of massive social services. Yet after the 1965 escalation of the Indochina war, this task became increasingly difficult. The cost of the war rose from $51.6 billion in 1964 to $82.5 billion in 1969, adding many billions to the budget deficit. Increased interest rates failed to deal effectively with inflation as business actually stepped up borrowing for capital improvements. When the balance of trade showed a deficit, foreigners wondered how the United States could pay for its excess of imports. Some, anticipating a devaluation of the dollar, drained gold bullion from American vaults.

The drawbacks of expansive government spending had been demonstrated inadvertently. According to Keynesian theory, the government should have avoided overheating the economy by increasing taxes to meet the rise in defense spending. Politically, however, it was a dangerous step: Americans would not endure sacrifices for this war. During 1967 the administration proposed instead a $7 billion income tax surcharge coupled with spending cuts; it hoped also to persuade gold raiders that the United States would seriously defend its paper currency. After seventeen months of delay, the surtax became law, accompanied by a $6 billion cut in federal spending. It was too late: the dollar remained in trouble and inflation continued.

Civil rights. At the pinnacle of its greatest impact, the black movement began to split apart under pressure from its left wing, which was committed to direct action, and its right, which wanted legal change. Martin Luther King's centrist position—mass protest to gain stronger legislation—held the unstable coalition together for a time. In 1962, under federal protection, SCLC marchers walked the fifty miles from Selma to Montgomery, Alabama, and nearly fifty thousand joined them at the state Capitol to petition for black voting rights. Johnson soon sent a strong bill to Congress. King's stirring promise, "We shall overcome," which Johnson himself used in an address to the nation, and the still fresh memory of John Kennedy convinced legislators quickly to pass the measure. The Voting Rights Act of 1965 empowered the Attorney General to send federal examiners to register black voters wherever he believed

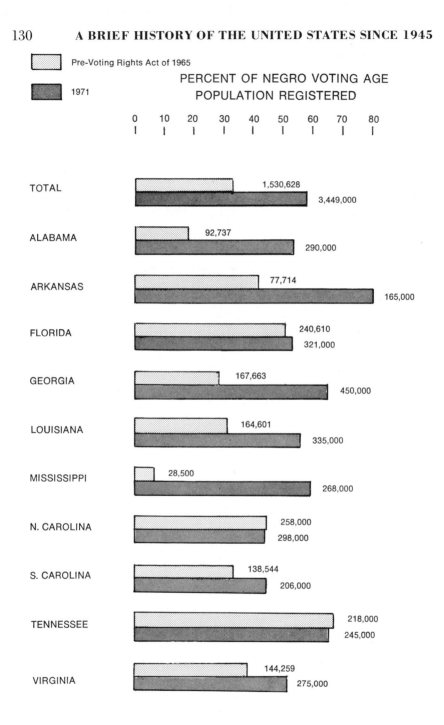

Pre-Voting Rights Act of 1965

1971

PERCENT OF NEGRO VOTING AGE
POPULATION REGISTERED

0   10   20   30   40   50   60   70   80

TOTAL — 1,530,628 / 3,449,000

ALABAMA — 92,737 / 290,000

ARKANSAS — 77,714 / 165,000

FLORIDA — 240,610 / 321,000

GEORGIA — 167,663 / 450,000

LOUISIANA — 164,601 / 335,000

MISSISSIPPI — 28,500 / 268,000

N. CAROLINA — 258,000 / 298,000

S. CAROLINA — 138,544 / 206,000

TENNESSEE — 218,000 / 245,000

VIRGINIA — 144,259 / 275,000

REGISTRATION OF NEGRO VOTERS IN THE SOUTH

Pictorial Parade/EPA.

James Meredith began a march through Mississippi in June 1966 to encourage Negroes to vote. When Meredith was shot near Hernando, Mississippi, other blacks and white sympathizers continued the march.

their rights were being abused. This important and highly effective act closed an era; legal action did not go much further.

Since blacks continued to suffer urban poverty and white hostility, more radical and more disruptive tactics soon emerged. One path led to five years of race riots in America's urban centers. Despite judicial triumphs, presidential efforts to eradicate poverty, and growing sympathy from many whites, daily life in northern ghettos mocked hopes for a better future. Black unemployment was three times that for whites; minority per capita income remained almost one-third less than the national average. Slumlords refused to improve tenements, and suburban prejudice prevented flight from the city to the suburbs. Both bigotry and fear of economic competition prompted skilled workers to preserve their lucrative jobs by restricting new members, especially blacks. Housing patterns wedged blacks into decayed, crime-ridden schools. Martin Luther King's dream of an integrated society seemed more and more irrelevant; white liberals spoke, but society did not act.

Frustration and a growing willingness to strike back fashioned race violence across the country; in 1964 a "long, hot summer" afflicted northeastern cities. It began on July 18 when New York City police officers arrested the leaders of a demonstration outside Harlem police headquarters and tried to disperse the rest of the crowd. The attempt soon degenerated into a guerrilla war between policemen and young blacks. After a patrolman shot and killed an assailant who had just lobbed a molotov cocktail at his car, Harlem residents took to the streets. For nearly a week, looting punctuated legitimate demands for a civilian review board to deal with charges of police brutality. The violence eventually petered out, and authorities adopted a few token reforms. A curiously similar pattern—incidents between police and black youths that escalated into large-scale protest, rioting, and property destruction—worked itself out in Rochester, Philadelphia, Newark, and two other cities in northern New Jersey. The FBI reported that "social and economic conditions" in the black ghettos had provoked the disturbances, but its analysis avoided the question of police culpability.

Racial turmoil became more chilling in 1965: blacks lashed out against white control of their ghettos, especially their schools and local businesses. In August, residents of the Watts district of Los Angeles rioted after renewed incidents of police brutality. This time cosmetic reforms did not placate the growing mob, which attacked white-owned property throughout the huge ghetto. Thousands of national guard troops and city police finally restored order, but only after thirty-four deaths, over a thousand casualties, and $40 million in damage.

Race riots culminated in a city that, like Los Angeles, had done much for its minorities—Detroit. During July 1967 the black ghetto erupted into days of warfare. More than forty died; hundreds were injured; fire gutted nearly a quarter of the city. Tanks and machine gunners roamed the town to attack snipers. Once again, government attributed the catastrophe to poverty and unequal economic opportunity. But, ironically, the ghettos in Watts and Detroit were relatively better off than black neighborhoods in other cities—they had more jobs, higher wages, and an open political system.

White liberals drew up more programs for reform, but events elsewhere undermined their hopes. Although Congress enacted Johnson's Great Society—vast federal projects to restore cities, build low-rent housing, retrain workers, and provide health services and education—a white "blacklash" dimmed the vision of legislated equality, and the Vietnam War robbed the federal treasury of necessary funds. This double obstacle convinced many blacks that only racial unity could wrest the American dream from white monopoly. While black conservatives sought political office, militants turned to more radical solutions. Stokely Carmichael, a SNCC leader, had sounded the alarm in 1966: "The only way we gonna stop them from whuppin' us is to take over. What we gonna start saying now is black power." At first his call evoked only a mood of resistance and minority pride. Then, as neither government reform nor direct action improved everyday conditions, the vision of an independent black existence came to intrigue many blacks, particularly the young. Political power in rural counties and urban ghettos could aid sharecroppers and slum-dwellers; black leaders must gain control over local government. Consumer cooperatives could ensure the success of black enterprise, perhaps itself communally owned. Black power advocates reinforced racial pride with such slogans as "black is beautiful," organized their own schools in the ghettos, and demanded special Black Studies courses in the colleges. Racial self-help beckoned to those who despaired that middle-class whites would ever accept an integrated society or an egalitarian economy.

If the black power movement eschewed integration, it also rejected the other half of King's formula—nonviolence. Extreme separatists, like the Black Panthers, a group founded by Huey Newton and Bobby Seale in Oakland, California, in 1966, used terrorist tactics to carve out and defend geographical isolation. Carmichael urged, "Kill the honkies," and he rid SNCC of its white members, dismissing them as "colonial administrators." His successor in SNCC, H. Rap Brown, went even further. During the summer of 1967, he urged blacks to "get your guns" and "burn whitey out." Listeners in Cambridge, Maryland, and Dayton, Ohio, apparently did just that; fires broke out in both cities hours after Brown's speeches.

The militants soon began to devour themselves in excesses (the Black Panthers, for example, of which Carmichael was also a member, expelled him as a CIA agent), and another, more productive movement temporarily displaced them. Black nationalism, particularly that preached by leaders of the Black Muslims, Elijah Muhammad and Malcolm X (who refused to use a "slavemaster's" last name), did not reject violence against whites but focused primarily on racial improvement. Condemning all whites as "agents of the devil," Muslims believed that God would resurrect blacks, who had suffered so much in this world. The sect required a puritanical, almost ascetic morality of its followers. Elijah Muhammad preached a reverse racism: no mixing of blood "with any un-alike people" and creating of a separate territory for an exclusively black nation.

Despite the allure of separatism, many blacks still dreamed with Martin Luther King, Jr., of an integrated, peaceful society of human dignity and equal opportunity. Then, on April 4, 1968, a sniper assassinated King in Memphis. The black leader was organizing a protest in behalf of striking garbagemen when James Earl Ray, possibly in collaboration with white supremacists, shot him as he stood on the balcony of his motel room early in the evening. Sorrow followed by anger swept black ghettos across the country. Despite

President Lyndon B. Johnson signs the Civil Rights Bill of 1968 in the East Room of the White House.

Pictorial Parade/EPA.

a televised appeal for nonviolence from President Johnson, riots broke out in more than forty cities. The holocaust gripped Washington worst of all: the troops that patrolled its streets could not prevent looting and widespread arson. Congress quickly passed the long-stalled Open Housing Act, which forbids discrimination in most real estate transactions. Several months later, however, the government ignored the Poor People's Campaign, a huge demonstration King had organized before his death. The Vietnam War, priorities elsewhere, and growing white backlash prevented further reform, a situation that played into the hands of black militants.

That Violent Year, 1968

Johnson's power was less solid than it seemed. The President told a labor union meeting, "You never had it so good," and superficially at least he was right. Yet many Americans resented the changes he had forced on them and the demands he had made on the country's collective psyche. Blacks anticipated equality; parents waited for their soldier sons to return home; everyone wondered whether inflation would knock down living standards. Then, too, the seams of society were weakening as more and more citizens accepted violence as a legitimate tool to challenge perceived injustices. Everything festered during 1968, the year when a presidential election should have demonstrated the government's adaptability to the new situation. Unfortunately, old institutions appeared to prove only that they were, in the then current phrase, "irrelevant." When one of America's greatest leaders, Martin Luther King, Jr., fell to an assassin's bullet, national catharsis extended far past a few moments of tears. A vague sense of doom enveloped the country: where would it all end?

Three men offered answers. Senator Eugene McCarthy of Minnesota detested the Vietnam War and the mushrooming power of the White House. A small group of renegade Democrats, led by Congressman Allard K. Lowenstein of New York, persuaded him to enter the New Hampshire primary. There, on March 15, 1968, after an unusual campaign of poetry reading, personal handshaking tours, and public musings about his philosophy, the former English professor nearly defeated Johnson, polling more than 40 percent of the vote. One day later, Robert Kennedy announced his candidacy, pledging to end the war and fulfill expectations raised by the social experiments of the mid-sixties. Kennedy won a string of primaries during the spring. Realizing that the albatross of Vietnam precluded a second term despite his magnificent domestic achievements, Johnson took himself out of the race on March 31 in a dramatic televised speech. Thereafter, Kennedy steadily gained, although McCarthy supporters denounced him as a ruthless opportunist ("Where was Kennedy in the cold snows of New Hampshire?"). Meanwhile, Governor George Wallace of Alabama, symbol of resistance to integration, attracted a different pocket of discontented voters with references to "exotic liberals" and "bureaucrats who carry their lunches to work in their briefcases."

Just after Kennedy won the California primary on June 5, virtually assuring his nomination, an assassin killed him in the Hotel Ambassador in Los Angeles. Moments earlier, he had told campaign workers, "I think we can end the division within the United States, the violence." An elaborate funeral followed only two months after that for Martin Luther King, Jr., whose plain wooden coffin was hauled by a team of mules from his father's church in Atlanta. Eugene McCarthy now appeared dispirited. Instead of campaigning, he spent days writing poetry or resting at a Benedictine monastery. He did little to rally his followers and seemed not to want the nomination. Like George McGovern in 1972, McCarthy showed that it was insufficient to have a good heart and the "right" instincts.

The nation badly needed spiritual sustenance. Hubert Humphrey, nominated easily at the Democratic convention even though he had not won a single primary, ignored the brutality the Chicago police used against youthful demonstrators at the convention and strangely called for a new politics, "the politics of joy." Richard Nixon, self-resurrected from political oblivion by years of grassroots politicking, seemed content to allow advisers to manufacture a new image of him. This "New Nixon" vowed to end the war, bringing "peace with honor," but refused to reveal his "secret plan" for fear of scuttling its usefulness. The transparent ploy bothered many voters, and after Humphrey hinted at American withdrawal from Vietnam during a speech in Salt Lake City, the smiling Democrat gained in the polls.

Nixon nearly lost a reasonably safe election. Without the third-party candidacy of George Wallace, Humphrey probably would have won since more than two-thirds of the Governor's supporters were registered Democrats. Nixon secured 301 electoral votes, but his two opponents together won 10.5 million more popular votes. Angering no one, once again running an issueless campaign, Nixon had "played it safe." The country's tensions, it seemed, would either have to go quietly away by themselves or explode in the streets.

◀ 6 ▶
FOREIGN AFFAIRS 1960-1975

ALTHOUGH THE pattern of domestic reform, consolidation, and new departure that characterized the first fifteen postwar years had repeated itself in the second fifteen years, in the realm of foreign affairs America's experience proved much different. The sixties and seventies tended to reverse rather than repeat the earlier design. Relations with the Communist powers swung through a thirty-year cycle from alliance to hostility to détente. Departing from the rigidity of the first decade and a half of Cold War, Kennedy vaguely looked for diplomatic breakthroughs that his successors, especially Richard Nixon, took up with enthusiasm and success. Western Europe moved from dependence in 1945 to self-assertiveness by 1975, while America's vaunted financial supremacy waned rather than waxed. As the rest of the world recovered from the destruction of war, America's role in international affairs took on different dimensions.

Even as Presidents met the new conditions of a changed world, America's accelerating intervention in Southeast Asia blotted out much of the nation's awareness of traditional concerns. (See Chapter 7, "Vietnam.") War in Vietnam, like Topsy, "just grew," and once grown, loomed over the country's conscience, good intentions having been distorted into dogged determination. The experiment of guerrilla war eventually backfired and, perhaps fortuitously, finally drew a boundary to America's great power.

New Frontiers Overseas

When the Democrats returned to power in 1961, the new President reoriented American thinking about the nature of national power. Argument within the party between proponents of Truman's militant, harsh prescriptions and those, like Adlai Stevenson, who favored more hopeful, internationalist alternatives was subdued when Kennedy took an altogether new tack. After discovering that its campaign rhetoric about a "missile gap" was unfounded— Eisenhower had efficiently applied America's advanced technology to strategic deterrence—the Democratic administration turned to the emerging dilemmas of the third world. A fresh phase in history was opening in those nonwhite areas of the world, mostly former colonies of western European nations. The need for modernization, particularly economic and social reform, appealed to confident New Frontiersmen, who liked to think they could generate humanitarian and material progress everywhere. Kennedy and his advisers formulated an integrated, constructive approach to foreign affairs, which also served to unify his party.

The grand design.   Afraid of Soviet expansion in the third world, liberal Democrats advocated long-term developmental aid and political support for "progressive" regimes to neutralize the impulse toward desperate measures and to mold economic growth in the shape of American capitalism. Kennedy's more militant advisers also formulated the tactics of counterinsurgency to deal with Communist-inspired "wars of national liberation," as Khrushchev called them. Sophisticated elite troops trained in political warfare would block radical violent change in the third world.

Kennedy incorporated these innovative techniques into an even larger vision. If the United States were to lead a "revolution of rising expectations," it must become economically strong at home and end embarrassing social injustices. Racial reforms would identify the United States with the hopes of nonwhites everywhere. Dynamic programs to ensure domestic prosperity might convince others of capitalism's strength. More foreign trade and lower tariffs could rectify an increasingly adverse balance of payments and strengthen America's bargaining power with a revitalized western Europe. The Democrats expected that each of the factors in their equation —counterinsurgency, developmental aid, domestic social reform, and economic integration—would maximize national power and reassert America's unquestioned leadership. The pursuit of globalism, if more complex than Truman's, was no less aggressive, no less determined.

The Alliance for Progress dramatized all the elements of Kennedy's grand calculations. To counter the appeals of Communist short-cuts to prosperity and social justice, he proposed on March 13, 1966, "a ten-year plan for the Americas." Only five months later, the nations of the New World, except Canada and Cuba, signed the Charter of Punta Del Este, and began the work of modernization. Latin Americans wanted to use the stimulant of vast credits from the United States to reform landholding patterns, diversify their extractive economies, and restore price stability. Their goal was a growth rate of 2.5 percent per year. Basic health services, minimum education standards, and decent housing would break the vicious circles of poverty and backwardness. Washington hoped that the judicious use of loans would sustain reformist regimes and break oligarchic ones.

Although apparently a perfect instrument for New Frontier diplomats, the Alliance ignored the strength of intrenched, feudal patterns and foundered native rejection of Yankee values and ways of life. Because few in Washington recognized the immensity of the task, the Alliance for Progress soon bogged down, its hopes for rapid economic growth stymied by a population explosion and a flight of local capital abroad. Similar problems also plagued the Agency for International Development, which operated in Africa, Asia, and Latin America. Increasing costs provoked congressional opposition, particularly among southern legislators already angry with Kennedy's mild racial reforms. After the Test-Ban Treaty of 1963 eased fears of Russia, liberal Democrats could not prevent major slashes in foreign aid programs.

The limits of power. New Frontier diplomacy faltered in its grand design, and grappled rather unsuccessfully with the day-to-day crises of world affairs. Kennedy soon became aware of the limits of

American power: "We must face the fact that the United States is neither omnipotent nor omniscient . . . and that therefore there cannot be an American solution to every world problem." The Bay of Pigs adventure was a chastening experience that confirmed this attitude. On taking office Kennedy did not put a stop to Central Intelligence Agency plans already underway to train fourteen hundred Cuban exiles and transport them into the Bay of Pigs, off the southern coast of Cuba. Instead, he allowed himself to be persuaded by the CIA that a disgruntled population would greet this makeshift force as liberators of Fidel Castro's regime. On April 17, 1961, the invasion began. Castro's planes, however, quickly gained control of the air and the rebels' supply ship *Houston* went aground. Havana routed the invasion within three days. Some CIA agents and State Department officials advised direct intervention then, but Kennedy rejected any use of American soldiers. Crises elsewhere precluded any major commitment, which in any case would only aggravate an already bad situation. Senator J. William Fulbright reasoned that "The Castro regime is a thorn in the flesh, but it is not a dagger in the heart." Kennedy eloquently accepted responsibility for the disaster; "Victory has a hundred fathers, but defeat is an orphan," he remarked.

Subsequent episodes in Laos and the Congo convinced Kennedy that the superpowers must seek tolerable compromises rather than ideal solutions. Worried that his decision not to commit American troops at the Bay of Pigs would encourage wars of national liberation elsewhere, Kennedy decided to foil a Communist-led guerrilla movement in Laos. Although the United States and Russia had supplied the contending sides, neither power wanted to escalate its limited commitment. Neutralization was the obvious solution, but Washington and Moscow could not control their Laotian counterparts. After fourteen months of negotiation, Kennedy finally threatened to bring in Marines. The Communist Pathet Lao insurrectionists decided to compromise, and in mid-1962 each side accepted a coalition government under Prince Souvanna Phouma and promised Laotian neutrality in foreign affairs. Even though the settlement soon collapsed—the various factions again fought among themselves and North Vietnam supplied the Pathet Lao—the Laotian tangle never again seriously disrupted relations between the United States and the Soviet Union.

Kennedy also used the complicated Congo crisis of the early

1960s to secure Russian acquiescence in a policy of limited engagement in areas outside essential national interests. Immediately after the Belgians left their Congolese colony in July 1960, the Congolese army, which was not controlled by the local government, mutinied, and Brussels sent back its troops to "protect" European lives and property. The President of the native government, Joseph Kasavubu, asked for aid to quell the army mutiny from the United States, Russia, and the United Nations. Both Eisenhower and Kennedy wanted to keep the Soviets from meddling, but they did not want to get permanently involved. So Washington supported UN action to maintain order until a viable governing coalition emerged. Then the pro-Soviet Premier, Patrice Lumumba, revolted against the central government. Although President Kasavubu captured Lumumba, who was then mysteriously murdered, the rebellion continued with Soviet help.

At this point, Katanga province, the rich copper mining area of the Congo that supplied most of the tax revenues for the new nation, tried to secede. Since its leader, Moise Tshombe, was pro-Western, his rebellion perplexed the United States. But rather than partition the Congo, Kennedy urged unification under UN auspices. This makeshift policy fell apart when neither diplomacy nor soldiers could convince Katanga to stop its revolt. Meanwhile, radical Communist propaganda attracted more and more Congolese. Finally, the UN peacekeeping force abandoned its neutrality and squelched Tshombe's regime. Throughout this labyrinthine struggle, both the Soviet Union and the United States avoided provocative action that might have escalated the dispute or involved them directly. Each country shunned victory, content simply that its opponent did not succeed.

Two crises: Berlin and Cuba.   Unlike Kennedy, Khrushchev was not ready to generalize this delicate formula as the basis of Soviet-American relations. Freezing the balance of power would favor the Americans who surpassed the Russians in conventional forces, strategic nuclear weaponry, and industrial potential. The Kennedy administration had even increased the gap, especially in elite ground forces, like the Green Berets, and in expensive technological devices, like Polaris submarines. To correct this lopsided balance, and counter hard-liners at home, Khrushchev embarked on a deliberately aggressive course. During his summit meeting with Kennedy in June 1961 at Vienna the Soviet premier refused to guarantee the status quo. Khrushchev argued that it was dangerous to oppose discontent and that his country would aid genuine popular, Communist movements. In any case, with so many third world nations experimenting with new measures of political and economic organization, no status quo really existed.

Khrushchev's determined pursuit of an actual balance of power led to two great crises, each potentially lethal. During the Vienna summit, the Russians had come close to threatening Kennedy with war if the West did not abandon its control over West Berlin. The city had troubled the Communists for years. Three million refugees, mostly young people, had slipped out of eastern Europe through this portal. Its black market drained large sums of scarce currency away from East Germany. Britain and America had poured hundreds of millions of dollars into the reconstruction of their sectors; West Berlin's prosperity hurt Soviet prestige. At the end of June 1961, Khrushchev proposed a general peace conference to divide Germany formally and neutralize West Berlin, while preserving Communist control of all access to the city. If the United States did not agree, the Soviet Union would conclude a separate peace with East Germany on these terms and support Walter Ulbricht's efforts to incorporate the entire city into his East German regime.

Determined to shore up his international credibility, Kennedy accelerated American rearmament and called up many units of the national guard. But mobilization and tripled draft quotas were only to serve a diplomatic purpose, for the President wanted to negotiate the issue. Although Khrushchev spoke of "thermonuclear holocaust" in early August, the Russian leader acted more cautiously. He sealed off East Berlin, at first only with barbed wire, but made no attempt to interfere with Western access to the rest of the city. Later the Communists built an eight-foot cement wall around their sector. Kennedy accepted the technical violation of four-power control and the compromise the Berlin Wall represented: the economic drain on eastern Europe would halt, West Berlin would remain Western. Khrushchev dropped references to a separate Russian peace with East Germany.

A greater threat against Kennedy's effort to freeze a favorable balance of power came in the fall of 1962. By the middle of October, CIA reports confirmed that Soviet technicians were building medium-range missile bases near the western end of Cuba. Kennedy and a dozen or so of his closest advisers debated America's course for nearly a week. Most of them agreed that the United States must thwart any alteration in the balance of power that might encourage more Communist advances elsewhere. Yet how should America respond without provoking war with the Soviet Union or killing thousands of people? What would the effect be on relations with Latin America? The President rejected any surprise air strike or an invasion of Cuba, largely because Robert Kennedy insisted that the United States should not violate its tradition of fair play and respect for individual life. As well as being morally unacceptable, either action might create more problems than it solved. A bombing run, for example, could miss some missiles, which panicked Cubans might then launch against American cities. But Kennedy was determined to rid the island of its offensive air weapons.

An intentional vagueness within the White House kept Soviet opponents off-guard. Then, on October 22, Kennedy announced in a televised address that he would prevent any more missiles from reaching Cuba by imposing a naval quarantine of the island. In private, the administration hinted at compromise: if Russia removed its weapons, Washington would pledge not to invade Cuba. The blockade began on Wednesday, October 24. At the United Nations, Adlai Stevenson relentlessly hounded the Soviets "to save the peace." Russian ships bound for Cuba stopped in mid-Atlantic, either to pick up a submarine escort or to await instructions. The next day, while American newspapers headlined imminent catastrophe, an official from the Soviet embassy offered to settle the crisis on the basis of Kennedy's *quid pro quo*. That evening, an emotional letter from Khrushchev confirmed this arrangement.

On Saturday, October 27, the Russian Premier abruptly demanded the removal of American missiles in Turkey. Robert Kennedy told the Soviet Ambassador that "the point of escalation is at hand" but preferred compromise. Once the Cuban problem was settled, the United States might "reconsider" the question of the Turkish bases. Meanwhile, the President had replied officially to Khrushchev's first message, ignoring his intervening proposal. On Sunday morning, the Premier promised to withdraw all offensive weapons from Cuba, a process completed in three weeks despite Castro's protests. The United States vowed never to invade, nor help others to invade Cuba. Several months later, the White House quietly dismantled obsolete missile bases in Turkey.

Contemporary critics and a few later historians faulted Kennedy's use of national power during the Cuba crisis. They accused him of needlessly risking nuclear war over what was, they argued, only a question of prestige. Missiles close to the United States would not have seriously disturbed the strategic balance, since bombs from central Asia threatened American cities just as much as from central Cuba. In fact, the nearby rockets might actually swing American public opinion in favor of meaningful disarmament talks. Kennedy's defenders challenged each point. Given America's strategic superiority, the Soviet Union would risk only bluster, not war. Castro's revolution, if protected by Soviet power, might spread throughout Latin America, undermining America's hegemony there and checking the Alliance for Progress. Then too, the Russians could not guarantee that Castro would not launch his missiles. Nuclear rockets in Cuba required only thirty minutes to reach most of America's major military bases, thus tipping the balance of mutual deterrence that prevented overt Soviet challenges to American power. That Khrushchev went so far as he did proves the seriousness of the situation Kennedy faced, these defenders argue, and the need for strong measures.

Rapprochement. Whatever the larger implications, Kennedy's elegant diplomacy during the Cuban missile crisis had left open a path of retreat for Khrushchev without sacrificing American national interests. The episode clearly bothered the Russians. Whether their aggressive thrusts in 1961 and 1962 resulted from a desire to improve the East-West balance of power, to test a new, young President, to counter Chinese criticism of Moscow's faintheartedness, or to excuse domestic failures with foreign triumphs, Khrushchev spoke for all the Politboro when he candidly admitted that "if [the United States] is now a paper tiger, it has atomic teeth." China's recent behavior added to the Russians' leaders troubles. During the fall of 1962, Mao Tse-tung had attacked India, overrun Tibet, and built missile installations and atomic plants in Sinkiang. Against the rhetoric of an ideological debate between an "opportunist" Moscow and an "irresponsible" Peking, Sino-Soviet differences widened into an hostility of "two revolutions, two leaders, two empires, and two races." Russia cautiously turned once again toward détente with the United States.

The Kennedy administration, scared by the nuclear confrontation over Cuba, more than ever desired a stable relationship with the Soviet Union. On June 10, 1963, during a commencement address at American University, the President called for a peace of mutual tolerance. Polite courtesies turned into concrete rapprochement during the summer. A direct telephone wire, the so-called hot line, linked Moscow and Washington, a testimony to their mutual responsibility for world peace. On July 25, 1963, Russia, America, and Britain initiated a Test Ban Treaty, which forbid atomic testing underwater, in the atmosphere, or in space. (The agreement did not cover underground tests because the Soviets vetoed necessary on-site inspections.) Although some Senators opposed ratification, Secretary of Defense McNamara insisted that from a military point of view, the treaty actually prolonged America's technological superiority.

Kennedy hoped that the two powers could agree tacitly not to challenge each other's vital interests. But prospects for such a détente succumbed with Kennedy's death and Khrushchev's enforced retirement. Yet the impulse toward coexistence survived because everyone realized that hostile, ruthless competition was suicidal and in fact unnecessary. Both countries sought peace and world stability; mutual security required mutual respect, not the absolute insecurity of nuclear confrontation. More crassly, the Soviet Union found that it could not challenge America's overwhelming military, political, and economic dominance, at least during the early 1960s.

LBJ's World

Kennedy's legacy, however sophisticated, did not long survive. His successor, Lyndon B. Johnson, altered policy in a number of areas. Military force more and more substituted for accommodation with local realities in the third world. In the Congo, for example, Johnson backed the once-shunned Tshombe, the Prime Minister of Katanga province, in his efforts to exterminate Communist rebels. This blatant interference—almost a half billion dollars equipped Tshombe's mercenaries—angered Africans everywhere and critically embarrassed the United States when his army, under General Joseph Mobutu, overthrew the civilian Congolese government on November 25, 1965.

Washington's maneuvers also soured in Latin America. The Alliance for Progress, already in trouble in the face of complexities and congressional penury, nearly collapsed when the President resorted to armed intervention in the Dominican Republic. During April 1965 a leftist military clique ousted the ruling Cabral regime, which almost two years earlier had itself overthrown the constitutionally elected Juan Bosch. The new coup wanted to restore Bosch, but a conservative military faction under General Elias Wessin-y-Wessin took to the streets. When the pro-Bosch group seemed about to establish its authority, Wessin appealed to the United States. Apparently under the impression that only the Marine Corps could prevent "another Cuba," Johnson dispatched a large contingent to "protect American lives and property." The next year, with eight thousand troops still present, the Dominicans elected a moderate government, and Bosch left for Spain. The episode aggravated Yankee-phobia throughout the western hemisphere and tarnished hopes for cooperative reform there.

The fragile Soviet-American détente faltered as well. The rest of the world refused to submit to a bipolar system run by the two superpowers for their own benefit. Moreover, the lessening of tension between the two giants crumbled the cement that had held both East and West blocs together. Moscow's effort to construct a self-sufficient trading area in Communist Europe distorted local development. Discontent spread when Russia imposed its own oppressive political and cultural uniformity on the variegated region. In 1968 the Czechs revolted rather than submit to further economic exploitation and political rigidity. Only the Red Army managed to hold the country in Russia's empire. Even more serious was the virtual collapse in Sino-Soviet relations. Angered by Mao's accusation that they had betrayed the world revolution to pursue national interests, the Soviets began to talk about a preventive strike to knock out China's nuclear capacity in Sinkiang. Extensive border clashes, sometimes involving thousands of soldiers, broke out in Manchuria during 1969. Instead of challenging the West, the Soviets turned toward these more immediate problems within the Communist bloc.

Meanwhile, America's prestige in western Europe shattered. Endemic strategic and economic conflicts, more than Washington's irrationality in Asian jungles, struck at North Atlantic unity during the 1960s. Regionalism created an alternative to the Atlantic partnership. Ever since the mid-1950s, France, Germany, Italy, and the Benelux countries had moved toward economic integration. The six countries merged their coal and steel resources into a "Common Market," thus accelerating production while thwarting future German rearmament. By 1957, the same nations had broadened the arrangement to include other products, primarily heavy manufactures and raw materials. Dreams of common monetary and foreign trade policies and hopes for the free flow of labor and investment became realities during the next decade. Although open to all countries, the European Economic Community (EEC) did not for many years include England. London preferred to organize its own trade association with Scandinavia and Portugal, one that would not interrupt its economic relations with the British Commonwealth. Then too, most continental powers, especially France, feared British overlordship and rejected its bid to join in 1965. Despite this temporary setback, the development of a strong Common Market accelerated dissatisfaction with America's parochial military policy and political aims.

Invigorated by a new constitutional order, the Fifth Republic, and a strong President, Charles de Gaulle, France led the movement toward regionalism. De Gaulle wanted to dismantle the bipolar world and reestablish a European system, which France would dominate. Fearing that Washington would sacrifice French interests to superpower amity, de Gaulle took France out of the NATO alliance and built an independent nuclear force. The success of his policy depended on West German support. Although Kennedy and Johnson wooed Bonn with plans for a multilateral nuclear force (MLF), East-West détente had eroded Germany's fear of Russian attack, the basis for its docile reliance on Washington. De Gaulle cleverly pointed out that unification of Germany was impossible so long as America dominated western Europe. A German understanding with Russia would open up markets in eastern Europe for the Rhineland's industries. That Bonn responded more to this vision of the future than to Washington's reflected Germany's national interests, not de Gaulle's theatrics nor America's preoccupation with Vietnam.

The Johnson presidency curiously distorted American foreign policy. Although the new chief executive trumpeted his desire to continue Kennedy's programs and in fact rehabilitated his predecessor's languishing domestic social and economic reforms, he drastically altered Kennedy's approach overseas. An imperial vision returned, and with it a growing readiness to solve complex

political dilemmas by military force. His deepening, almost bewitched involvement in Southeast Asia halted the movement toward
multipolarity. America's concern for western Europe and Russia, its
central national interests, waned. The East-West détente did not
progress toward arms limitation or increased trade. Washington
somehow felt that the Soviets should facilitate peace in Vietnam,
but Moscow could neither dictate to Hanoi nor abandon a Communist regime. America's outsized commitment did ease Russian
diplomacy elsewhere, however, especially in the Middle East, and it
deflected China from its Russian borders to tend its southern frontiers.

Johnson also ignored rising tensions within the NATO alliance
and the erosion of America's financial hegemony over the capitalist
world. Unlike the arrested détente with Moscow, which could be
revived, the disintegration of the Atlantic partnership, particularly
its economic crisis, was cumulative and perhaps irreversible. The
Vietnam imbroglio, as with all self-righteous blunders, tallied great
costs. Grandiose aims and military solutions reversed two decades
of evolutionary adjustment.

Nixon and the New World Order

If Johnson had sown the wind, his successor, Richard M. Nixon,
reaped the whirlwind, not only in Vietnam, but in Europe and
throughout much of the third world. The breakup of tightly controlled blocs, together with America's preoccupation in Vietnam and
Russia's concern with China, created a new maneuverability for
middle-sized powers. Israel had already shown the way during its
six-day war against the Arabs in 1967. The nuclear countries would
not risk atomic war to reverse a *fait accompli*. Five years later, in
1972, in response to threatening army maneuvers, India attacked
Pakistan and converted Bangladesh, its populous eastern province,
into a client state. Once again, neither the United States nor the
Soviet Union dared to become directly involved. In 1974, the
"superpowers" could only preside nervously over a renewal of
Greece's struggle with Turkey for control of Cyprus.

In Latin America, where many people looked for an alternative to
both Castroism and capitalism, Chileans elected a Marxist President, Salvador Allende, in October 1970 to begin the work of peaceful, democratic reform. Although plagued by strikes and attempted

coups, Allende's regime slowly chipped away at Chile's poverty and the power of an almost feudal landowning class. But when rising prices threatened middle-class living standards, the usually quiescent military overthrew the regime in September 1973. One month later, Argentina tried to narrow the gap between rich and poor by restoring former dictator Juan Perón, although his unexpected death the next year obscured the country's eventual course. Clearly, the western hemisphere no longer blindly followed Washington's prescriptions and, like more and more of the third world, defined their own future.

A sense of waning globalism pervaded the Nixon administration. Republicans dismantled Truman's dream of a prosperous West-European–East-Asian bloc supported by United States military and economic might. They really had no choice, for the imperial impulse had fallen apart. Vietnam corroded America's self-righteous mission to remake the world in its own image. But if the frustrating, ultimately unsuccessful war shortened Washington's reach, Vietnam did not precipitate a retreat into isolation. President Nixon and his adviser on foreign affairs, Henry Kissinger, who became Secretary of State in 1973, ended ideological diplomacy and relied on a more realistic appraisal of national power. They argued that America should participate in, not dominate, world events. Parity, not superiority, would guide military policy. The administration returned to the traditional concerns of American diplomacy —the Atlantic alliance and the problems of East-West détente.

The Atlantic alliance.   While careful diplomatic maneuvers plotted rapprochement with a mellowing Russia and a still militant China, more immediate economic pressures forced the new administration to deal with an endemic monetary crisis and redesign relations with western Europe. The United States had financed its postwar hegemony on credit. Although the country always exported far more than it imported, military expenditures and overseas investment created extensive deficits in the balance of payments. From 1950 to 1972, U.S. gold reserves declined more than 50 percent to less than $10 billion. Because American gold and American commercial debts were the only major source of liquid capital in the world, many governments used dollars as reserves against their own currency. Central banks discounted dollar obligations and thereby created immense sources of capital for private European banks. Such

"Eurodollars" financed the continent's economic revival. Rather than suffer a paper loss on the value of their dollar reserves or restrict domestic credit, most nations supported the dollar throughout the 1960s. The United States acted, in effect, as a world bank, supplying currency in payment for foreign goods.

Unfortunately, after 1970, war-induced inflation struck at America's ability to sell high-priced products abroad; instead, Europe had to inject more and more paper dollars into the world economy. Too much of a good thing forced some countries, like West Germany, to revalue their currencies upward in an effort to discourage American buying. Although Nixon apparently hoped that Japan and England might also adopt this solution, both countries flatly refused. The Japanese did not even maintain the yen's convertibility, thus trapping American assets abroad and further aggravating the monetary pinch. Domestic deflation would have remedied the situation, but the Republicans could not even balance the budget or halt price rises. Nixon finally devalued the dollar by nearly 20 percent in two stages, increased tariffs, and sold surplus goods at bargain prices to raise foreign exchange. Since inflation continued and overseas military spending actually increased, a speculative raid against the dollar developed during 1972 and 1973 that drove the price of gold to three times its official valuation in the United States, a grim vote of no confidence in America's financial future.

The monetary crisis heightened European nationalism. Although student riots had brought about de Gaulle's resignation in 1969, they could not destroy his regime. The new premier, Georges Pompidou, continued an independent foreign policy, particularly with China and the Middle East. France, along with West Germany, dominated the Common Market. The combination of newfound prestige and prosperity sustained the Gaullists in power until 1974, and even influenced their more conservative successors under Valery Giscard d'Estaing to continue evolutionary domestic reform and an expansive foreign policy.

Germany's gross national product reached $6,600 per capita in 1972, the world's highest. For the first time in more than a century, the Germans were on good terms with the French. Then Socialist Chancellor Willy Brandt launched *ostpolitik*, a careful effort to repair relations with Russia and open up eastern Europe for German exports.

Bonn established diplomatic relations with East Germany in 1972 and later recognized Poland's frontier at the Oder-Neisse line, thus settling old disputes with Warsaw and Moscow.

At the same time, Britain abandoned its world role and became a regional power. Prime Minister Harold Wilson trimmed imperial obligations east of Suez during the late 1960s. After tedious negotiations, Britain joined the Common Market in 1972. While gaining access to Europe's markets, England lost its preferential trading system with the Commonwealth. Edward Heath, the Conservative Prime Minister who presided over the historic change in British policy, argued that membership would stimulate manufacturing and reduce unemployment. England's nuclear armaments freed Europe from dependence on Washington, and the new economic unit of the Common Market was the world's most powerful, both financially and productively.

The Nixon administration reacted slowly to these trends, if only because it could hardly stop them. The President's visits to western Europe and Romania in 1969 were symbolic gestures to register America's hopes for economic détente with its allies and political détente with its opponents. But dramatic events elsewhere always postponed any serious reconsideration of general European policy. Relations within the Atlantic community remained cordial, but a new era had dawned. In 1973 the long-awaited European Security Conference convened, with NATO, neutral, and Communist countries present. Its goal, a continental peace cemented by close economic ties, would permit Russia to concentrate on its China problem and western Europe to escape American tutelage. Although Nixon grandiloquently dubbed 1973 "The Year of Europe," a tacit recognition of previous neglect, Watergate scandals cut short a portentous beginning during his summit meeting in Iceland with Premier Pompidou. Chancellor Brandt's visit to Washington later in the year ended inconclusively, largely because of continued economic differences. America's relations with western Europe were always friendly, but the mid-1970s repeatedly confirmed that divergent interests had dulled the former comradeship.

Détente.   The United States and Europe may have drifted apart, but the Republicans revolutionized America's dealings with its most dangerous opponents, Russia and China. Severe tension, even open fighting between the two Communist nations, facilitated the new departure, since Moscow and Peking feared each other more than they did the United States. Nixon returned to the devices of summit diplomacy and personal, heavily publicized state visits, pursuing regional balances of power. In Southeast Asia, America demon- strated its resolve to remain a Pacific power, but gradual troop reductions in Vietnam foreshadowed both Washington's future re- straint and a settlement ultimately acceptable to the Communists. Preparations for the Strategic Arms Limitation Talks (SALT) con- firmed Russian-American intentions to avoid mindless escalation of omnipotent terror; the purchase of vast stocks of American surplus wheat with Soviet gold illustrated the benefits—and pitfalls—of cooperation. Although the Vietnam War postponed the thaw in rela- tions, Nixon's trips to Peking and Moscow in 1972 not only an- nounced détente but also reconciled the American people to a radi- cal change in their foreign affairs.

The route to the Communist capitals was tricky and always un- certain. During 1970, when relations with the Soviet Union momen- tarily soured over another crisis in the Middle East, Nixon signaled a new interest in China. He began to refer to the "People's Repub- lic," not "Red China." The two powers set up a private line of communication through their Polish embassies. In 1971, Nixon eased trade and financial restrictions against China and talked more and more openly about his desire to visit Peking. Kissinger met secretly with Premier Chou En-lai in July, and the President an- nounced that he would travel to the People's Republic within the year. Months of small courtesies followed. When Chinese ping-pong players decimated American amateurs, the good will flourished. Nixon shook hands with Mao Tse-tung in Peking on February 22, 1972, and for the next seven days carefully controlled festivities with Chinese officials, although not with the Chinese public, ended two decades of mutual neglect.

While television sets in the United States reported every cere- mony and unquestionably strengthened Nixon's image as a world statesman, negotiators privately reorganized the basis of Sino- American relations on present realities, not past animosities. The United States accepted Chou's contention that Chiang Kai-shek's island refuge, Taiwan, was an integral part of the People's Repub- lic; in return, the Chinese tacitly agreed to negotiate a solution and not to incorporate the province forcefully. Although American troop withdrawals from Vietnam had already reassured Peking's leaders,

Chairman Mao Tse-tung, President Richard Nixon, and Henry Kissinger confer during Nixon's visit to China in February 1972.

Nixon pledged that "foreign domination shall never be visited upon any independent country in this world," a formula that satisfied America's fears about the future of Indochina and China's anxiety about Russian aggression. Indeed, both powers vowed that neither "should seek hegemony in the Asia-Pacific region and each is opposed to the efforts by any other country to establish such hegemony."

This self-denying ordinance ratified the Nixon-Kissinger commitment to a multipolar future, but the dangerous reality of superpower confrontation between the United States and the Soviet Union still dominated the present. Both nations had more to gain from cooperation than from hostility: stability would not only ease nuclear terrors but also strengthen their diplomacy elsewhere. Yet the Moscow summit between Nixon and Brezhnev could not wipe out the past. Meeting daily from May 22 to May 29, 1972, the two leaders found no compromise concerning Vietnam or reciprocal trade relations. Several proforma treaties concerning joint ecological and space projects lent an aura of substance to an otherwise unproductive summit. The two nations agreed to disagree, but each recognized that the more complex world of the 1970s required mutual tolerance for its rival's legitimate national interests.

The first concrete sign that the United States had accepted a less expansive role in world affairs came during the SALT talks. An arms race could have undermined the tenuous nuclear parity established between the two superpowers during the sixties, especially if a technological breakthrough by one side upset the stability of mutual deterrence. The never-never-land quality of SALT calculations aimed at balancing offensive weapons—a trade-off, say, between the multiwarhead (MIRV) Soviet super-missile, the SS-9, and America's similarly equipped submarines, like the Trident II. A system like antiballistic missiles (ABM), which could defend against these offensive weapons, would upset the balance. Thus the Moscow Agreement of 1972, which President Nixon signed during his summit talks, outlawed extensive deployment of ABMs.

Negotiations resumed in November 1972 on the much more difficult task of equalizing the Soviet's superior ICBMs (intercontinental ballistic missiles) against America's more sophisticated MIRVs. Reconciling domestic military bureaucracies proved as difficult as compromising international stalemates or technical problems. Yet SALT became an ongoing process that itself stabilized relations. Brezhnev visited the United States in 1973, and Nixon returned to Moscow for Summit III a year later. Neither meeting brought an arms agreement, but a steady flow of ritual treaties—cosmetic agreements about cooperative cancer research and a joint space launch, for example—reinforced the notion that even if solutions never came on greater issues, the Cold War had changed into a cold peace.

Republican foreign policy in the Middle East.   Nixon-Kissinger diplomacy and the enforced lessons of Vietnam pointed to a less grandiose future for the United States, but to one perhaps more consonant with its national interests. Multipolarity and economic diversity had erased the simpler imperial years; now Washington would seek to protect, not propagate, the American way of life. As formerly unified blocs disintegrated, Nixon and Russian leaders faced potent challenges closer to home.

While the Soviets eyed China and America struggled with unexpected economic limitations on its global power, the third Arab-Israeli war broke out in October 1973. Although some evidence indicates that Russia may have encouraged Egypt and Syria to regain military territory occupied by Israel since 1967, Moscow refused direct aid after Jewish soldiers quickly surrounded Egypt's Third Army on one front and seemed ready to take Damascus, Syria's capital, on another front. After Washington supported Israel, the Arabs boycotted all shipments of crude oil to the United States and western Europe, hoping to isolate Israel diplomatically.

Anxious to end a blockade that threatened economic chaos or worse, and realizing that Russia's on-again, off-again policy had discredited Moscow among most Arabs, Kissinger took up a virtuoso shuttle diplomacy. After six months, culminating with thirty days of constant travel, he produced a disengagement on both fronts by May 1974. The Arab embargo ended. When Nixon visited all three countries the next month, he promised each peaceful aid, including nuclear technology. Clearly, the United States had reoriented its Middle Eastern policy, treating equally both Arab and Israeli, in hopes of upholding its prestige and guaranteeing its oil supplies from the area. Détente with the Communists not only liquidated the bipolar world of the 1950s, but also permitted a more flexible pursuit of national interests.

◄ 7 ►

VIETNAM

THE KISSINGER-NIXON reorientation of America's foreign policy responded partly to the needs of a changing world and doomsday technologies, but especially to the nation's ten-year war in Southeast Asia. That ultimately frustrating conflict challenged America's long-proclaimed mission to spread liberal government and a humane capitalism throughout the world. This far-away war also questioned the parameters of power, the morality for propriety of ground combat against guerrilla warfare and air assaults against more primitive societies. America lost a sense of innocence in Vietnam's unfamiliar rice paddies. Many wondered whether domestic upheavals simply mirrored the ritual violence of a televised war, and whether an increasingly meaningless struggle sapped the country's moral strength. The war in Vietnam called into question America's purpose, its power and prestige, and eventually even its belief in itself. Asian jungles provided the stage for a nation's coming of age.

France and the First Indochina War
France first entered the Indochina peninsula during the 1850s and subsequently colonized it for French aggrandizement. In 1930 a

group of dissatisfied intellectuals and leftists among the small native middle class was organized as the Communist party by Ho Chi Minh. When they called for land reform and rebellion against the French, France ruthlessly suppressed the group within a year. During the Japanese occupation of Indochina (1940–45), however, Ho created a united front of anticolonialists, the Vietminh. In August 1945 revolution spread across the country. The Vietminh formed a provisional government, and Ho declared an independent republic, using Thomas Jefferson's famous Declaration as his text.

Although President Franklin D. Roosevelt had favored the principle of colonial self-determination, he did not oppose the demand of the Fourth French Republic under General Charles de Gaulle that all former French territories be returned after the war. In the last months of 1945, Anglo-French occupation troops installed a puppet cabinet in Saigon. Instantly the Vietminh launched a guerrilla counteroffensive in what soon became a war of colonial reconquest. Dreams of empire and a belief in its military superiority misled France into repudiating a compromise agreement worked out with Ho in early 1945 and launching what became the first Indochina war. This military offensive developed in two phases. From 1947 to 1950 France committed hundreds of thousands of soldiers and vast amounts of scarce materials, but Vietminh dominance in the countryside and the Communist control of the nationalist movement survived. In its second phase, which ended in 1954, the entire complexion of the war changed. Vietminh military strength grew while desperate French generals took increasingly ill-advised risks to defeat the guerrillas. Paris no longer justified the war in terms of colonial restoration but as an anti-Communist effort in support of the "legitimate" government under Emperor Bao Dai. Yet, France still refused to grant political independence or to begin economic reform—further undermining the Emperor's credibility, already strained by his transparent acquiesence to French policy. Meanwhile, more and more nationalists joined the Vietminh as the only alternative to collaboration.

With Mao Tse-tung's victory over Chiang Kai-shek and the appearance of the People's Republic of China in late 1949, Washington's disinterest in Indochina suddenly ended. President Truman was determined "to block further Communist expansion in Asia." Accordingly, in February 1950, the United States extended massive military aid to the French. The National Security Council justified the new policy largely in terms of the domino theory: if Indochina were "lost," Thailand would be next; if the Communists succeeded in Southeast Asia, they might then reach out either for India or for the rich islands of the Pacific. Remembering the fall of Austria, Czechoslovakia, and other European countries to Hitler after Britain tried appeasement in 1938, diplomats too easily substituted communism for fascism and Asia for Europe. American leaders believed the best way to defeat the Vietminh would be to set up a non-Communist nationalist regime, but Paris always rejected any compromise that might risk its future control over Indochina. Because he needed French support in European affairs, Truman reluctantly financed the French against the rebels.

Contradictions plagued Western goals, and frustrations soon blocked their military efforts during the last four years of the first Indochina war. French generals found that superior firepower and orderly combat were of little use against guerrilla forces who knew the land and fought a slow war of attrition. France's armies could not control the countryside or even move very far from the main roads. After eight years of steady attack, the insurgents still held their stronghold in an area north of Hanoi and Haiphong. Late in 1953 General Vo Nguyen Giap moved the bulk of his Vietminh forces toward Laos in an attempt to win territory and lure French divisions under General Henri Navarre away from their coastal redoubts. Certain that he could at last trap the Communist main army, Navarre converted a small frontier outpost at Dien Bien Phu into a major fortress, concentrating nearly twenty-five thousand of his best troops there. He built an airstrip to supply the fort and set up massive artillery batteries. In spite of such preparations, not only did Giap's forces still outnumber the French two to one, but also with the aid of China and thousands of Vietnamese who backpacked ammunition into the remote area, the Vietminh assembled superior firepower around the hills of Dien Bien Phu. Bombing strikes could not destroy the well-hidden Communist embankments, which soon knocked out the French airstrip. Giap slowly encircled the outpost with trenches, and during the first week of May 1954 the garrison fell to his army. France had gambled that a dramatic victory would demoralize its enemy; instead, the unexpected disaster ended any hopes for a French military conquest.

Enter the U.S.A.

The Eisenhower administration seriously considered a tactical air strike to save Dien Bien Phu and active intervention to bolster the entire French effort, which it accepted as an anti-Communist campaign. Murmurs from Britain and opposition from important Congressmen, including Senate Majority Leader Lyndon B. Johnson, shook the President's resolve, but Republicans abandoned a direct military commitment only after the French government itself refused to go on with the war. In the meantime, the powers involved in the Indochina imbroglio—France, Britain, Russia, China, the United States, and representatives of Ho Chi Minh's Hanoi-based government and Bao Dai's puppet regime—had already agreed to negotiate a settlement.

The 1954 talks in Geneva became increasingly complex: Britain and Russia were most concerned about France's future military role in Europe; China hoped to secure international respectability; America's sulking Secretary of State, John Foster Dulles, did not want to compromise at all, certain that the West should, and could, defeat the Communist guerrillas. Surprisingly, after only six weeks, the powers reached agreement, largely because the Soviet Union and China forced Ho Chi Minh to accept Western terms for the independence of the three Indochinese states of Laos, Cambodia, and Vietnam. None of the new states was to permit foreign troops or bases on its soil or to join outside alliances. Vietnam itself, temporarily divided into North and South at the 17th parallel to facilitate military disengagement, was to hold nationwide elections within two years that would determine the country's permanent political future.

This outcome satisfied neither Dulles nor Eisenhower. The Secretary of State had already vowed "to do everything short of belligerency" to save Vietnam, or at least part of it, from communism. Refusing to ratify the Geneva Accords, Washington launched the search for a non-Communist alternative that was to hypnotize three subsequent administrations. The State Department announced that the United States would treat North and South Vietnam as independent, separate entities. Then, in September 1954, Dulles negotiated the Southeast Asia Treaty Organization (SEATO), a milder version of the European NATO alliance, since it pledged action only "in accord with constitutional process." The original signatories, France, Great Britain, the United States, Australia, New Zealand, the Philippines, Pakistan, and Thailand, later agreed to protect Cambodia, Laos, and South Vietnam—none formally members of SEATO. Convinced that disengagement would mean the gradual fall of all Southeast Asia to communism, Eisenhower shipped vast economic aid to the native, but increasingly elitist, South Vietnamese leader, Ngo Dinh Diem, who had become President after Emperior Bao Dai was deposed in 1955. In 1956 the administration unofficially backed South Vietnam's official break with the Geneva settlement. Dulles gave explicit approval for Diem to call off elections, which the nationalist Communists would have won, and to organize a separate government. This series of actions irrevocably committed Washington to defend the new anti-Communist state, but the gamble seemed worth a limited risk.

At first, the new nation appeared altogether viable. Between 1954 and 1957, generously financed by America, the country made substantial economic progress and even achieved some land reform. Diem suppressed gangsterism in Saigon and brought the religious sects under control, many of whose leaders had set up independent fiefdoms in the countryside. Lyndon Johnson even thought that Diem might become "the George Washington of South Vietnam." But Diem never attained broad popular support, and his regime adopted increasingly repressive tactics: his own henchmen replaced local village elders, a relocation program was launched that degenerated into political witchhunts, and land redistribution schemes were sabotaged in favor of absentee landlords. In particular, Diem's Catholicism alienated the predominately Buddhist nation, especially its intellectuals, and his dependence on the United States angered nationalists.

Predictably, Diem's oppressive policies provoked a new revolt. Led by Communists, the National Liberation Front (NLF) linked together South Vietnamese natives who opposed Diem. They called for land reform, democratic government, and local village rule, but at first their activities did not seriously threaten the Saigon regime. By 1959, however, widespread frustration with Diem's dictatorship, together with surreptitious North Vietnamese support for the rebels' military force, the Viet Cong, had reversed the situation. Only billions of American dollars and a growing corps of American advisers fended off popular discontent and maintained the ruling clique in Saigon. Washington could not push reforms on Diem, for he only met American requests with threats to turn the country over to the

Viet Cong. So American aid to Diem escalated, and Hanoi strengthened its support to the insurgents, primarily by training recruits. Then, after completing the first phase of its industrial program in early 1960, North Vietnam sent more and more materials south along the famous Ho Chi Minh Trail through Laotian mountains and Cambodian jungles.

By the end of the 1950s, the Eisenhower administration had dispatched some eight hundred Americans to Vietnam. Although Eisenhower "could conceive of no greater tragedy than for the United States to become involved in an all-out land war in Asia," Dulles announced that "the free world would intervene in Indochina rather than let the situation deteriorate." If American troops did enter the battle, he pointed out, "our prestige would be involved to a point where it would have to obtain victory." The President managed to avoid being caught in this trap of self-justifying war, but his Secretary of State had foreshadowed the obsessive certainties and inevitable escalations of the 1960s. Eisenhower himself found no solution to the puzzle, which his successors attempted to solve by sending in more and more American troops.

Crisis in South Vietnam

In the early sixties Diem's government became weaker still. Efforts at modernization ceased and even retrogressed as he pursued an unchallenged power. His regime had aggravated the political situation in the countryside, and its persecution of Buddhists crystallized opinion against him in Washington. The ruling family persuaded the legislature to pass laws requiring Buddhists to obey Catholic religious laws. Beginning in May 1963 the Buddhists organized strong protests, culminating in self-immolations, which Diem's sister-in-law, Madame Nhu, dismissed as "barbecues." Diem's brother led attacks on Buddhist temples and pagodas throughout South Vietnam in August in a futile attempt to curb their growing popularity. These raids alienated the urban middle class, most other religious sects, and intellectuals everywhere. Clearly the United States had to abandon Diem. Secretary of State Dean Rusk wired the American Ambassador in Saigon that Washington would support a coup that had a "good chance of succeeding," a blatant interference in the affairs of a sovereign state. Accordingly, Ambassador Henry Cabot Lodge actively collaborated with a cabal of generals who, acting on their own, assassinated the President in October and set up a new government under Major General Nguyen Khanh.

The overthrow marked the "Americanization" of the Vietnamese conflict: an American goal, a non-Communist South Vietnam, rather than the need to settle internal differences now dictated the purpose of the war effort. Leaders in Washington and their agents in Vietnam acquiesced in, and perhaps abetted, the military coup against Diem not because he was corrupt but because he was ineffective.

Despite such unsavory events, America's commitment had grown imperceptibly. Saigon's excesses spurred thousands of southern insurrectionaries to join the NLF and to take the trek north for military training. In response, the Kennedy administration sent artillery and fighter-bombers to South Vietnam, then more and more American advisers—fifteen thousand by 1963. Washington also approved a clandestine war against North Vietnam. Kennedy ordered secret agents to sabotage lines of communication around major urban areas. Amphibious landings and military raids against North Vietnamese territory and Communist outposts in Laos took place under American direction and sometimes included American soldiers. Initially, these tactics appeared successful: in 1962 the Viet Cong suffered a temporary setback.

Kennedy's Commitment

Once well established as the principle, American aid and troop support could hardly be held in check, either in size or purpose. Apparently aware of the open-ended nature of his decision, Kennedy compared sending soldiers to Vietnam with having a drink: the effect wears off and you have to have another. Then too, by 1963 sixty Americans had died in Vietnam. Those who advocated further escalation could employ the effective argument of redemption: for what had these men died? Certainly Kennedy had doubts, insisting shortly before his assassination, "In the final analysis it is their war." His apologists insist that he would have avoided a full-scale conflict.

But Kennedy had also remarked that America's withdrawal would mean the collapse of Southeast Asia. The war in Vietnam served ideological purposes; it would demonstrate to the Russians that wars of national liberation, in Chief of Staff Maxwell Taylor's words, were not "cheap, safe, and disavowable," but "costly, dangerous, and doomed to failure." Yet counterinsurgency required native support, and the Kennedy administration concentrated instead on military victory.

By November 1963 when President Johnson took office, he had few political alternatives. He inherited not only the war itself but also Kennedy's principal advisers on foreign affairs. The United States had some sixteen thousand troops in the country, and South Vietnam's new government depended completely on American economic and military aid. Yet the Diem crisis might have presented a final opportunity for disengagement. Attorney General Robert F. Kennedy urged such a course during a cabinet meeting, and *Time*'s editors suggested the possibility of neutralizing all of Southeast Asia. But Secretary of Defense McNamara and General Taylor had visited Vietnam in September and told Kennedy on October 2 that much of the American task there would be completed in fifteen months. They guessed that perhaps a thousand troops could return home by the end of the year. With a relative hiatus in Cold War confrontations elsewhere freeing the nation to act in Southeast Asia, pursuing the war seemed practical, prudently weighing cost against advantage.

Johnson and Indochina

Johnson himself approached Vietnam on the basis of his knowledge of the Second World War and Korea, and he quickly identified the problem as one of halting aggression. America must assist the South Vietnamese, he said in 1964, "to win their contest against the externally directed and supported Communist conspiracy." Contrary to views expressed by later critics, this confusion over the nature of South Vietnamese politics was no willful misconception, but a simple determination "to protect our interests and keep our promises." This equation of American interests with "taking a strong stand" pointed toward self-perpetuating war, and neither Johnson's advisers nor Washington's bureaucracy interrupted this momentum.

The past also haunted Johnson. The Kennedys had esteemed success and an aggressive style; nay-saying became an admission of a faint heart. Perhaps a vigorous effort in Vietnam could redeem the drabness and failure of Cuba, Laos, and the Congo. Then too, government itself was not neutral. Senior officials guarded the reach and prerogatives of their agencies; middle-level workers followed orders. If a policy decision went against the military, for example, generals often leaked their side of the problem to allies in Congress or to the press. In this seductive situation, bureaucratic gamesmanship compounded wishful thinking at the White House.

The second Indochina war. Circumstances in both the United States and South Vietnam during 1964 made inevitable the beginning of the second Indochina war. Diem's disastrous legacy of unresolved problems, together with his elimination of political opponents, created a political vacuum in South Vietnam. While a musical chairs of military juntas undermined the anti-Communist effort, the Viet Cong made rapid, large-scale gains. In response, Washington became more and more interested in bombing North Vietnam as a substitute for the unsuccessful counterinsurgency campaign in the South. Johnson found a pretext for such an attack in the Gulf of Tonkin crisis of August 1964. The covert Kennedy war against North Vietnam had included secret operations, code-named 34-A, against shore installations. American-supported Saigon forces had just completed one such raid when the spy-ship *Maddox* violated the twelve-mile limit claimed by Hanoi in the Gulf of Tonkin. North Vietnam, probably assuming the destroyer part of the 34-A raid, sent several torpedo boats into the area. The *Maddox* fired on the approaching North Vietnamese ships, which then returned several volleys. Two days later, on August 4, as the *Maddox* and another destroyer, the *C. Turner Joy*, cruised in the same general area, they reported a second attack. But intense darkness and malfunctioning sonar and radar equipment may have made overanxious naval captains only imagine this second "attack," which may have been simply a North Vietnamese scouting mission. In any case, no evidence proves an attack took place.

President Johnson publicly denounced this "unprovoked aggression" and used the mood of crisis to extract approval from Congress of a document (written many months before) that came to be called the Gulf of Tonkin Resolution. It authorized "all necessary measures" to check further Communist advances. Lacking full knowledge of events in the South China Sea and sharing the President's misconceptions about the situation in Saigon, a nearly unanimous

Senate adopted the de facto declaration of war, 88-2. Only two members, Senators Wayne Morse of Oregon and Ernest Gruening of Alaska, questioned its ultimate purpose or the advisability of such an open-ended commitment.

Freed of domestic restraints through a dramatic gesture demonstrating internal unity, the administration further Americanized the war. During the last months of 1964, Pentagon and White House officials debated whether to bomb North Vietnam on a regular basis. Initially the United States had announced a "reprisal policy": American planes would attack North Vietnam only after a specific incident. The first such reprisal had come on August 5, 1964, when the air force bombed PT boat bases in the North after the naval clash in the Gulf of Tonkin. But as military effectiveness in the South steadily deteriorated, the administration reversed itself and relied more and more on systematic air attacks against North Vietnam as a substitute for direct attacks against Viet Cong units in the South. In an even more curious reversal, nearly everyone in Washington now assumed that the Communists must be destroyed before Saigon could begin major reforms, whereas it was economic and political abuses that sustained the Viet Cong rebellion. Both contradictions stemmed from a subtle alteration in America's purpose: the war in Vietnam was now a test of the credibility of America's global anti-Communist mission.

The 1964 presidential election reinforced everyone's confusion. Johnson postured as a peace candidate, calling his opponent "trigger happy," even while he himself was planning major escalation. Few Americans then understood the sinister implications of White House delusion or even cared very much about Vietnam.

By January 1965 the Democrats had molded the policies and attitudes that would escalate the war to include United States ground combat troops, all-out air attacks on North Vietnam, and consistent rejection of diplomatic compromises. On one level, planners anticipated that an extensive use of GIs would improve morale in South Vietnam and might perhaps bring a military victory there. Johnson also hoped that the conflict would "contain" China and prevent an Indonesia–North Vietnam–China–North Korea bloc that might slowly squeeze the United States out of East Asia. On another level, however, the President justified the war more and more for what might be called its "demonstration effect." The United States must at all costs avoid defeat, not only to prevent the dominos from falling in Southeast Asia, but also to convince Communists everywhere of America's resolve to deter aggression. The conflict thus transcended Vietnamese issues and became a crusade for indeterminate, almost mystical goals. Yet wars of national liberation generally break out because of domestic failures, not as the result of intrigue by a Communist world conspiracy. Johnson's growing obsession with South Vietnam did more to disturb America's allies than to reassure them.

While Washington's soldiers and diplomats sought victory, South Vietnam itself degenerated into chaos. Disagreements over military tactics and economic policy continually widened fissures in the junta that had replaced Diem. Even after two generals, Nguyen Van Thieu and Nguyen Cao Ky, emerged on top, the regime continued to ignore land reform and the social tensions that fed the Viet Cong insurgency. Diverted by the chimera of military success, both the junta and the U.S. command could never strike at the causes for Communist strength in the countryside. On the other hand, Johnson rejected the quick, massive attacks against North Vietnam and the Viet Cong advocated by the Joint Chiefs of Staff as dangerously provocative to China. The President anticipated that a calculated, steady increase in force would convince both opponents that they could not win. In February 1965 he ordered sustained bombing of North Vietnam, ostensibly in reprisal for a Viet Cong attack on American installations at Pleiku. He poured more and more combat troops into South Vietnam to protect marine and army outposts and to aid Vietnamese units threatened by attack. Johnson then authorized independent action by American units; the first "search and destroy" mission involving large numbers of United States soldiers took place June 27-30, 1965, several miles northwest of Saigon.

Quagmire. Washington planners soon discovered that America was not omnipotent. No one had foreseen the massive troop needs in Vietnam; everyone underestimated the enemy's ability to build up reserves of men and materials; guerrilla methods bewildered commanders trained for large-scale wars of maneuver. Experts began to argue that American forces would have to outnumber Viet Cong–North Vietnamese troops by about ten to one. Yet every time Washington increased its effort, so did the enemy. Overly optimistic reports from political and military advisers buoyed up hopes for a

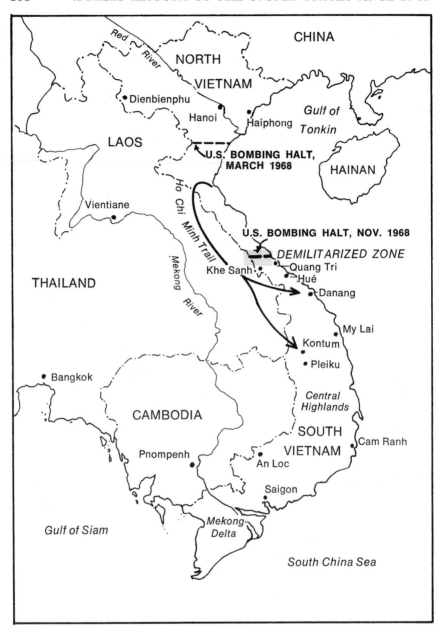

VIETNAM

solution by force, however, and Johnson pressed on in an ever-widening war during 1966 and 1967. A mystique of nomenclature sustained the illusion of force: "body counts" replaced territorial control; enemy dead somehow proved that the United States, in Johnson's words, "was winning the hearts and minds of the Vietnamese people." The "slow squeeze"—Pentagon jargon for the narrow band of force necessary to defeat little Communists without provoking big ones like China and Russia—replaced traditional military doctrine and ruled out diplomatic compromise. Secretary of Defense McNamara consulted his computer and its statistics. Every day he divined victory from "kill ratios," the "cost effectiveness" of bombing runs, and colored graphs that quantified political support in the villages. But no amount of creative accounting could change reality. By early 1968, Hanoi had fielded roughly 135,000 men in the South; the United States about 550,000. Yet double that number would be required just to offset Hanoi's troops, and the bulk of enemy strength came from Viet Cong units within the South.

Determined to "negotiate from strength," the President rejected early opportunities to meet the enemy at the conference table. As early as July 1964, U Thant, Secretary General of the United Nations, suggested reactivating the Geneva Conference. The French, now under de Gaulle's shrewd leadership, quickly agreed, as did the Soviet Union, North Vietnam, and Communist China. But Johnson, fearful that a conference might restrict his options, answered, "We do not believe in conferences called to ratify terror." Only nine months later, during a speech at The Johns Hopkins University, he apparently relented. The United States would attend a peace conference and speed plans for an Asian Development Bank to rebuild Southeast Asia. Johnson did sincerely hope for peace, but not if it meant jeopardizing the war's demonstration effect. His continued demand for a non-Communist regime in Saigon was tantamount to a North Vietnamese–Viet Cong capitulation. When the Communists repeatedly dismissed Johnson's efforts to achieve at the bargaining table what he could not win in the field, the President interpreted each rebuff as further "proof" of aggression.

Such naivete eventually turned into cynicism, most vividly exposed by the thirty-seven day bombing pause against North Vietnam in December 1965 and January 1966. To check critics at home, Johnson ordered a halt to the air war and sponsored a far-flung diplomatic offensive. Yet the President's closest advisers realized

Photo by Ghislain Bellorget. Black Star.

Soldiers of the 173rd Airborne Division in action near Saigon in 1967.

that his terms remained those of victory, not compromise; he undertook the charade largely to justify renewed escalation since the
"Rolling Thunder" bombing operations had not materially impaired
Hanoi's ability to make war. When bombing resumed in February
1966, ostensibly because Ho Chi Minh refused to negotiate, its purpose had changed: the air force would dam the flow of supplies from
the North to the Viet Cong rebellion rather than attempt to knock
Vietnam out of the war. At the same time, Johnson dramatically
escalated the ground war. For nearly two more years, the world
witnessed America's effort to save a country from communism by
destroying it.

As he sought a will-o-the-wisp victory, the President encountered
two other obstacles: the Saigon dictatorship, whose existence
mocked his concern for a democratic, progressive regime; and a
swelling tide of discontent within the United States. At a meeting

with Thieu and Ky in Honolulu during February 1966, he extracted promises that the Saigon junta would begin social reform. The problem required delicate diplomacy, for if Johnson threatened to cut off American aid to force compliance, the two Vietnamese leaders could abandon the nation to the Viet Cong. The generals remained the President's only option. When the massive United States build-up of 1966 temporarily eclipsed Communist progress, the junta permitted nationwide elections for a Constituent Assembly. Unfortunately, they rigged this "constitutional convention": no Viet Cong delegates attended, and the generals quickly asserted their personal control over the new government apparatus. Reinforced by Johnson's eagerness for military victory, President Thieu and Vice-President Ky ignored rural complaints, and their rule grew increasingly arbitrary.

Johnson was able to smoke-screen reality in South Vietnam, but domestic opposition proved less malleable. Although most Americans at first had accepted this latest military crusade, the public never understood its larger purposes, and events soon soured even their illusions. Americans began voicing frustration at the inconclusive struggle. The more the United States bombed North Vietnam, for example, the more Ho dispersed his industry, infiltrated the South, and whipped up war fever. Fears about reactions in Russia and China may have prevented an assault against the major port, Haiphong, but even its complete destruction would not have ended the Viet Cong insurgency. Strategic bombing could not alone force a military decision, nor could the air force interdict supplies flowing south along the Ho Chi Minh trail. This route was a path, not an Interstate highway; its location, even its existence, was largely problematical. Since the bulk of war material moved at night in small vehicles or on human backs, American "damage" could be easily repaired or simply avoided.

The ground war, despite repeated reinforcements, was as frustrating as the bombing. By 1968 half a million troops guarded major cities and rural outposts; yet the Communists still controlled most of the countryside. When American units fanned outward on a search and destroy mission, Hanoi's regulars avoided combat and Viet Cong guerrillas simply hid among the population. Vastly improved "kill-ratios" could not offset Communist recruitment and North Vietnamese infiltration. Johnson's program to win the people of Vietnam ideologically was no more successful. To pacify the countryside, Washington planners fashioned the strategic hamlet program. Troops would move into a village and protect it by building a fort and garrisoning it with soldiers. Although the tactic protected inhabitants from Viet Cong attack, the spectacle of farmers living under American guns in barbed-wire enclosures provoked memories of concentration camps, not visions of a free, democratic state. Both political and military victory seemed to elude American armies.

As these frustrations caused public support for Johnson's crusade to wither, a growing protest movement questioned its larger purpose. In 1967 Senator J. William Fulbright, chairman of the Foreign Relations Committee, and the one who had guided the Gulf of Tonkin Resolution through the Senate, attacked "the arrogance of power" in the administration. "Power," he observed, "tends to confuse itself with virtue." America's history gave the United States a dangerous sense of omnipotence and self-righteousness, he believed, which, at its worst, had resulted in the terrifying miscalculations of Vietnam. Bureaucratic "world-saving" in Asia assumed that Western institutions and political methods could soothe the tensions created when an alien culture experienced rapid modernization. If Fulbright and other liberal critics worried about mistaken purpose, a mushrooming antiwar coalition questioned the war in moral terms. During October 1967 at a rally in Washington, 200,000 Americans marched against the war. An important part of the Democratic coalition had rejected Johnson's leadership and the war fueled the growth of a vigorous left, which threatened to destroy the party.

Tet, de-escalation, and Vietnamization. During 1968 public pressure and a military emergency forced Johnson to change his techniques, though not his anti-Communist objectives. Most Congressmen and senior officials realized that the United States would not be able to win the war in Vietnam for many years, if ever. Bombing had only strengthened the enemy's resolve to fight. North Vietnam was probably the most stable country in Southeast Asia. An army of willful peasants operating without an air force or heavy artillery had confounded traditional military techniques. The Americans, it seemed, were in serious trouble.

Then, during the Tet new year celebrations, Viet Cong units attacked some thirty major cities throughout South Vietnam on the night of January 29. Saigon and the American embassy nearly fell;

Communists occupied the former capital, Hue, for several days. Their troops, who accomplished the mission in secrecy and with dedication, contrasted with President Thieu's inept forces. "It was," as the Chairman of the Joint Chiefs, Earle Wheeler, said, "a very near thing." Only a brutal counteroffensive restored the cities to allied control. Tet marked a new threshold of violence and cruelty. The Communists slaughtered thousands during their brief occupation of urban areas and dragooned hundreds of villagers into their guerrilla army. Americans, frustrated by the failure of mechanized combat to secure conquered territory, more and more made war on the people of South Vietnam.

Faced with an altogether new situation, General William Westmoreland, the American military commander, immediately flew to the United States and asked for 200,000 reinforcements. This action prompted a major review of policy in Washington. The President could not order seven more divisions to South Vietnam without endangering American commitments elsewhere and producing severe monetary and fiscal strains on an already taut domestic economy. Johnson would have had to mobilize the reserves and increase taxes, both steps requiring congressional consent. He knew that neither the legislators nor the general public would acquiesce in such drastic measures. At this stage the President also seems to have realized the futility of escalation. When General Westmoreland explained that he could not guarantee victory even with the additional troops, Johnson replied, "Then where will it all end?" Seeking an answer, the President entrusted the search for an alternative, for "the lesser of evils," to a study group chaired by a personal friend, Clark Clifford. Since no military victory was in sight, the Clifford committee focused on Secretary of Defense McNamara's proposal for a negotiated settlement, which included a coalition government for South Vietnam.

The drift toward compromise intensified as the United States Army itself balked and home front sentiment grew decidedly antiwar. Demoralization in the military found expression in two divergent forms. The disaster of Tet created near hysteria among some military men and cultivated a need for revenge, for some sort of victory. General Westmoreland, when asked about the huge civilian casualties resulting from indiscriminate bombing and shelling, replied, "Yes, but it does deprive the enemy of the population, doesn't it?" Since "body count," not territory, defined the terms of war in Vietnam, the step to the mass murders at the South Vietnamese villages of My Lai and Song My was short. Here and elsewhere company commanders like Lieutenant William L. Calley, Jr., and their troops lost all sense of proportion and inflicted atrocities on the civilian population not revealed to the American public until three and four years later. But the sense of frustration also led to withdrawal and to breakdowns in discipline of another sort: widespread drug use, slacking, desertion, and even occasional mutinies mirrored the growing malaise.

Meanwhile, domestic events further narrowed Johnson's options. Early in March 1968, antiwar presidential candidate Senator Eugene McCarthy carried more than 40 percent of the vote in the New Hampshire Democratic primary, a stunning rebuke to an incumbent President. The next day, Senator Robert Kennedy began his campaign for the nomination and pledged to end the war, calling it "immoral and intolerable to continue." Intellectuals like George F. Kennan thought Johnson was "in a dream," while Max Lerner bluntly concluded, "To fight a war of corpse statistics on Asian terrain, with China's endless millions in the background, is to move ever farther away from the world of reality." Soon the party abandoned the man who had led it to a landslide victory four years earlier. On campuses throughout the nation, protests against the war became more and more unrestrained. A need to unify his party and the country convinced the President not to escalate again.

In a dramatic television appearance on March 31, 1968, Johnson officially announced a change in his tactics. First, Westmoreland would receive only one-tenth of his recent request, or twenty thousand troops. Second, to signal its intent of serious peace negotiations, the United States would halt bombing north of the 20th parallel. And finally, to reinforce his sincerity, the President declared he would not run for reelection. South Vietnam would progressively take over active prosecution of the war, an approach President Nixon later dubbed "Vietnamization." Unfortunately, a desire for victory still flawed Johnson's impulse toward compromise. The President believed that the Tet offensive had severely weakened Communist ground forces and that a new spirit of efficiency in South Vietnam would enable the Saigon regime to defeat the Viet Cong insurgency. He did want to negotiate, though not along the lines suggested by McNamara. His acts—the de facto limit on American troops, the bombing restriction, and the beginning of

Vietnamization (Thieu promised to conscript 135,000 additional troops)—moved toward peace, but an American peace for an American objective: a non-Communist South Vietnam.

Negotiations begin. To insure that the bombing would stop and probably to see what sort of deal the United States contemplated, Hanoi replied favorably to Johnson's offer for talks. For several weeks the two opponents debated an appropriate site for the negotiations, each advocating a city where local feeling would support its position. Hanoi finally suggested Paris, presumably to take advantage of de Gaulle's growing anti-Americanism. World opinion favored this site, and Johnson could not refuse. On May 10, 1968, peace talks opened at the Majestic Hotel, with Xuan Thuy representing Hanoi and W. Averell Harriman, a former ambassador to Moscow, leading the United States delegation.

For five months the diplomats deadlocked over a question of timing. Thuy insisted that meaningful talks could begin only after Washington pledged not to resume bombing raids against North Vietnam. Johnson had his representatives counter that he would continue attacks across the Demilitarized Zone (DMZ) to protect American troops and asserted that the question of permanent cessation of the raids should be part of a settlement. The President repeatedly called for "reciprocity" from Hanoi—a mutual winding down of the war and coexistence between the Thieu-Ky regime and the National Liberation Front. Slowly Johnson came to understand that since the United States, not North Vietnam, wanted to compromise, he could not insist on reciprocal concessions. By mid-October 1968, however, Harriman and Thuy had worked out an arrangement: the United States would halt all bombing north of the 17th parallel, and Hanoi would "by its silence" allow the Saigon regime a part in the negotiations and would not increase its aid to the Viet Cong.

In an attempt to boost Hubert Humphrey's chances in the November presidential election, Johnson planned to announce this settlement, but he reckoned without his South Vietnamese allies. Thieu wanted to destroy the Communists, not deal with them. Mindful of its precarious control, his regime maneuvered to prevent any agreement between Hanoi and Washington that might reduce American aid. Thieu also apparently believed that he could get better terms from a Republican administration. Stymied by Thieu's reluctance to join multilateral talks, Johnson announced the total bombing halt anyway. This obvious disunity among allies cast a cloud over Harriman's fledgling settlement. After Nixon's victory in November, a long struggle over minor procedural details—including the shape of the bargaining table—dominated the Paris talks until February 1969. Leaving his successor with a war and an undiluted commitment for a non-Communist South Vietnam, Johnson also left him a diplomatic tool, the Paris peace talks, and a military weapon, Vietnamization, to pursue that commitment.

Nixon and Indochina

Nixon used both tactics, but changed the objective. The new President and his foreign affairs adviser, Henry A. Kissinger, wished to come to terms with the Communist world, not to challenge it. Vietnam blocked détente. Kissinger argued that the United States should simply withdraw, insisting only on a "decent interval" before the South Vietnamese replaced the unpopular Thieu. Nixon disagreed; he believed that American power could still force a compromise that would allow Thieu a "good chance" of permanent survival. For the next four years, the administration practiced both diplomacy and Vietnamization; Nixon reinforced South Vietnam's self-sufficiency with massive American military and economic aid, while Kissinger pursued peace directly with North Vietnam and the Viet Cong at private meetings in Paris. Yet this double-edged method of extricating America from the Vietnam War still represented an effort to forestall other wars of national liberation and restore America's prestige rather than deal with Vietnam's immediate needs.

The local realities, not America's larger goals, ultimately determined the fate of Republican prescriptions. The crass immorality and endemic weakness of Thieu's dictatorship undercut Washington's bargaining strength. War wrecked economic modernization. The regime alienated peasants and cynically exploited urban poverty. Land redistribution programs were in near collapse. Inflation reduced city-dwellers to frustrated insecurity, dependent on the unpredictable spending of Americans. To prevent desertion, conscripted Vietnamese soldiers were sent far from home, but provincial troops fought only sluggishly, if at all, in unfamiliar regions. Thieu maintained his power only through political suppression:

"tiger pens" (make-shift jails dug in the ground) silenced opponents, a palace guard terrorized the national legislature, censorship muzzled the press. A once politically sophisticated people lapsed into existential quiet. America's client simply had no internal support.

The Nixon Doctrine. Nixon tried to preserve South Vietnam from external threats, but growing American discontent defined the limits of his assistance. In 1969 he had announced the Nixon Doctrine: American support but not American men would block further Communist advances in Asia. This promise of "no more Vietnams" did not satisfy many citizens more anxious for peace than for an American victory. Even though he cavalierly dismissed massive public protest marches during October and November 1969, opinion polls showed that "Middle America" no longer supported apparently futile slaughter. The administration decided to begin a steady withdrawal of American ground troops at an average of about twelve thousand per month. (The last American combat soldiers left South Vietnam in 1973, the same year that conscription ended in the United States.) At the same time, Nixon improved the quality of whatever military forces were left in South Vietnam and stationed a vast naval fleet in the China Sea and an air armada in Thailand. American money financed a huge expansion of Thieu's army. He achieved his purpose, for the decrease in combat troops ameliorated domestic unhappiness with the war, while American firepower— and American expenses—actually increased. Nixon thought that these more unobtrusive devices, together with whatever combat soldiers remained in Vietnam, could force an acceptable compromise from the Communists.

During March 1970 a coalition of Cambodian generals under Lon Nol overthrew the neutralist government of Prince Sihanouk. Nol immediately asked for American aid against North Vietnamese infiltrators who had repeatedly violated his country's neutrality by supplying the Viet Cong via the Ho Chi Minh Trail. The southern guerrillas themselves often retreated into the sanctuary of Cambodian neutrality when hard-pressed by American or South Vietnamese troops. Nixon ordered ground attacks on Communist supply depots in Cambodia and air raids against the Ho Chi Minh Trail on April 30, 1970. American and South Vietnamese troops stormed into the Fishhook and Parrot's Beak regions of Cambodia. Although they captured vast amounts of supplies, the soldiers failed strategically, unable to find Communist headquarters or engage the insurgents' "main force." Material losses may have delayed further enemy attacks, but the month-long incursion did not prompt the Communists to negotiate.

In the United States, meanwhile, widespread student strikes protested the invasion and condemned Nixon's demagogic vow, "I will not be the first American President to lose a war." Stung by public rebuke, Nixon pledged not to send American soldiers on offensive missions outside Vietnam again, a decision reinforced by the collapse of morale within the army itself. Less than a year later, however, during February 1971, U.S. forces aided a Vietnamese invasion of Laos, again in search of supplies and elusive enemy divisions. This attack too foundered; newspaper photographs showed panic-stricken Vietnamese soldiers rushing for safety aboard American helicopters. The military option to give Thieu "breathing space" disintegrated.

Henry Kissinger and Le Duc Tho.   Nixon turned to his other tactic—negotiation in Paris through Henry Kissinger. The sometimes flamboyant former professor had reached a compromise with his North Vietnamese counterpart, Le Duc Tho, on a wide range of issues, including a cease-fire, mutual withdrawal of troops, prisoner exchange, and free elections. But Hanoi, having countered America's thrusts in Cambodia and Laos and about to launch its own counterattack, insisted on the removal of President Thieu. Despite months of patient bargaining, Kissinger could not modify this demand, which would have robbed the United States of any semblance of success. The impasse reflected a central dilemma: if Thieu remained, his dictatorship would subvert any "free elections," but if he left, the Communists, the only organized political party, would dominate the country.

Once again, each side resorted to military measures. At the end of March 1972, General Vo Nguyen Giap—the same man who had defeated the French almost eighteen years earlier at Diem Bien Phu—committed 90 percent of his troops to a triple-headed invasion of South Vietnam. The Communists quickly captured Quang Tri province in the North and threatened Hue; another thrust toward Kontum nearly split the South in two, while the third attack overcame An Loc, only thirty miles from Saigon. Immediately, Nixon resumed heavy bombing of military targets in North Vietnam, but the advance continued so rapidly that by May it seemed possible that the invaders might conquer all South Vietnam. Meanwhile, Kissinger reported that his private talks in Paris remained deadlocked. Determined that the United States would not become a "pitiful, helpless giant," the President mined North Vietnamese ports and increased bombing even though most military targets were already destroyed.

Hanoi, too weak to carry on without continued help, realized that it must negotiate only when the Russians did not call off the planned Soviet-American summit. Accordingly, private talks again resumed in Paris, but Le Duc Tho seemed hopeful that he could use American dissatisfaction with the war and the approaching presidential election to pressure Nixon into abandoning Thieu. Thus, late in October, he agreed to a cease-fire, but publicly interpreted the settlement in such a way that, unless Nixon made some overt gesture, American silence would have signified the end of Thieu's regime. Despite Kissinger's emotional announcement that "peace is at hand," Nixon broke off talks and sent a vast armada of nine hundred bombers over all North Vietnam. The imminent destruction of the country convinced Hanoi to accept an American compromise: Thieu would remain but the Communists would not abandon their recent gains. Kissinger and Le Duc Tho quickly arranged a cease-fire "in place," to be supervised by an international commission of neutral powers. The peace agreement was signed in January 1973, and beginning in February, Hanoi gradually repatriated American prisoners of war as Washington withdrew its last fifty thousand soldiers from South Vietnam.

The United States and Indochina: A Balance Sheet in Red

The peace agreement did not terminate either the second Indochina war or America's participation in it. Thieu's future remained uncertain. Any coalition in Saigon required a third party, not simply an untenable compromise between the generals' junta and the Viet Cong. But six years of war dictatorship had nearly wiped out Thieu's leftist opponents and the Buddhist neutrals. Fighting continued unabated in Laos and Cambodia. Although Washington wrote off the mountain kingdom of Laos after the Pathet Lao recaptured the strategic Plain of Jars, American airpower supported Lon Nol's effort to chase the Communists out of Cambodia. By August 15, 1973, when Congress cut off funds for more bombing, guerrillas had surrounded the capital, Phnom Penh, on three sides. Yet, as happened so often before, a weakened enemy could not make a final, conclusive push, and Cambodia balanced for two more years between two forces, each on the edge of victory or defeat. The persistence of war even in South Vietnam, where repeated local violations prompted Canada to withdraw from the control commission, reinforced the impression that only the confrontation between Hanoi and Washington had ended in 1973, not the dilemmas of Southeast Asia. By fall, a too-familiar process had escalated reprisals for accidental clashes into sustained military action. Both sides in the civil conflagration—President Thieu's urban machine and Communist insurrectionaries in the countryside—proclaimed the beginning of the third Indochina war, an unhappy epitaph for America's long efforts. By 1975, more than 250,000 more people had died, and almost a million had been forced from their villages.

If indecisive in Southeast Asia, Washington's ten-year crusade decisively changed American politics, wrecked the nation's economic stability, and undermined its self-confidence abroad. During the late 1960s, the Vietnam War became to many a symbol of America's sickness, an amoral country bewitched by power, engaged in pursuing profit amid slaughter. An antidraft movement encouraged young men to resist serving in the armed forces, if necessary even to leave the country. More than seven thousand fled to Canada, and tens of thousands refused combat training, performing instead alternate, nonviolent service as conscientious objectors.

Peaceful protest, based on the war's uselessness or its sinfulness, changed to violent, left-wing dissent against liberalism. The 1968 student strike at Columbia University inaugurated an anarchic pattern. Serious rebels, whether loosely organized in local groups or part of the national cacophony of the Students for a Democratic Society, frequently abandoned "middle-class" restraints. Arson, bomb killings, and irrational hatred of authority figures soon alienated most Americans and fissured "the movement." But not before official efforts at suppression. By 1970 the process threatened to rip the country apart: protests against the Cambodian invasion triggered reprisal killings by national guardsmen and police in Ohio and Mississippi and mass marches by "hard-hat" workingmen in New

York City. The White House harassed dissenters in the name of national security; though public passions soon cooled, no one realized that President Nixon's lieutenants had adopted the disregard for the law their opponents had displayed.

The impact of the Vietnam War on America's economy proved more tangible and perhaps more lasting. Both Republicans and Democrats financed the most costly conflict in the nation's history by grand-sale borrowing, as much as $130 billion. By adding to the supply of currency and at the same time diverting industrial production into war material, the prices of consumer goods rose inexorably. More and more Americans bought cheaper foreign goods, and investors everywhere shied away from the overheated domestic economy. Government borrowing, inflated prices, and an adverse balance of trade—the first since 1945—fueled an international dollar crisis and finally forced the United States to devalue its currency 18 percent during 1971-72. But the war-induced domestic inflation could not so easily be exorcised. Distortions in the economy would require years of difficult adjustment. Events in Vietnam had affected Americans, their politics, their economics, and even their attitudes about the future, perhaps to as great an extent as the United States had altered Vietnamese history.

◄ 8 ►

POSTWAR AMERICAN SOCIETY: DIVERSITY AND CHALLENGE

MOST OF THE broad trends of American history since the Second World War tended to standardize and nationalize American life. Industry moved into almost every part of the country. Everyone watched television, shopped at supermarkets, carried credit cards. Pockets of provincial style broke down under restless migration. Yet complaints about a too homogeneous culture were overdrawn. Despite the uniformities of life, an increasing number of discreet groups emerged, bent on their own style of living, their own perception of the world, and their own politics. Affluence and the widening range of goods and services that the economy provided actually opened up new possibilities for diversity—as the teenagers of the fifties had already demonstrated.

Having feared that such currents of diversity had vanished from American life, many at first rejoiced over each manifestation that the country was less predictable than was thought. The "radical right" was one of the first groups in the postwar era to achieve notoriety for dissent from the consensus. Young radicals in the sixties also attacked that consensus from a much different perspective. Almost too quickly, however, the problem became not one of conformity, but of lack of social cohesion. The model of a conforming society was replaced by an image of America as a collection of disputing, even warring factions, divided by cultural distinctions —the long-hairs against the cops and hard hats, the "corporation liberals" against the male chauvinist establishment, the "silent majority" against vocal minorities.

Both views of American society exaggerated accurate perceptions about it. No subculture, no spokesman could speak for all women or all blacks or all members of the silent majority. And neither were we all conforming Americans trying to be as much like each other as possible. The truth lay somewhere between the two views, but only the clash of groups and the pressures of large trends in society would determine exactly where.

The Radical Right

In the thirty years following the Second World War, groups that advocated extremely conservative political philosophies or crusaded almost religiously against "godless communism" maintained varied, but constant, activity. Collectively labeled the "radical right" by scholars, such movements had deep roots in the American past, but they updated their compaigns in the 1960s and 1970s to establish a front on contemporary issues. Of the dozens of rightist groups, few achieved any notable size, and most cloaked their actions in secrecy. Yet on particular issues they occasionally exerted considerable pressure, the very existence of the more extreme cadres frightening many citizens.

The radical right was by no means isolated from certain main currents of thought in the postwar period. The national fixation with security against communism in the late forties and early fifties had lent extreme conservatives unaccustomed respectability. Congressional witchhunts, carried on by the House Un-American Activities Committee even after McCarthy's demise, contributed to irrational anticommunism. For a time, the warnings and alerts the rightist groups sounded seemed to be accepted by a sizable portion, perhaps a majority, of the American people. Speakers like Senator Thomas Dodd of Connecticut and Representative Walter Judd of Minnesota graced anti-Communist rallies of the fundamentalist crusade into the 1960s. The columnist William F. Buckley, Jr., directed a respected intelligence toward the defense of conservative causes. Within the military, many highly placed officers sympathized with the far right; one general, Edwin A. Walker, had to be dismissed in 1958 when he insisted on training his troops in extreme anticommunism. These people, and many more who simply did not resist, contributed significantly to ultraconservatism.

While older ultraright concerns like religious fundamentalism and anti-Catholicism maintained an important place in the platform of some groups, the dominating concern of most far right organizations during the sixties was the cleansing of American life from "radical" influences. They were convinced that the United States was crawling with Communists and their sympathizers, and a few even feared imminent Russian invasion. Servicemen's associations, such as the Veterans of Foreign Wars, supported readiness campaigns and promoted individual ownership of weapons. Since far-right tactics often copied military practices, some groups developed guerrilla warfare drill, using weapons along with the training methods of the armed forces. The most extreme groups gathered caches of guns and ammunition, sometimes with the help of the National Rifle Association, and made plans to resist any Communist takeover. A Baptist minister, the director of one guerrilla group that thought terrorism might weaken the morale of invaders, suggested that Communists be decapitated and hung headless in trees near highways.

The best known and perhaps the largest paramilitary organization called itself the Minutemen. Founded by Robert Bolivar De Pugh of Norborne, Missouri, in 1959, the Minutemen trained local guerrilla units and gave instruction in the use of mortars and antitank guns. To maintain secrecy, De Pugh's organization operated under a variety of names in different areas. During the early sixties, the group intermittently received unwanted publicity when discoveries of illegal weapons depots led to the arrest of many of its leaders.

The most important far-right group of the early 1960s was the John Birch Society, named in memory of the "first victim of World War III," an American pilot shot down over China while fighting Mao Tse-tung's Communists. Candy manufacturer Robert Welch founded the Society in 1958; within several years it became the most active, most efficient, and best known ultraconservative organization. The Society's income neared $2 million annually by 1963, and its well-scattered membership exceeded fifty thousand. A central office in Belmont, Massachusetts, employed forty-one staff workers; thirty-five full-time "coordinators" journeyed throughout the nation, assisted by seventy partially paid "volunteers." Several Congressmen openly boasted membership.

Welch wielded an unquestioned authority over the Society. Democracy, either within the organization or outside, was to Welch "merely a deceptive phrase, a weapon of demagoguery, and a perennial fraud." In prescribing techniques for Birchers, Welch consciously copied many of the methods developed by the Communist party. "The founder" suggested, for instance, the use of front organizations to disguise the true goals and support of some Birch Society groups. He outlined ways to heckle speakers and disrupt meetings. Birchers were told to charge publicly any suspected individual with being a Communist, regardless of his actual sentiments. Convinced that "Reds" already controlled most of the United States, Welch declared that Franklin Roosevelt had been guilty of "deliberate treason" and accused Dwight Eisenhower of "consciously serving the Communist conspiracy for all of his adult life." He even told his followers that "the largest single body of Communists in America is in our Protestant clergy." Despite ridicule and condemnation from many quarters, the John Birch Society continued to nourish a shriveled and sour patriotism into the seventies.

Groups on the far right remained alert for local battles. Afraid that Communist propaganda would convert the unsuspecting, extreme conservatives tried to ban many books in public and school libraries. In the front line of the campaign against tainted texts stood the Minutewomen of America. In Sapula, Oklahoma, these militants burned books that apparently countenanced socialism or sex. In San Antonio, Texas, they wanted to brand numerous books with a large red stamp, indicating that the authors had "Communist sympathies." Albert Einstein's scientific works, Dorothy Parker's short stories, Thomas Mann's novels, even Geoffrey Chaucer's *Canterbury Tales* (in an edition illustrated by the suspect Rockwell Kent) all deserved branding. A member of the Indiana State Textbook Commission argued that since "Quakers don't believe in fighting wars," books about them should be removed from the schools as "Communist." The same person objected to *Robin Hood* because taking from the rich and giving to the poor showed obvious Communist implications. Some extremists attacked the *Girl Scout*

Photo by Declan Haun. Black Star.

Goldwater supporters in Portland, Oregon, during the 1964 presidential campaign.

Handbook, condemning its approving reference to the Public Health Service and its hopeful attitude toward the United Nations. This proved evidence enough for the American Legion at its 1954 convention to call the *Handbook* "recognized un-American propaganda." Later the Legion, together with the National Association of Manufacturers, tried to ban textbooks that did not wholeheartedly support capitalism. Several states passed laws against "seditious" teaching, and some schools summarily fired a few teachers for "disloyalty." A growing national concern for quality education in the years after the launching of the Russian Sputnik strengthened the hand of educators, and by the mid-1960s, the threat of censorship had greatly diminished.

While these silly paranoias often discredited the far right, it was the assassination of John F. Kennedy in Dallas in late 1963 that permanently alienated most citizens from militant conservatism. Many adults in Dallas had expressed an open hostility toward Kennedy during his visit, encouraged by newspaper advertisements placed by anti-Communist organizations, and some school children even cheered when they heard of the President's death. Birchers and rightists like Carl McIntire, a fundamentalist minister, tried to exploit the Marxist connections of the assassin Lee Harvey Oswald, arguing that he had acted under orders of "the world-wide Communist conspiracy." But many Dallas residents and like-minded citizens throughout the nation had had enough. They blamed the whole climate of fearful extremism in America for the President's death.

Despite this setback for anticommunism, a less harsh conservatism reached its apogee in the middle of the 1960s. Many people had still not accepted the New Deal reforms of Franklin D. Roosevelt. These cadres of true believers, determined to turn the clock back, labored for months to seize the 1964 Republican nomination for Senator Barry Goldwater of Arizona, one of the few politicians that most ultraconservatives backed. Goldwater supporters argued that masses of citizens usually did not vote because the parties did not offer a true choice. The candidate challenged much that had previously been taken for granted in American life: social security programs, public power companies, even free lunches for school children.

An ignominious defeat left many on the right with the feeling that the country was beyond saving. For the remainder of the decade, only the defense of America's role in Vietnam aroused much rightist activity. Most conservatives returned to religious fundamentalism or drifted toward the racist populism of George Wallace's presidential politics. And when pieces of their philosophy seemed to gain acceptance in the Nixon administration, conservatives nevertheless found themselves undercut first by the President's dramatic turnabout in relations with the major Communist powers and then by the Watergate scandal and impeachment hearing.

The Search for New Religions

The role of the church as an identifying niche faded in the sixties. Rival allegiances beckoned; many Americans were more likely to think of themselves as construction workers, radical feminists, or speed-freaks than as Protestants, Catholics, or Jews. Then too, church activism made traditionalists shudder. Liberal denominations and some individual church leaders became active in the civil rights and antiwar movements. A few, like Episcopal minister James J. Reeb, were murdered in the South while working for civil rights. Some churches inaugurated important new programs to aid the poor; volunteers performed a variety of services in downtrodden neighborhoods. Several radical clergymen, of whom the brothers Daniel and Philip Berrigan became the most famous, dramatized Christian protest, harboring draft evaders at their church altars and destroying military records. Such activities seemed to drive away prospective members, for the percentage of communicants actually declined. Critics objected to the intrusion of political and social controversy into church life, but activists insisted that their crusades were analogous to the religious revivals of the nineteenth century and the example of Jesus Christ himself.

Then, during the late 1960s and early 1970s, American religion generally backed off from activism. Evangelicalism and a new focus on individual spiritual cares replaced social reform. Groups of "Jesus freaks" sprang up among young people in California and the Deep South. But a self-righteous intolerance among members, added to the lack of compassion and the profiteering of many group founders, rapidly alienated most of the public. The experience of the activist sixties convinced many that religion seemed most useful yet least popular when it faced squarely the moral questions posed by modern American society.

This crisis of purpose among Protestants paralleled a debilitating crisis of authority within the Catholic church. Good Catholics were expected to obey religious doctrine without question. Yet in the sixties not only parishioners but also priests and nuns openly violated church rulings. Many Catholic women who took birth control pills placed personal and social concerns above the explicit decision of Pope Paul VI. A few priests married, flouting canonical law. Others participated in political activities, such as burning draft cards to protest the Vietnam war. In 1973 the Vatican felt it necessary to remind even Bishops that the Pope was infallible and that they should obey without hesitation.

The Catholic church also faced major obstacles in maintaining its parochial schools. Parochial enrollments more than doubled between 1940 and 1960, and after that bettered percentage increases for public schools in every year for the next decade. With such rapid growth, the demand outgrew the supply of priests and nuns from Catholic teaching orders, forcing church schools to hire lay teachers at higher salaries. There were also pressures to build new schools, purchase new equipment, and improve curriculum.

By the late 1960s the financial crisis reached an acute level. Church leaders, unable to find sufficient support within their denomination, looked to state and federal governments for aid. Since the Constitution of the United States clearly specifies the separation of church and state, tax revenues could not directly subsidize religious schools. Yet Catholic leaders still hoped to obtain some kind of financial transfusion, arguing that if church schools closed, a sudden tide of some ten million children would flood the public system and place a huge burden on all taxpayers. Several states responded to the church's pleas by indirectly supporting parochial schools with subsidies for textbooks, school lunches, and busing. But in 1973 the Supreme Court ruled that all such laws violated the doctrine of separation of church and state. A few Catholic schools closed almost immediately and more shutdowns seemed inevitable.

Students and the Left

In the 1960s, university students, for the most part apolitical in the previous decade, challenged a wide range of government policies and cultural practices in America. The young voiced their dissent through a plethora of loosely organized groups and experimented with unconventional social patterns in their daily lives. Militants on both the right and the left were usually among the most intelligent and articulate students. The conservative philosophy of groups such as the Young Americans for Freedom limited their activity, for by agreeing with most faculty members and administrators that universities were islands of learning that should not become deeply involved in politics, right-wing students undercut their own ability to organize and express political opinions. Students on the left, believing that the university was part of the larger society, felt no qualms about making political protests to affect university policies.

Young people who became leftist activists in the 1960s were an older version of the upper-middle-class, suburban high school students of the late 1950s. (See chapter 4, pp. 107–108.) Deliberate training in self-confidence and responsibility had given them the independence to scorn parental norms. Pressured to do well both socially and intellectually in high school, they had won the teen-aged academic sweepstakes by gaining admission to high quality and prestigious colleges. In their social sciences and humanities seminars, self-confidence and self-righteousness soon changed into a potent corrosive.

Student activism. Three movements of the fifties nurtured and shaped student activism during the next decade. The black peoples' struggle for equal rights introduced thousands of young men and women to picket lines, sit-ins, and protest marches. Students involved in fighting for this clearly moral cause often had the backing of liberal professors and their usually liberal parents, but they learned some lessons that would displease their elders. Faced with the violent reaction of some southern whites to civil rights workers, for instance, a few students concluded that democracy did not work in America. Instead, elements of the established system used violence to maintain their control. An especially important influence on later activism was the Student Nonviolent Coordinating Committee, whose programs and techniques of organization reappeared in support of many causes.

A second movement also contributed personnel and fervor to the new activism. Peace groups opposed to nuclear testing and the proliferation of nuclear weapons enjoyed fleeting prominence in the

Kennedy years. Organizations such as SANE—the Committee for a Sane Nuclear Policy—virtually disappeared after the signing of the Test Ban Treaty in 1963, but as Vietnam became a major issue "peaceniks" added bulk to antiwar ranks. Pacifist philosophy stood at the heart of moderate protests against the draft and America's involvement in Vietnam, while pacifist religious and lay groups, like the Quakers, contributed money, facilities, and manpower to many anti-Vietnam campaigns.

A third force, more a climate of opinion than an organized group, fed the youthful rebellion of the sixties, but it resists precise definition. The cultural experimentation championed most virgorously in the fifties by the beats expanded into the "youth culture" of the 1960s. When a newspaperman coined the word "hippie" in 1965, it was used interchangeably with "beat" for a time before becoming dominant. Another writer defined hippies as "no more than Beats plus drugs," and certainly drugs influenced many young people. Timothy Leary, a former Harvard psychologist, used his beat connections and years of professional experimentation with drugs to declare himself the "high priest" of a drug religion.

But Ken Kesey, with the proceeds of a briskly selling first novel, brought drugs more directly to the new generation. Traveling with his whacked-out band of followers called the Merry Pranksters, Kesey preached the joys of LSD he had learned while a subject of drug experiments at a VA hospital. The Merry Pranksters drove their gaudily painted bus into the Haight-Ashbury area of San Francisco in 1965 to put on the first of what Kesey called "acid tests." Hundreds of people gathered to have their ears assaulted by the pounding rock of a group called The Grateful Dead, their eyes stunned by spectacular strobe light shows, and their heads turned round and round by Kool-Aid spiked with still-legal LSD.

"Acid-rock," psychedelic posters, and festivals of indulgence in music and drugs soon characterized a unique culture of disaffiliated young people. The newer youth culture commercialized itself rapidly and extensively. By the late sixties, stores across the nation stocked a range of mass-produced psychedelic trinkets aimed at "counterculture" consumers, an ironic comment on America's aimless affluence.

Fed directly and indirectly by these three movements—black civil rights, war protest, and the drug counterculture—youth activism came into its own with the first major political outburst on an American campus in 1964. The Berkeley Free Speech Movement (FSM) was directed largely by veterans of the civil rights Mississippi summers and by former Peace Corps volunteers. Triggered by an ill-considered university decision to ban political solicitation in an area used by students to recruit for civil rights activities, the FSM introduced widespread civil disobedience and riots to the academic world. Despite the cries of anarchy from California conservatives, the FSM did not want to destroy the university or subvert American society; instead, student demands centered around familiar liberal themes of free speech. Yet FSM also taught administrators and students that they had little in common.

Radical groups. The student movement in the later 1960s fostered so many groups with so little structure that it is difficult to pinpoint leaders, philosophies, or even trends. Over a period of years, the Students for a Democratic Society (SDS) came closer to being the organizational center of the student left than any other group. SDS first appeared in 1960, the continuation of the Student League for Industrial Democracy (SLID), an old socialist youth group. But it was not until early 1962 that SDS began to take on its characteristic form. Two University of Michigan activists, Al Haber and Tom Hayden, campaigned vigorously to make SDS a nationwide organization advocating a broad radical program, not just a collection of local groups responding to single issues and events. Hayden and Haber stirred enough interest to bring hundreds of activists from all over the country to a convention at Port Huron, Michigan. Once there, they approved a manifesto drafted by Hayden. "The Port Huron Statement," which became a major intellectual landmark of the student left, still aimed at reforming existing institutions, but it also introduced new themes, soon to be familiar in the liturgy of protest: hostility toward bureaucracy, a rejection of anti-Communist ideology, hopes for community and participatory politics, and, most important, the use of universities as a base for radicalism.

Until 1965, the student movement remained a minor limb of the civil rights struggle. SDS largely copied SNCC's techniques and methods of political action. Both groups experienced danger in the South and learned to distrust the federal government. SNCC abandoned cooperation with liberals during this period and adopted "community politics"—local control of government institutions

—for the poor as its program. Rapidly assuming SNCC's distrust of moderate reformers, SDS made an effective call for participatory democracy within the universities. The desire for power over their own activities aroused many students and faculty members frustrated by the impersonality of the "multiversity," and it gave white radicals a cause that was independent of the black movement.

As American involvement in Vietnam deepened in the midsixties, student activists focused more and more on the war. Still small in membership and influence, SDS called in April 1965 for a demonstration in Washington against Johnson's policy in Southeast Asia. The organizers received a pleasant shock when fifteen thousand people showed up, giving SDS wide publicity and considerably boosting its strength. Aroused by a dramatic escalation of the war in early 1966, a wide variety of campus groups across the country set up Vietnam teach-ins. Recognizing an opportunity, SDS took up antiwar protest as its chief tactic, virtually ignoring the goals of the Port Huron Statement.

Beginning in December 1966 at Berkeley, SDS supported a series of confrontations with campus recruiters for the armed forces, for the CIA, and for Dow Chemical, the makers of napalm. Leaders organized draft resistance, urging eligible men to dodge or refuse military service. By 1967 demonstrations and marches involving thousands of students and sympathizers had occurred in several cities, with SDS often supporting protests organized by others.

In the spring of 1968, SDS became deeply involved in a new tactic. At Columbia University and elsewhere in the following years, activist students seized university buildings to dramatize demands and provoke confrontation. Usually the demands combined local issues with the call for an end to ROTC military training and university complicity in the war through defense research. Harried administrators reacted unimaginatively by calling in police, which only aroused large numbers of students to protest along with the original few. In some cases, the force of the larger turmoil provoked reforms in the university. And the building seizures focused intense national attention on the issues involved.

The new activism forced the question of morality into discussion of public and university issues. University growth must be balanced against the effect of expansion on surrounding communities; the welcome financial boost of Department of Defense research funds had to be considered against the destruction wrought by the new

Photo by Claus Meyer. Black Star.

Columbia students protest the action of New York City police, who were called in by university administrators to quell the campus uprisings in 1968.

weapons in Vietnam and elsewhere. If student radicals were sometimes absolutist and authoritarian, faculties and administrations
were often unforgivably slow in recognizing the validity of radical
challenges. By the end of the decade, professors and presidents
alike recognized, in many cases for the first time, that the liberal
university must justify its social role while defending its traditional
concern with open inquiry. By making Americans aware of the attitude that sustained established institutions, student activism at
the very least gave the nation an education.

SDS unity was tenuous, for its various factions bickered over
tactics and even purpose. Some SDS people, also members of the
Maoist Progressive Labor Party (PLP), stressed the traditional
Marxist class struggle and wanted to organize workers in production, transport, and communications industries. Other SDS members emphasized the enlistment of educated workers such as engineers, technicians, and teachers. These various differences in
philosophy and tactics fractured SDS into several narrow and ineffective factions by 1969.

By that time, a unique new group had gained prominence—the
Youth International Party, or "Yippies." Organized primarily by
Jerry Rubin and Abbie Hoffman, the Yippies decried the dullness of
serious leftist activism. Merging politics with the cultural revolt of the
young, they aimed to provoke excitement, shock, and fun through
deliberate unconventionality. The Yippies called for a "Festival of
Life" at the 1968 Chicago Democratic Convention; once there, they
nominated a pig for President and threatened to dump LSD in the
water supply. Political slogans became campus cultural clichés;
easy talk about the coming "revolution" could suggest both the
approach of the millennium and the wish for a fairy godmother.
Haphazard use of left rhetoric in rock songs, on posters, and at
cocktail parties evaded political meaning. Even if revolution only
appeared in chic conversation, leftists and Yippies did frighten conservatives. Officials, businessmen, and even middle-class families
seemed worried that somehow those foul-mouthed, long-haired
"students" might actually elect that pig President.

The climactic year 1968 brought the remarkable presidential
campaign of Eugene J. McCarthy. Thousands of college students
trimmed their hair and donned their best clothing to "get clean for
Gene" and take part in what the media labelled a "Children's

Crusade." McCarthy symbolized antiwar protest, but he also represented a route to reform through established channels. His supporters still believed in democracy and the possibilities of the American system, but some had this belief literally beaten out of them during a "police riot" at the Democratic convention in Chicago. Then the nomination of Hubert Humphrey, who had not won a single primary, cooled the desire of many young people for national political participation. Their remaining energies seemed to turn inward to work for reform within their universities, or—for those early activists growing older—within their professions.

The age of enthusiasm gradually waned, but the quieter radicals of the 1970s promised a long-term impact perhaps greater than that of their predecessors. Radical political philosophy—major reforms in the capitalist economy toward production for social need rather than private profit—and humanitarian concern for individual liberty became almost fashionable in urban centers, academic communities, and some ethnic groups. Madison Avenue advertising executives pumped the country full of media campaigns based on the freedom, the innocent fun, and self-indulgence of youth.

That serious discussion of the country's future could so easily be coopted into an affluent style or empty conversation convinced many that meaningful protest in the United States was impossible. Yet the pleasures of wealth and the security of comfortably accepted rhetoric did not thwart the struggle for personal dignity. The black movement of the sixties soon spread among other minorities, like the Mexican-Americans and Indians, who used similar tactics of racial pride, organization, and white liberal support to achieve, if not an integrated society, at least an increased measure of self-respect. The feminist movement was even more characteristic of the new revolt of the seventies, for it emphasized practical short-term gains more than the cosmic concerns of earlier radicals. Still, the sixties had convinced most Americans that the calm complacencies of an earlier age hid injustices that should be exorcised. By 1975, Americans had drifted far from the calm predictability of life in the 1950s.

Women

In the fifteen years following the war, magazines and books, movies and television programs taught American women that fulfillment lay in a suburban home with children to care for devotedly. The mother who cooked elaborate but always nutritious meals, who sewed many of her own and her children's clothes, who kissed away the bruises of her husband and her tots—this homemaking wonder became the ideal woman of the fifties. Until Betty Friedan's *The Feminine Mystique* appeared in 1963, few had considered the scope or the consequences of this passion for domesticity. Girls learned to make themselves attractive to boys before either were old enough to care; school-sponsored dances began in junior high, and going steady followed soon after. All this training in securing a mate worked exceedingly well. The average marriage age for women fell continually during the 1950s, dropping below twenty by the end of the decade.

Just as the intellectual girl collected few dates in high school, the "overeducated" woman supposedly repelled men. Women entered college to earn a husband rather than a degree, speaking more admiringly of an "M.R.S." than a B.A. Two-thirds of women attending college in the mid-1950s dropped out—many to marry, others fearing too much education might hamper their prospects for marriage. In proportion to men, fewer women attended college in 1960 than in 1920. Even college graduates increasingly accepted the role of housewife and mother, having four or five children instead of one or two. With careers for women immediately suspect, traditional female professions like nursing and teaching suffered a shortage of new recruits. Although one-third of American women worked, most held temporary or part-time jobs that required little skill. Frequently women received less pay than men for the same job; protective legislation delimiting hours and conditions of work further restricted their earning power; and women seldom gained promotion to top-level positions.

Women's groups concerned over economic and legal discrimination on the basis of sex had succeeded in getting Congressmen to introduce an equal rights amendment to the Constitution as early as 1923; beginning in 1944 both major parties included recommendations for such an amendment in their platforms. But little was accomplished. The first significant federal action on women's rights came in 1961 when John Kennedy set up the President's Commission on the Status of Women. Skeptics suggested Kennedy wanted to gain votes and at the same time avoid the party platform endorsement of an equal rights amendment by naming a commission that would recommend against it. The commission's report, *American Women*, released in late 1963, presented statistical data and specific recommendations. The commission report accepted the assumption that women had primary responsibility for housekeeping and childrearing, whether or not they held jobs. While recognizing widespread occupational and legal discrimination by sex, the commission suggested that specific laws and a new reading of the Constitution would solve these problems and advised against an equal rights amendment. Despite its restraint, the report stirred greater concern among women over their rights and provided information, techniques, and momentum for feminists who later challenged the entire traditional image of women's role in society. Within the federal government, President Kennedy established, in accordance with the report, the Citizens' Advisory Council on the Status of Women, which has been an official force for change since its inception in 1963.

Two laws passed in the early 1960s took steps toward ending some kinds of job discrimination against women. The Equal Pay Act of 1963, an amendment to the Fair Labor Standards Act, required that men and women receive the same pay for equal work performed under identical conditions. The law was reasonably well enforced, but it did not cover executive, professional, or administrative personnel and until 1966 applied only to private business. Title VII of the Civil Rights Act of 1964 prohibited discrimination on the basis of race, color, religion, national origin, or sex by private employers, employment agencies, and unions. Originally intended to combat racial rather than sex discrimination, the law weathered various hagglings that delayed effective enforcement of its provision concerning sex. The Equal Employment Opportunity Commission (EEOC), established to administer Title VII, wavered over definitions of what jobs could properly be limited by sex and struggled to clarify its authority in relation to state legislation.

Women's rights groups maintained pressure on the federal government to step up the attack on sex discrimination. The National Women's Party, founded in 1913 to battle for suffrage, changed course after women obtained the vote in 1920 and became a single-issue party fighting for an equal rights amendment. Another group with a long history, the National Federation of Business and Professional Women's Clubs (BPW), organized in 1919, lobbied for women's rights and provided members for a number of federal committees and commissions.

Despite the existence of these groups, several women in government positions saw the need for a new and more militant organization to fight for women's rights. For example, during early 1966 the categorization of newspaper want ads by sex developed into a hot issue, and many women believed that the EEOC was uninterested in this or any other question regarding women. So in June 1966, members of the National Conference of the State Commissions on the Status of Women met with several women officials from the federal government in Washington, where they heard the controversial feminist Betty Friedan discuss the possibility of a new action group. The result was the formation of the National Organization for Women (NOW), a militant feminist group (which soon came to be considered moderate) that opposed sex discrimination in all aspects of American life. Through demonstrations and private arm-twisting, NOW immediately set to work banishing sex-segregated want ads and other forms of occupational discrimination. In its first few months NOW had considerable effect on politicians frightened by this new and potentially powerful force.

Although often remembered for its picketing of "all male" bars and attacks on "male chauvinism," NOW devoted much time and energy to unspectacular efforts for justice within the channels of law and politics. In February 1968 NOW filed suit against EEOC to force it to uphold all of Title VII; later it brought legal charges against thirteen hundred corporations for sex discrimination. From the beginning, NOW lobbied for government support of child-care centers. During the 1968 elections, the organization presented presidential candidates with a list of questions on women's rights. By the early seventies, the group had entered nearly every area of feminist activity. On August 26, 1970, NOW organized a national Women's Strike for Equality to commemorate the fiftieth anniversary of women's suffrage. Their slogan, "Don't Iron while the Strike is Hot!" reflected feminist disaffection with woman's traditional role in American society.

At its founding, NOW served as an umbrella group for feminists of all persuasions; reasonably conservative women seeking only equal pay for equal work shared membership with radicals committed to remolding American society. Tensions naturally developed, and meetings were sometimes torn by violent arguments over issues and tactics. A new problem developed in 1970 when Gay Liberation activists encouraged homosexual women to demand acceptance and public support from women's groups. Worried that NOW would be regarded as a lesbian organization, many members sought to avoid the issue of homosexuality; a statement from Aileen Hernandez, president of NOW in 1970-1971, took a moderate position that satisfied neither side. By the mid-1970s, however, declarations of mutual support came from gay and women's organizations. And despite serious splits, NOW expanded steadily to over one hundred fifty chapters with several thousand members.

Meanwhile, student activism of the sixties had incubated a more radical strain of protest. Women working in civil rights groups found themselves cooking, cleaning, and typing, but seldom participating in policy decisions or strategy sessions. A small group of SNCC women, for example, met to discuss their role and wrote a paper called "The Position of Women in SNCC." Stokely Carmichael quipped that "the only position for women in SNCC is prone," reflecting a deep prejudice that women would not forget. Female workers in other leftist groups discovered similar male attitudes; men seemed to stop listening when a woman rose to speak.

The first small groups of radical women gathered in Chicago and New York in 1967; within months such enclaves of protest developed in other cities. Few groups gained substantial size and many lasted only a short time before disbanding or reforming. A protest against the Miss America Contest in 1968 brought the radical groups national attention and new members. Within the next three or four years, radical feminists produced scores of manifestos and plans for action. Some fought bitter internal battles, weakening the power of an already fragmented movement. But one of the most lasting and widely used techniques developed by these women was "consciousness-raising," in which small units of ten or fifteen women discussed their personal experiences as well as their social roles. Although some members were so caught up in personal problems that they forgot social needs altogether, the technique allowed many women all over the country to gain insights and a sense of unity.

From the beginning, radical women's liberation suffered from an ideological split among its members—the "politicos" and the "feminists." Politicos came largely out of leftist political activism, and most of them sought social and political revolution. They generally adopted the Marx-Engels belief that the family, as the first institution of private property and the division of labor, served as a source of oppression. Feminists, though no lovers of capitalism or the traditional family structure, argued that social values defined by males and stereotyped sex roles were the real causes of women's status problems. Eliminating male-female social and economic differentiation, not just attacking the economic system, would produce freedom. Politicos charged feminists with being counterrevolutionary in trying to alter rather than overthrow the established system.

Neither faction met the particular challenge of enlisting black women in the movement. Radicals echoed critics' charges that traditional women's rights groups spoke only to the problems of middle-class whites, but few black women became involved in radical feminist organizations. Racism was a more vicious prejudice and a more immediate problem in their lives.

Unity in the women's movement proved elusive. NOW women, mostly older, came from government offices, state commissions, and the professions; younger, more radical women usually had backgrounds in civil rights work or New Left politics. Radical women tended to condemn anyone more moderate than they, even while proclaiming the solidarity of women as an exploited class. NOW militants attacked NOW conservatives; radical feminists criticized all women's rights groups; politicos shrilly rejected the validity of feminist positions. In 1969 and 1970 particularly, militants even attacked their own strongest members; desiring an egalitarian movement, they condemned anyone who showed leadership as a "power seeker" or "elitist." Purges—described by one feminist as a "frighteningly vicious anti-intellectual fascism of the left"—contorted radical women's groups and scattered their influence.

Despite disarray on the left, women finally persuaded Congress in March 1972 to pass the Equal Rights Amendment (ERA). "Equality of rights under the law," the proposed constitutional amendment reads, "shall not be denied or abridged by the United States or by any State on account of sex." Approval came rapidly from twenty-two states and slowly from a few more; yet by the beginning of 1975 the future of the amendment lay in doubt, for it was still five short of

Photo by Dennis Brack. Black Star.

Abortion on demand was a rallying point for all factions of the women's movement in the early 1970s. This rally in Washington, D.C., in November 1971 attracted large numbers of demonstrators.

ratification by the necessary thirty-eight states. Early legal arguments on such issues as selective service for women, child support,
alimony, and public accommodations seemed to favor the amendment, suggesting that all problems could be easily worked out.
Some lawyers disagreed, however, pointing out that specific legislation could best handle instances of discrimination and predicting
mass legal confusion if thousands of laws were challenged under
ERA. The longer the amendment stayed before state legislatures,
the weaker appeared its chances for ratification.

Women did achieve some victories. For many years civil liber-
tarians had demanded the free dispersal of birth control information
and materials and the repeal of restrictions on abortion. But the
women brought real power to the fray and soon forced repeal of
abortion laws in several states, including New York. In 1973 the
Supreme Court ruled (in *Roe* v. *Wade*) most state restrictions on
abortion unconstitutional when applied to the first six months of
pregnancy. The battle did not end with that decision, but activist
women had achieved a major advance with the help of the Court's
"nine old men." The federal government also required that businesses demonstrate positively a lack of sex discrimination by hiring
women under so-called affirmative action programs. In 1972 the
feminist writer Gloria Steinem secured financial support from the
Ford Foundation to publish a glossy magazine, *Ms.*, which not only
propagandized for feminist reforms but also tried to make women
aware of sexism in American society. The magazine flourished and
the title itself appealed to many women, who substituted it for the
"Miss" or "Mrs." in their names. To those who objected, women
pointed out that "Mr." had long protected the anonymity of a man's
marital status. Still, many other women defended male-female distinctions and declared themselves proud to be housewives. They
denied feelings of oppression and maintained an individualistic
aloofness from activist groups. Whatever their politics or social
opinions, women became considerably more aware of their condition and their options by the mid-seventies, and feminists continued
to challenge the traditional ethos that forced sex roles on citizens.

The Environment, Consumers, and Economic Growth

In the late sixties and early seventies, as Americans worried
about the divisions visible in American society, a new concern for
the environment and consumer interest in the quality of goods and

services seemed to offer rallying points for bringing Americans together again. Here were common needs of pressing urgency on which all men and women of good will might agree. People might combine to clean things up rather than break them up, save resources rather than waste them, beautify the nation rather than see it deteriorate. But such tasks proved more difficult than expected, for people soon learned that they had challenged one of America's most sacred cows: maximum economic growth. What seemed to be reasonable reforms only lengthened the list of divisive questions that faced Americans.

The great expansion of American industry during and after the war consumed the nation's resources with frightening speed, belching smoke into the air and dumping wastes into the water as byproducts. Even before the concept of "ecology" gained currency in the late 1960s, densely populated areas recognized mounting environmental problems. In the midst of their considerable financial, transportation, and racial problems, urban areas faced rapid deterioration of two absolutely vital natural elements: air and water. Los Angeles "smog" became a national joke. When more than water came out of the tap and when eyes burned from particles in the air, only the diagnosis was clear.

Factory smoke and automobile exhaust fumes accounted for most of the damage to air quality. Sulfur dioxide, nitrogen oxide, ozone, and carbon monoxide poured from smokestacks and tailpipes; their chemical reactions—frequently intensified by bright sunlight—suspended dangerous gases in the atmosphere. If a stationary weather front left a stagnated air mass over a city, instead of moving the toxic particles away from heavily populated areas, tragedy could occur. As early as 1948, a "killer smog" took twenty lives in Donora, Pennsylvania, leaving five thousand others seriously ill. Los Angeles' peculiar geography, a valley surrounded by mountains, also guaranteed perpetually "unacceptable" air quality once suburbs ringed the area. Such cities as Birmingham, Alabama, shut down all industrial activity when masses of highly polluted air threatened public health. But perhaps the greatest costs lay in the slow workings of the corrosive acids in the air. Human health deteriorated under the constant burden of a foul atmosphere. Lung cancer was twice as common among urbanites as among rural people. Pollution aggravated the slow choking of emphysema. In major cities bronze statues developed a pitted surface as did the stone faces of buildings. Offending cars suffered ironic punishment as airborne acids peeled away their paint. The spectacular sunsets possible in a particle-filled atmosphere offered precious little compensation for all these urban sores.

But by the mid-1970s there seemed at least a chance of curtailing industrial air pollution. Solutions to reduce massive industrial pollution included filters and electrostatic precipitators in smokestacks to screen out most particles and the use of low sulfur fuels in factories. When, for example, Consolidated Edison of New York City switched to "cleaner" fuels, the pollution rate decreased nearly a third. Some of these changes were made voluntarily, others under public pressure or legal edict; some were subsequently abandoned, especially after shortages of oil forced many power companies to return to high sulfur fuels like coal.

The automobile—the major culprit in poisoning the atmosphere in most large cities—proved a stubborn foe. As suburbanites moved farther and farther away from the city, an enormous increase in the number of people commuting offset any benefits gained from early automobile antipollution devices. Even the forced introduction of emission control valves on new cars in 1974 promised no major relief, for the gadgets tended to deteriorate rapidly. Detroit car manufacturers showed more interest in obstructing controls legislation than developing a low-pollution product. Mass production of automobiles run by steam, electricity, or a clean combustion seemed unlikely in the near future.

A variety of industrial abuses contributed to water pollution. The oceans of the world, used as a dumping ground for centuries, suffered new assault from a rash of oil spills. Thousands of gallons of thick, sticky crude oil escaped from tankers or from off-shore drilling operations. Near Santa Barbara, California, in 1969, a reddish-brown coating of oil covered beautiful beaches and destroyed many sea birds. Such tragedies might be called accidental, but the destruction of aquatic life and water quality by systematic mistreatment of wastes seemed far more controllable. Growing industries demanded a greater and greater volume of water, which seldom returned to lakes or rivers undirtied. The muck of manufacturing wastes turned the beautiful Hudson River in New York into a swamp. In Dayton, Ohio, and Houston, Texas, some streams actually caught fire, burning for several days at a time. Not only wastes, but thermal pollution—the increased temperature of a return flow of water—radically altered the ecological balance that supported life. As factories, offices, and homes called for more power to operate machines, air conditioners, and a vast array of electrical gadgets, conventional hydroelectric plants reached out hundreds of miles to supply sufficient electricity.

Although atomic power plants seemed to offer a dynamic solution, alert citizens pointed to their carelessness with heated water and the dangers of radioactive contamination. In 1973, newspapers cited Atomic Energy Commission information that underground tanks storing atomic wastes produced in the manufacture of nuclear weapons had in fact leaked; here was a frightening new source of pollution impossible to filter or wait out.

Even increased farm production exacted a price. Widespread use of insecticides and chemical fertilizers endangered both man and animal. Indiscriminate spraying killed not only weeds but nearby plants and wildlife as well; then these chemicals drained into streams. During 1963, for example, farming and industrial wastes killed five million fish in the Mississippi River. The chemicals used in growing food crops helped arouse a considerable interest by the late 1960s in health and organic foods produced without such aid.

The disposal of sewage, always a problem for cities, too often meant simply emptying it into the nearest body of water. When forced to accept massive loads of raw sewage, New York's huge harbors became a breeding ground for maggots and harmful bacteria, threatening disease and epidemic. Effective sewage treatment plants required substantial investment by the already financially overburdened cities, but public concern and some much-needed federal aid from Johnson's Great Society programs convinced many cities to undertake the task. Sewage problems also afflicted America's spanking new suburbs. About one-third of the houses built in them depended on septic tanks. Although economically necessary and environmentally safe in areas of sparse settlement, the large-scale use of cesspools in housing developments threatened water purity in the entire area. Seepage could contaminate any well within miles.

The common use of synthetic detergents threatened both ground and running water supplies. Such detergents are not biodegradable; unlike organic products, they cannot be broken down by bacterial action. To complicate the matter, most detergents easily flow through filters and are almost infinitely expandable; high-sudsing detergents falling fifteen stories in an apartment building may enlarge themselves seventeen thousand times. Governments in some areas dependent on ground water—like Long Island's Suffolk County—have banned detergents completely to preserve drinkable water. The heavy concentrations of phosphates in these laundry products created another problem. Acting as a super-fertilizer, phosphates alter the oxygen content of water and speed the growth of aquatic plants, accelerating the aging of a lake or river by building up layers of decayed plants.

With all these menaces to purity, cities often found it difficult to ensure an adequate supply of drinking water. Major urban areas have had to tap water sources hundreds of miles away. Los Angeles' tentacles of supply clutch at the mountains of Nevada and reach for the wetter regions of northern California. Reservoirs last when the rains come; but, drought or no drought, New Yorkers get water in restaurants only if they ask. As the nation's population expanded, the demand for water naturally increased; some areas found themselves reusing water many times or limiting nonessential supplies.

Cities also encountered increasing difficulty in disposing properly of their garbage. Although more people naturally created more garbage, each individual not so predictably also produced more trash over the years. In 1940, an American averaged about two pounds of garbage per day; by 1965, the figure had reached three and one-half pounds. People bought more, and what they bought was more elaborately packaged. Convenient and attractive packaging usually meant more cardboard, cellophane, and aluminum foil for the trash barrel. Some cities dumped their refuse in the ocean, while others burned garbage in an open field. Both polluted the environment and angered those unlucky enough to live near stinking waters and smoking acres of trash. Sanitary land-fill—a method of building up low-lying areas with alternate layers of packed garbage and soil —provided relief for some municipalities, but there were only a limited number of holes to fill. A rational challenge to the garbage problem in the late 1960s called for the recycling and reuse of paper and metal waste. But used material often proved more expensive to produce than new, and reprocessed fibers did not retain their original strength.

Certain maxims became clear after several years of problems of air and water pollution, sewage treatment, garbage disposal, and the like. High levels of production created high levels of pollution and waste. Solutions were neither simple nor cheap. The society wishing to escape its own filth would have to invest considerable time and money. More significant, individuals might well have to practice restraint and conservation, perhaps even suffer inconvenience. Few Americans seemed willing to accept this mortgage on material comfort for health and survival.

The complexity of ecological problems and the expense of reform quickly enlisted the federal government in remedial action. Spurred on by conservation groups like the Sierra Club, an environmental preservation society dedicated to protecting "open spaces" from industrial and suburban sprawl, Congress passed the Clean Air and Water Quality Acts in the mid-1960s. Then in the seventies, government tried to force citizen, city, and businessman into compliance with a long list of regulations. But each avoided major clean-up campaigns, pleading that neither the money nor the technology existed to end pollution. Consumers wanted energy-intensive products, local governments could scarcely meet current financial demands, and industry feared a decline in profits. Yet the federal government persisted. In December 1970 President Nixon reorganized scattered agencies concerned with ecology into a centralized bureaucracy, the Environmental Protection Agency (EPA). EPA brought suit against polluters, but not until Congress passed a $25 billion authorization over the President's veto could vigorous clean-up programs begin. Even though many states passed pollution control laws and citizens propagandized the cause through "Earth Day" rallies, the driving force of pollution—industry's concern with profits and consumer greed—remained to challenge the future of America's environment.

The environmentalists of the seventies spawned a new interest in consumer protection. The Consumer Federation of America, an amalgam of nearly two hundred state consumer organizations and labor unions, lobbied for new laws to give recourse to citizens victimized by frauds, poor products, or high credit costs and for strict enforcement of consumer protection laws already in existence. Ralph Nader won prominence in the mid-sixties with his book *Unsafe at Any Speed*, a thoroughgoing condemnation of Detroit's automobile industry. Then he put together a research staff, nicknamed Nader's Raiders, that publicized abuses in mining safety, pension funds, food adulteration, and many other fields. A former Secretary of Health, Education and Welfare, John Gardner, set up

Common Cause, an organization eventually totaling one million members, whose contributions financed legal suits and muckraking studies on behalf of consumer rights and political reform.

By the mid-seventies, "consumerism" was solidly entrenched. Like the environmental movement, however, it challenged the long tradition of maximum economic growth and material affluence. Perhaps Americans will at some point become more attuned to the quality than to the quantity of life in their country, but whatever the future, complacent acceptance of an unrestrained industrialism seems unlikely.

◄ 9 ►

IMPERIAL PRESIDENCY: THE NIXON YEARS

RICHARD NIXON, a secretive man whom friends called "a loner," came to the presidency in 1969 without much experience as a political administrator. His congressional career had focused on exposing Communists; during the fifties he had merely marked time, as do all Vice-Presidents; in the sixties he had worked as a tax lawyer in New York City. None of his closest advisers—John Ehrlichman, H. R. "Bob" Haldeman, John N. Mitchell, and Henry A. Kissinger—were drawn from government. Only Kissinger possessed a technical expertise in his role as chief adviser on foreign policy; the Harvard professor had long studied history for clues to a stable international system. Haldeman, the President's chief of staff, was an advertising executive who had packaged a "new Nixon" for the 1968 campaign. He viewed most Congressmen, even Republicans, as adversaries or potential enemies. Fanatically loyal to his boss, Haldeman withheld disturbing news from the President in order that, he claimed, "Nixon might think clearly about a few great decisions." Ehrlichman and Mitchell acted as "super-administrators," overseeing trouble spots; like Haldeman, they reinforced the President with words he wanted to hear.

Nixon himself believed that with these four men and a strong cabinet, "domestic affairs would pretty much take care of themselves," and he could concentrate on foreign matters, especially ending the Vietnam War and easing relations with the Soviet Union and China. Indeed, economics and congressional politics bored him. In any case, he believed government too intrusive. With his constituency of worried middle-class Americans, "the silent majority," anxious for surcease from the alarums of the sixties, he moved toward a quiet, "low-profile" approach. That way he could pursue the role of world statesman.

Nixonomics

But domestic problems, especially economic ones, hounded Nixon's administration. His first task was to bring skyrocketing inflation under control. Years of huge war deficits, together with consumer belief that prices could only go up, generated a self-sustaining spiral of inflation. The President's approach to slowing this rate was a standard one, and at first it met with general approval: he intended to use restrictive government fiscal policy and Federal Reserve monetary policy. This meant that the Federal Reserve would almost completely halt increases in the nation's money supply, causing interest rates to jump upward and making credit difficult to obtain.

Yet instead of merely "cooling" the economy, Nixon's fiscal policy turned it downward, creating a decline in production and a sharp rise in unemployment. The real GNP (which eliminates the effect of price increases) gained only 2.5 percent in 1969 and declined 0.6 percent in 1970. While industrial production nosed downward, unemployment figures climbed until they reached a high 6 percent by the end of 1970. And in spite of the antiinflationary policy, real prices rose 5 percent in 1969 and 5.5 percent in 1970, the largest increases since the Korean War years. By the end of 1971 it was clear that the nation had stumbled into a serious recession, even while inflation continued. Economists spoke of this new phenomenon as "stagflation"; others called it "Nixonomics."

End of the Wall Street boom.   The ending of the economic boom of the sixties hit Wall Street hard, for the good times had been very good indeed and "the Street" had lost any notion that lean years might follow the fat ones. The financial community had changed its style too much to remember its troubled past. In 1960 the typical Wall Street entrepreneur was still a gentleman in the traditional mode: well-bred, generally of Protestant or German-Jewish stock, possessing the proper educational and family credentials. By the end of the decade a new breed had risen to the top of the financial world; their credentials varied widely, and they wielded power through their aggressiveness, financial acuity, and successful performance. These new entrepreneurs came to symbolize the 1960s on Wall Street—fast-moving years of high style, quick profits, and rapid growth.

Two new types of investment defined the character of the sixties boom: frankly speculative high-performance mutual funds and a new species of business organization, the conglomerate. High-performance mutual funds—sometimes called "go-go funds"—provided a way to manage and invest other people's money for quick high returns and relatively large managerial commissions. By taking high risks and skillfully manipulating stocks, investment managers made it possible for small-scale amateurs to increase their investments by as much as 40 percent in a year. By the end of 1965 three million people held mutual funds, their holdings totaling $35 billion.

Conglomerates, like Gulf and Western or James J. Ling's LTV enterprises, usually started as small companies that expanded rapidly by merging with or absorbing other businesses. Because they strung together a wide range of differing, noncompetitive companies, "conglomerateurs" avoided violation of antitrust laws. Like mutual funds, these new investment vehicles yielded swift high profits, frequently dealt in new growth fields such as computers, and operated under the direction of one or two men. With their reputation for growth, they could even threaten old and established firms. In the past, mergers generally meant the big fish swallowing the little ones, but in the sixties the process would often reverse itself; holders of stock in older firms coveted the greater growth potential of the young industries and were increasingly willing to trade their safe holdings for more glamorous and speculative possibilities. A major result of that process was an increase in the enormous capital concentration dominating America's economy. Billion dollar corporations had increased their share of the total national assets from 26 to 46 percent and reported huge profits.

The quick fortunes, financial coups d'etat, and sheer volume of activity of the stock markets during these ten years came to an abrupt, almost devastating end. The Wall Street crisis of 1969-70 resulted from high speculation and risk taking, stock and profit manipulations, and gross inefficiencies in accounting. Both the volume of shares traded and stock prices dwindled rapidly, and over one hundred brokerages, many of them old and established like Hayden Stone, went under either through merger or by liquidation. President Nixon's attempts to help only compounded the difficulty; by loosening restrictions on the market, he removed many of the controls that kept it in check. External factors also worried investors: Nixonomics, recession, continuing federal deficits, an accelerating gold drain as America's balance of trade worsened.

Contrasted with the 90 percent decline in the stock market crash of 1929, its fall in 1970 seemed relatively minor—only 30 percent. But the Dow Jones industrial average on which that figure is based surveyed blue chip stocks, not the more speculative issues that had beguiled most investors. Using realistic indicators, one study suggested that the actual market decline during the year passed 80 percent. And paper losses, some $300 billion, were ten times those of 1929. While not so severe as the depression that followed the 1929 crash, there was an economic malaise after 1970, one in fact far more substantial than official sources acknowledged.

One major difference separated the crash of 1929 and the crisis of 1970: the earlier crash wrecked entire fortunes but in this newest panic few people suffered grievously. Most stockholders had invested only a few thousand dollars or had purchased shares in mutual funds, rather than single stocks, which showed far greater losses. Even the big losers survived. Texas financier H. Ross Perot, for example, absorbed losses on paper of $450 million in a single day. He had built his fortune rapidly in the 1960s until he was one of the six richest men in America. His data processing company had assets of about $10 million in 1968, but stock speculation forced the price of its share up to 160, making Perot worth about $1.5 billion. Even after his loss he was still a billionaire!

The bumpy economy. The economic situation obviously demanded more substantial measures, and President Nixon responded with his New Economic Policy. Phase I of this four-phase plan began on August 15, 1971, with a ninety-day wage and price freeze, the establishment of a Cost of Living Council to administer the freeze and plan for Phase II, the imposition of a 10 percent surcharge on most imports and a variety of other tax measures to stimulate the economy, the suspension of the right to convert foreign-held dollars into gold, and widespread cuts in federal expenditures. The following November, Phase II went into effect with a program of mandatory but more flexible controls, which allowed ,price rises of 5.5 percent but restricted most wages to 2.5 percent increases. The difference, Nixon hoped, would encourage business expansion and boost production.

Still, at the end of 1971 the economic picture remained cloudy. For the first time.in the twentieth century, the nation had a trade deficit, with imports exceeding exports at an alarming annual rate of around $1.7 billion. A combination of circumstances—the outflow of gold from the United States, foreign speculation against the dollar, and an increase in the balance of payments deficit—forced Nixon to devalue the dollar by 8.57 percent. The domestic economic scene shone little brighter: unemployment remained around 6 percent and the real GNP rose very slightly. Yet, one year later, at the end of 1972, recovery looked hopeful. Predictable costs had encouraged production and revived consumer spending, which in turn raised real GNP. The Nixon administration publicly took credit for this apparent prosperity, relieved that the President had not had to counter charges of economic mismanagement during the election campaign.

The "Second American Revolution": Revenue Sharing

In his 1971 State of the Union message President Nixon outlined a major reordering of the federal system. Calling for a "second American revolution," he urged that state and local governments take over social services, financing them with federal grants. As a result of this call, Congress passed the State and Local Fiscal Assistance Act of 1972, better known as revenue sharing, which authorized $30 billion over a five-year period. The money, two-thirds of which was earmarked for local governments and one-third for the states, could only be used in seven areas: public safety, environmental protection, public transportation, health and recreation, social services, financial administration, and libraries.

Revenue sharing met with sharp criticism because it distributed the money to areas on the basis of population rather than need, and it inadequately provided for social welfare programs. "Local control" could easily mean that spending would reflect race prejudices or needless affluence—one wealthy community built a golf course and bridle paths with this federal largesse.

Nixon defended revenue sharing as a step away from federal centralization and as an aid to financially pressed local governments. As budget cuts drained federal funds from social programs, however, disenchanted mayors and governors realized that revenue-sharing funds were not a bonus but only a pale substitute for previous federal grants. Democratic governors in particular labeled the whole program a "hoax" and a "snow job," for the Nixon administration eliminated several federal social welfare measures, such as the Job Corps training program. Nixon vetoed a plan for day care and an aid to education act, offering instead an Opportunities for Families Program (OFP) and the Family Assistance Program (FAP). FAP guaranteed an annual income of $1,600 to each family of four but gradually removed all aid when family income reached $3,920. OFP encouraged, and in many cases compelled, poor people to work while reducing their benefits by nearly two-thirds of the amount earned. In effect these measures—which the Democratic Congress rejected—would have severely cut back welfare spending, particularly funds going to dependent children, and would have forced mothers to work at a time when day-care facilities were being curtailed.

Civil Rights in the Nixon Administration

After the shocks of 1968, disillusionment and a sense of irony suffused the civil rights movement. Nixon quickly reversed over twenty years of White House activism. His conservative Attorney General, John Mitchell, permitted several school districts to delay integration and slowed efforts at cross-city busing to achieve racial balance. The President's new welfare proposals—a guaranteed cash income and inducements for the "working poor"—were calculated to benefit rural areas more than urban ghettos, and those who had jobs, not the unemployed.

Nixon then tried to remold the Supreme Court, the source of much advance toward racial equality, but his carefully chosen Chief Justice, Warren E. Burger, rigorously defended individual freedom against social or government infringements. The President's next nominations for a vacancy of the Court revealed his purpose more clearly. Both C. F. Haynesworth, Jr., and G. Harrold Carswell were southern judges with weak civil rights records; higher courts had consistently overturned their segregationist decisions. Although Nebraska Senator Roman L. Hruska suggested that Carswell's "mediocrity" would make the high court "more representative," his colleagues in the Senate rejected both men, and the NAACP declared Nixon "an enemy of integration." The President eventually appointed a total of four responsible conservatives—Burger, Harry A. Blackmun of Minnesota, Lewis F. Powell, Jr., of Virginia, and William H. Rehnquist of Arizona. If the remodeled Supreme Court did not wholly reverse its egalitarian precedents, neither did it extend them. In one critical area, busing, it had, by 1974, set limits that severely restricted this controversial solution to the problems of segregated urban education.

Then too, a new mood affected the 1970s. White liberals abandoned crusades and settled into apathy, convinced that reform must mark time during Nixon's administration and the backlash appeal of George Wallace. Disturbed by the excesses of violence and bizarre solutions espoused by fringe elements, most blacks adopted more constructive tactics. Black capitalism attracted some of them, but the dilemmas of ghetto business—poor consumers, high crime, and scarce capital—undermined independent enterprise, despite rhetorical support from President Nixon. Traditional politics proved more promising: black mayors governed Los Angeles; Cleveland; Newark, New Jersey; Gary, Indiana; and even Atlanta, Georgia, by 1973. A "Black Caucus" in Congress lobbied for favorable programs. Ghettos sought "community control" over schools and low-cost housing projects, although such efforts sometimes produced festering racial disputes as in the Ocean Hill-Brownsville section of Brooklyn. After the confusion of the sixties, radicals themselves turned more toward the prosaic problems of self-help than the dramatics of race war.

The great majority of blacks still sought a peaceful, integrated society, but their goal was bound up with the future of America's cities, where most of them now lived. Urban prosperity and racial harmony required more than uncoordinated local efforts, however; and neither a national moral commitment nor congressional appropriations seemed likely to materialize in the early seventies. A coalition of blacks, white liberals, and the federal government had mortally wounded legal discrimination, and perhaps tokenism foreshadowed racial harmony. But white prejudice and black poverty had not greatly abated—nor had black resentments.

Superficial reforms and liberal sensitivity had not eased the condition of the country's other minorities either—the Mexican-Americans, or Chicanos, and the Indians. Although both groups copied the tactics, and even the objectives, of the black civil rights movement, they experienced limited success. The Indians, for example, had no political power: numbering less than a million and scattered in remote, lightly populated western states, they had little support from eastern white liberals. Many tribes began to organize. The National Congress of American Indians lobbied for legislation, while the more militant National Indian Youth Council focused on achieving spectacular, short-term projects. These organizations, along with many regional groups, aimed to remove offensive symbols—as in 1967 when Indian pressure forced ABC television to cancel an inaccurate series about the Indian-fighter, General George Custer—and dramatized their desire for cultural nationalism. But discrimination persisted, and unjustified hopes eventually led to violence. For ten weeks in 1973 Indians occupied Wounded Knee, South Dakota, the site of a nineteenth-century cavalry massacre of innocent Indian women and children. Yet this protest against the paternalistic policies of the Bureau of Indian Affairs, which officially segregated Indians on reservations, provoked more white backlash than constructive change. No one seemed to care about America's most unknown minority.

In contrast, protest and white concern have radically changed the daily life of most Mexican-Americans. Long separated from American culture by race, religion, and language, the Chicanos lived an isolated existence, sometimes even outside the law. Although many were American citizens, hundreds of thousands of others had entered the United States illegally. Chaos at home and the prospect of high wages across the border lured Mexicans into Texas and southern California to work as unskilled laborers. Employers ruthlessly exploited such people since, if discovered, the government would deport them as undesirable aliens or "wetbacks." Yet even legal workers and Mexican-American citizens—well over five million people—suffered prejudice, low wages, and isolation. Inadequate education and urban poverty crowded many Chicanos into *barrios*

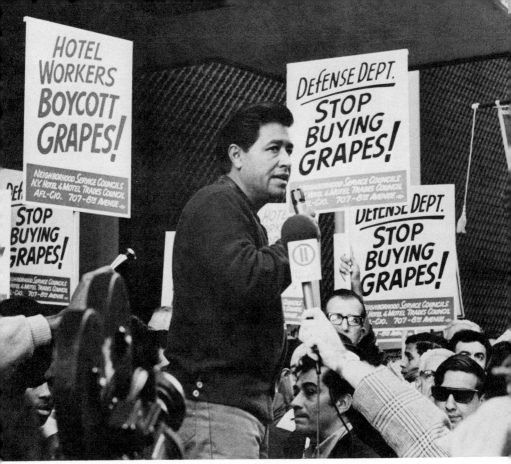

Bruce Anspach from Editorial Photocolor Archives.

Cesar Chavez speaking in New York City at a demonstration in support of the United Farm Workers' grape strike.

(ghettos), while white bigotry too often ruined the lives of second- and third-generation immigrants who lived in middle-class suburbs.

During the 1960s, there was an impetus for change on two fronts: local politics and regional economics. More and more Mexicans registered to vote and organized pressure groups, such as the Political Association of Spanish-Speaking People in Texas, and the Mexican-American Political Association in California. As in the black movement, community self-help projects put an end to ghetto apathy, and "black is beautiful" found its counterpart in "Viva la Raza!" (Long live the race).

The Chicanos also took up new techniques. In 1966 a charismatic leader, Cesar Chavez, organized a union of stoop laborers, workers who harvest ripe vegetables and fruit. This United Farm Workers of America immediately struck the giant Delano ranch in southern

California and demanded that all growers recognize the principle of collective bargaining. Chavez threatened to let the crops rot unless employers abolished child labor, provided decent housing, and raised wages. When the California growers brought in strikebreakers, Chavez appealed to the country not to eat grapes picked by "scab labor." *La Causa* spread nationwide. But while Manhattan matrons changed their dessert menus, the conservative Young Americans for Freedom flew a planeload of fruit to Hawaii "for all those starved for the sight of a California grape." The U.S. Army bought much of the crop for its soldiers in Vietnam and elsewhere. Stung more by unflattering publicity than by economic pressure, most growers relented. The next year, 1971, Chavez started another national boycott, this one against iceberg lettuce, to force more ranchers to deal with the UFWA. Although controversial, such direct action secured more immediate benefit for Chicanos than did other broader but less well-focused minority schemes to end discrimination and poverty.

The 1972 Election

Few voters and fewer politicians took George McGovern seriously when he began his campaign for the presidency a year and a half before the Democratic nominating convention. McGovern, a first-term Senator from South Dakota, was not well known; and his main issue, the Vietnam War, seemed an asset of diminishing value as Americans either grew conditioned to the fact of war or gauged its progress by the steady withdrawal of American troops. But in the 1972 primaries, only McGovern survived. The long-time Democratic front-runner, Senator Edmund Muskie of Maine, made a poor showing in the first primary—New Hampshire—largely because he inspired no enthusiasm and remained vague on most issues. From there he went downhill. Another presidential contender, Governor George Wallace of Alabama, campaigned vigorously in several states, winning primaries throughout the South and in Michigan, but his campaign ended on May 15 when he was shot in Laurel, Maryland, and left paralyzed from the waist down. Hubert Humphrey posed a major threat until McGovern's devoted precinct workers blitzed voters during the California primary. Suddenly, with that state's 271 nominating ballots, the unlikely candidate seemed unstoppable.

George McGovern was nominated for the presidency on July 13 by a national convention that, partly as a result of his leadership, gave greater representation to women, minorities, and youth. But the long struggle for the presidency culminated that evening. By the time McGovernites regrouped for the presidential race, their candidate had seriously faltered.

Senator Thomas Eagleton of Missouri, McGovern's vice-presidential choice at Miami Beach, became the center of a major controversy. At first nearly everyone viewed the personable Eagleton as an asset to the Democratic ticket. But in a press conference ten days after his nomination, Eagleton confirmed the rumors in Jack Anderson's newspaper column that three times between 1960 and 1966 he had been hospitalized for "nervous exhaustion and fatigue." On two of these three occasions he had undergone psychiatric treatment including shock therapy for "depression." Eagleton had disclosed nothing of this before his nomination. Even though somewhat stunned, McGovern foolishly announced that he supported Eagleton "one thousand percent." Within hours debate raged between Eagleton backers and those who believed his history of emotional instability made him unfit for potential presidential control over nuclear weapons. When this squabble appeared to be undermining the campaign, McGovern on July 31 dropped Eagleton from the ticket. By shifting in the space of a few days from total support of Eagleton to a near demand for his withdrawal, McGovern earned the image of a waverer, a stereotype he never escaped. McGovern than sought out several Democratic stalwarts to replace Eagleton before receiving a positive response from R. Sargent Shriver, a Kennedy kinsman and an energetic speaker. Despite Shriver's abilities, the reluctance of earlier choices to run with McGovern further weakened his candidacy. The Eagleton fiasco demolished the entire Democratic presidential campaign at its beginning.

Many voters viewed McGovern as a radical or as some sort of visionary because of remarks he made during the early primaries. His startling proposals for cutting $30 billion from the defense budget in order to finance welfare programs that would guarantee every American a minimum standard of living, his argument that the United States should get out of Vietnam simply by leaving, and his support of amnesty for draft evaders all seemed to many citizens the programs of a perhaps well-meaning but impractical and possibly dangerous candidate. The strong support given McGovern by the women's liberation movement and his willingness to forgive draft evaders and reform marijuana laws elicited charges that he was the candidate of "amnesty, acid, and abortion." And when McGovern attempted to modify or redefine some of his proposals during the summer, he only added fuel to the charges that he too often changed his mind and was, therefore, himself unstable.

Meanwhile, Richard Nixon remained calm, his "back porch" campaign all the more effective because the porch was attached to the White House. No element of suspense invested his renomination on August 23. Some early jockeying over the vice-presidential slot perhaps worried Spiro Agnew, who retooled his style for 1972—more poised, restrained, and independent. After the Republican convention, President Nixon cooly sent his staff and cabinet members out to do battle on the campaign trail while he nourished his own image as world statesman by traveling abroad or conferring with foreign leaders in Washington. He simply coasted toward November. Even one of the most bizarre political incidents in several decades aroused little voter reaction. On June 17, 1972, five men were captured in the Watergate building in Washington while attempting to bug the Democratic National Headquarters. Investigators quickly established definite connections between the five and President Nixon's reelection committee, but little more information leaked out before election day. No one, however, overlooked the fact, that on October 31 Henry Kissinger told reporters, "Peace is at hand."

The professionalism of Nixon's public campaign, and his reasonable claim to have brought "peace with honor" in Vietnam and to have fashioned a new, more productive relationship with Russia and China contrasted with the amateurish bumbling visible in McGovern's campaign. Voting became largely perfunctory. Despite the recent lowering of the franchise age to eighteen, only half of America's eligible citizens went to the polls, the lowest percentage since 1948.

As the pollsters had predicted, Richard Nixon won a landslide —60.8 percent of the popular vote and 520 of 538 electoral votes: only Massachusetts and the District of Columbia went for George McGovern. But in congressional voting, the Democrats picked up two seats in the Senate to pad their already weighty majority and held on to a comfortable margin in the House. The GOP lost one governorship, so that the state house margin favored the Democrats 31 to 19. President Nixon interpreted the results as a personal mandate for his style of governing and his conduct of foreign affairs.

The Second Term: President and Congress

Despite Nixon's triumph, growing tension between the White House and Congress corroded the President's effectiveness during his second term. Executive slights contributed substantially to the legislators' feisty mood. Governing with little regard for congressional opinion, Nixon's staff implied that their own ideas and opinions alone deserved preeminence. And power became increasingly centralized within the executive branch itself among a few favored aides. Cabinet members had limited access to the President, and congressional leaders found it difficult even to reach his staff members by telephone. Nixon's attempt in 1973 to create special domestic advisers corresponding to Henry Kissinger in the foreign policy area indicated a continuing drive to concentrate executive power.

It was only natural that Democrats would rebel at haughtiness and centralization in a Republican administration, but representatives of the President's own party also joined the clamor. And yet another complaint weakened Republican ties with the White House: in the 1972 campaign President Nixon had run alone; he had offered scant help to his party's candidates for Congress. Many Republican legislators came back to Washington feeling little obligation to help an administration that had ignored them. The issues before the new Congress provided ample opportunity for a bipartisan demonstration of legislative independence and vitality.

The President's method of achieving fiscal reform especially clashed with congressional aims. Aware that the United States had run up huge deficits annually, Nixon approached budget making during the mid-seventies determined to prevent increased federal spending. Defense appropriations remained sacrosanct, however, and actually increased as retooling began after years of war in Southeast Asia. This meant that the cut had to be made in other areas, including housing, job training, and education programs for the disadvantaged. Branding President Johnson's "War on Poverty" a failure, Nixon destroyed its command center, the Office of Economic Opportunity (OEO). Congressional leaders, encouraged by complaints from urban mayors, promised to fight this debilitation of social service programs. The spring of 1973 opened with a major struggle between President and Congress over national priorities.

Nixon's chosen weapon in this battle was the impounding of funds. To meet his personal goal of limited spending, Nixon simply held back money authorized by the legislative branch for federal programs. This action not only irked an already querulous Congress but also raised a significant constitutional issue. Claiming that constitutional powers over appropriations had been unilaterally abrogated, Congress joined in lawsuits to force the disbursement of the impounded funds. In 1972, for example, Congress had authorized several million dollars for water pollution control. Nixon vetoed the bill in October, but both houses produced the necessary two-thirds vote to override the veto. The President then refused to allow more than half the money to be distributed. In May 1973 a United States District Court ordered the government to make available to the states the full amount authorized by Congress. If this case set a precedent, Nixon's impoundings would be rejected as unconstitutional whenever tested. Yet Congress still had to contend with a President prepared to veto any appropriation he disliked, and it still had to muster a two-thirds majority to override the veto.

Economics Again

Phases III and IV. Pleased that Phase II controls had slowed the inflation rate to 3.5 percent annually and anxious to do away with "bureaucratic controls," Nixon virtually abandoned federal supervision of the economy in January 1973. Secretary of the Treasury George Schultz, who believed in minimal government regulation, became the President's chief economic adviser. Phase III, announced on January 11, removed nearly all restrictions on prices and wages and relied on voluntary cooperation from businessmen and workers. Phase III aimed to reduce inflation to under 2.5 percent by the end of 1974.

Many observers immediately expressed skepticism, and within three months their doubt seemed all too fully confirmed. Freed from controls, prices surged upward. During the first quarter of 1973, the cost of living rose 8.8 percent, mocking administration goals. Such inflation and the economy's uncontrolled expansion caused some experts to forecast recession for 1974-75. In March of 1973 alone, food costs climbed 3.2 percent, the largest monthly increase since such calculations began in 1952. Skyrocketing meat prices prompted consumers to participate in a loosely organized national meat boycott during April. Although its economic impact did not force prices down, the boycott impressively demonstrated consumer anger. President Nixon imposed a price ceiling on meats at the end of the first week of the boycott. Yet another phase, Phase IV, temporarily froze prices in July, but when most controls ended during the first months of 1974, the inflation rate jumped to 11 percent annually. Interest rates for ordinary business customers soared as high as 15 percent, the highest in the nation's history and a level that would soon provoke a huge slack in American production. Nixonomics—inflation and recession—still plagued the nation.

The international economy.   During this time the administration also tried to ease the dollar crisis and reduce domestic unemployment by increasing international trade. The Soviet-American Trade Agreement tripled trade with Russia: the value of the American exports rose from $500 million in 1969-71 to $1.5 billion in 1973-75. In 1972 the Soviet Union pledged gold bullion to pay for $1 billion of wheat to be imported during the next three years. This sudden demand for huge amounts of grain forced American wheat prices rapidly upward, adding to inflationary pressures. The Russians, in a maneuver many commodity speculators appreciated, then sold some of their grain futures on America's markets, sometimes doubling their money. Détente and capitalism, it seemed, could work both ways. The administration had hoped that opening the potentially huge markets of China could help restore a balanced prosperity to the United States, but that country's low buying power postponed any significant boost.

Attempts to stabilize international monetary relations were equally inconclusive. Foreigners worried that chronic federal budget deficits would force the United States to print more money to pay overdue bills, thereby making its dollar worthless. Moreover, since Americans bought more from other countries than their citizens purchased from the United States, the dollar was further weakened, just as a person who spends more than he makes finds his credit weakened. If this trade imbalance continued long enough, other nations might not accept American currency in payment for their goods—a technical state of international bankruptcy. So in 1973 Nixon allowed the dollar to "float," finding its own market value in relation to foreign currencies rather than fixing its value in terms of gold. The United States had already devalued the dollar in late 1971; this devaluation, combined with an upward revaluation of Germany's mark and Japan's yen, had made the dollar depreciate nearly 12 percent by 1973. Since American products could now be purchased overseas for fewer marks or yen while foreign purchases required more dollars, the American trade balance slowly improved through more exports and fewer imports. By 1974 the balance on current account—goods, that is, not financial services—showed a slight gain.

Yet some of the results were puzzling. The price of a Japanese color television set, for instance, increased only 3.5 percent, even though the yen was revalued by nearly 17 percent. The dollar's strength continued to deteriorate, forcing another devaluation in February 1973, this time by 10 percent. Worried that these aggressive measures would rob them of markets in the United States, several major European countries floated their own currencies against the dollar, pledging to keep them from fluctuating more than

---

The Arab embargo on crude oil forced filling stations to limit quantities of gasoline sold and curtail hours of service. Throughout the winter of 1973-1974, scenes such as this one were common.

Andrew Sacks from Editorial Photocolor Archives.

2.25 percent from one another. This arrangement aimed to make speculation unprofitable and dangerous. Nonetheless, international monetary stability in the mid-seventies seemed only a dream, for the monetary crisis continued, fed largely by America's uncertain economic future, its political disorientation, shortages and the high cost of oil, and speculation.

The Energy Crisis

In late 1973, the Arab nations of the Middle East embargoed oil shipments to the United States in retaliation for Washington's diplomatic support for Israel during the October war there. With high quality crude no longer available, American refineries could not shift their cracking procedures rapidly enough to meet expected winter demands for heating oil and gasoline. Prices shot upward, most of them doubling between November 1973 and mid-1974; meanwhile oil companies tallied record profits, apparently as a result of hoarding what reserves existed. The President called on Americans to conserve, and temporarily most did, cutting room temperatures to 68 degrees and slowing automobiles to fifty-five miles per hour.

Nixon also launched "Project Independence" to make the United States "self-sufficient in energy by 1980." Many doubted whether this goal was realistic, given the long lag-time to switch sources of power. But Congress did approve a giant pipe-line project to bring the oil of Alaska's North Slope from the Arctic to the western United States, and many localities granted oil companies permission to drill off-shore. (With cars lined up at the filling stations, concern for the possible effects of such policies on the environment faded.) Yet none of these stop-gap measures dealt with the overall problem of increasing demand for energy in an advanced technological nation amid obviously declining sources of energy.

◄ 10 ►

THE END
OF AN AGE

THE NIXON administration's grand ambitions to revamp the federal government in a way that would have given the White House effective power over the national purse, centralized decision making in the executive branch, and ended much of the welfare activities of five previous Presidents required an administration with great internal strength and broad public support. Instead, in early 1973 a devastating scandal crippled the entire executive branch, toppling Nixon and his administration in a way politically more final, constitutionally more definite, and personally far more tragic than anything in the sad final year of the Johnson era.

Watergate

Since the break-in at Democratic Committee Headquarters in the Watergate complex in June of 1972, suspicions and rumors of close executive involvement had circulated freely. Hard information emerged slowly, however; more than six months of probing and speculation by a few newspapers like the *New York Times* and the *Washington Post* preceded the first real breaks in the case. Federal

227

District Judge John J. Sirica worked skillfully to force exposure of wrong-doing in the Watergate tangle, but the five men caught at the break-in refused to give details and entered guilty pleas to avoid full testimony in court.

After their conviction in January 1973, Sirica handed out provisional maximum sentences to the defendants while hinting that prison terms might be reduced for those who told all to a grand jury. One, James McCord, Jr., a security officer for the Committee to Re-elect the President (CRP) who had once worked for the FBI and CIA, indicated a willingness to talk, so Sirica postponed sentencing him. Testifying before a grand jury, McCord implicated three high-ranking Republican officials in the planning of the Watergate bugging attempt: former Attorney General John Mitchell, at the time chairman of CRP (some newspapers used the acronym CREEP); Jeb Stuart Magruder, Mitchell's deputy; and John W. Dean III, counsel to the President. McCord also claimed that after their arrest the Watergate defendants received regular payments for their silence from Dorothy Hunt, wife of one of the accused men, E. Howard Hunt. When she was killed in a Chicago plane crash in December 1973, Mrs. Hunt was carrying $10,000 in cash.

Yet McCord's information did not provide the evidence a grand jury needed. Then on April 6, John Dean talked to prosecutors and supported much of McCord's testimony. Later that month Magruder also began describing his role in Watergate to Justice Department officials. As Mitchell and Dean in turn testified before the grand jury, more accusations began spilling forth in a complex and contradicting array implicating an ever-widening group of top officials in the planning of the Watergate break-in or its subsequent cover-up. Even Republican congressional leaders expressed growing anger and called for removing the "stench" about the White House.

On April 30, President Nixon announced on national television the resignations of his two top staff members. H. R. Haldeman and John Ehrlichman, both implicated in the scandal. John Dean also left the White House. Then Attorney General Richard Kleindienst resigned because, he said, close associates were involved in the Watergate case. In the same speech, Nixon also told his audience that he had had no knowledge of White House staff involvement until the month before, March 1973. While accepting responsibility for his subordinates' actions, Nixon mainly attempted to excuse himself from guilt and implied that the resignations would purify the White House. Consistent with his desire to deflate the scandal and to force other news into the headlines, the President avoided Watergate and tried to conduct his office as if nothing had happened.

But Nixon had to replace the official casualties. By mid-May at least twenty resignations resulting from Watergate and associated scandals decimated the White House staff. For a brief time, the nation had no Attorney General. Assistant secretaries in at least two cabinet departments quit. Acting FBI director L. Patrick Gray admitted destroying papers relevant to the case, and Nixon withdrew Gray's nomination. Many political leaders urged the President to bring new and untainted officials into his administration, but Nixon chose to reshuffle old officials whose integrity remained intact. Secretary of Defense Elliot L. Richardson, in office only briefly, moved to the Justice Department as Attorney General; Director of the CIA James Schlesinger filled Richardson's old post; William D. Ruckelshaus moved from the Environmental Protection Agency to head the FBI temporarily; General Alexander M. Haig, Jr., Henry Kissinger's deputy, took over as White House Chief of Staff; and John Connally, former Secretary of the Treasury, returned to the executive branch as a general presidential adviser. But more vacancies appeared regularly, including many unrelated to Watergate, and they were filled slowly. The scandals hampered the normal functioning of presidential bureaucracy and, eventually, created a crisis of confidence in government itself.

Several investigations maintained public interest in the case. A special Senate committee chaired by Sam J. Ervin of North Carolina began televised hearings on May 17 and soon heard new testimony from James McCord on cover-up attempts. Promising to follow every lead, the Ervin committee heard from all major actors in the Watergate drama, while its staff penetrated contradictory statements. Mitchell, Ehrlichman, and Haldeman denied guilt, even knowledge of what Dean, Magruder, and others had sworn was their involvement in "hush money" for the Watergate burglary and other campaign activities that Mitchell called "the White House horrors." When Dean had accused Nixon of participating in the cover-up, the White House press secretary denounced him as "a liar." Then a White House aide, Alexander Butterfield, told the startled Senators that Nixon had tape recorded most of the private conversations that

Senator Sam Ervin confers with members of the Senate special committee investigating the Watergate break-in.

took place in his White House office. Ervin pressed the President to turn over tapes that could settle the discrepancies between witnesses. But Nixon refused on the basis of "executive privilege," a valid constitutional argument though seemingly self-serving in this case. What, many citizens asked, did he have to hide?

In late October 1973, the so-called Saturday Night Massacre created, as one White House staffer later said, "a fire-storm of opposition." During the spring, Nixon had appointed as special Watergate prosecutor Harvard law professor Archibald Cox, promising him "full freedom of action." But Cox and his eager colleagues began probing not only Watergate matters but also 1972 campaign malpractices and the President's personal finances. Angered at such "fishing expeditions," Nixon ordered Cox's superior, Attorney General Elliot Richardson, to fire him, But Richardson resigned rather than bow to this new display of executive power. So did his deputy, William Ruckelshaus. Solicitor General Robert Bork agreed to remove Cox, but the three casualties of presidential ire symbolized for many Americans Nixon's arrogant, dangerous usurpation of power. Two days later, Congress began the first steps toward impeachment.

Other Scandals

Despite its preeminence, the actual Watergate case stood out only as the most striking of a cluster of scandals. In October 1973 Vice-President Spiro Agnew resigned, in effect admitting his guilt in taking bribes while in office rather than risk a possible jail term. The recently enacted Twenty-fifth Amendment to the Constitution provided a method for selecting a successor, and Representative Gerald R. Ford of Michigan was quickly installed. The episode, however, shocked and embittered many Americans.

As early as the summer of 1972 irregularities in Nixon's campaign finances had surfaced. CRP workers solicited large contributions to beat an April deadline for reporting campaign funding under a new election law; substantial sums were channeled through Mexican banks to disguise the identity of donors. After Nixon personally intervened to raise milk price supports, dairy interests contributed several hundred thousand dollars to his campaign. Both International Telephone and Telegraph (ITT) and the Seafarers' International Union gave generously and later received favorable government treatment. A strange affair involving the secret contribution of $200,000 by financier Robert L. Vesco made headlines in the spring of 1974. For the first time since the Teapot Dome scandals of the twenties, a grand jury indicted former cabinet members for criminal offenses. Attorney General John N. Mitchell and Commerce Secretary Maurice H. Stans—Nixon's chief campaign fundraisers —allegedly solicited Vesco's contribution with promises that a government investigation of the financier's shady stock maneuvers would end. Mitchell and Stans also were charged with six counts of perjury based on their earlier testimony before the grand jury. But the prosecution could not prove its charges, and a New York City jury acquitted the pair in May.

The large contributions of Vesco and others attracted great attention because of their connection with secret funds—funds that CRP officials used to finance the Watergate caper as well as a broad program of political espionage and skullduggery. Nixon workers faked letters of support for the President's policies and infiltrated opposition groups. An array of "dirty tricks" perpetrated against

Democratic presidential hopefuls in 1972 discredited many of that party's strongest candidates. Even more frightening, the Nixon administration had used government intelligence agencies to gain information about political groups and individuals, while top Nixon advisers had apparently formed their own espionage ring, "the Plumbers."

The secret activities of the White House staff emerged in time to ruin an attempt to prosecute two former government researchers, Daniel Ellsberg and Anthony J. Russo, Jr., who were charged with turning over to the *New York Times* during 1971 secret Defense Department documents on the Vietnam War. The Nixon administration clearly wished to punish Ellsberg and Russo for leaking these Pentagon papers. But in May 1973 a series of startling disclosures concerning government improprieties relating to the case brought their trial to a sudden halt. Some of the same men who burglarized the Watergate complex had the year before, on the orders of John Ehrlichman, broken into the office of Daniel Ellsberg's former psychiatrist in an attempt to find embarrassing personal information that might be used against Ellsberg. In the middle of the trial, Ehrlichman, then Nixon's chief domestic assistant, privately offered Judge Matthew Byrne the FBI directorship. The defense quickly labeled this approach an attempted bribe. Angered by the multiple irregularities, Byrne permanently dismissed all charges against Ellsberg and Russo. Later, Ehrlichman himself was convicted of perjury and obstruction of justice, his illegal tactics condemned as "dangerous to Constitutional government."

Whatever his personal involvement in these scandals—whether simple errors in judgment or conspiratorial plans against constitutional government—Nixon could not escape blame for creating a climate in which political espionage might flourish. Internal security had become a fetish, so the President encouraged domestic spying and his administration conveyed a totalitarian atmosphere. Rewarding loyalty more than competence or integrity, Nixon taught his staff to equate support for him with patriotism and opposition to his policies with subversion. Nixon's men did what they thought was expected of them, even planning sabotage against the Democrats. Too much aware of the glamour and too little experienced in politics, the White House staff pursued power and personal glory. They were, or so they thought, above the law.

Nixon's Reaction

Watergate and related scandals inflicted enormous harm on the administration. The confidence in President Nixon expressed by many Americans during the 1972 election steadily eroded during his second term. Signs of disenchantment appeared even among stalwart party members; Conservative New York Senator James L. Buckley urged him to resign "for the good of the Republic." Despite White House publicity efforts like "Operation Candor" designed to counter media revelations, opinion polls reflected widespread doubt in the President's honesty and his ability to govern. By entering government battles without the shield of popular support, Nixon further aggravated the split between Congress and the White House. Some legislators shunned his support after a special off-year election in Michigan during 1973 returned a Democrat to the House of Representatives—the first in twenty years from that district.

The President more and more avoided Washington in favor of San Clemente or Key Biscayne, while his administration responded only fitfully to mounting economic pressures. A spokesman almost admitted failure in mid-1974 when he said, "Americans will just have to live with high inflation." The scandals weakened America's bargaining position in international affairs. Trade and disarmament negotiations with the Soviet Union and other powers became considerably more difficult, as Nixon clearly hoped to use foreign successes to counter domestic critics. Financial experts even attributed renewed pressure on the dollar to the Watergate affair. Government was barely muddling through.

Although observers worried about the effect of a two-and-a-half year lame duck presidency, few questioned Nixon's hold on the presidency itself. Despite Senate inquiries and impeachment bills in the House, the chief executive was "stonewalling it," refusing to hand over any tapes other than the edited transcripts released in late April 1974, which Nixon had pledged "would tell it all." Nevertheless, special Watergate prosecutor Leon Jaworski asked the Supreme Court to force disclosure of more conversations, but this was an arduous, time-consuming process. Meanwhile, the House Judiciary Committee pursued a parallel impeachment investigation with what evidence existed.

Public faith in the President wavered; polls showed that a majority thought Nixon was probably involved in Watergate. Still, in late spring, most were not demanding his ouster from office. A Harvard law professor, for example, quipped that Nixon's lawyer, James St. Clair, was "doing a magnificent job of defending the President if he's guilty, but a lousy one if he's innocent!" For a time, Nixon's strategy of riding out his seventh crisis with a cool, grim determination to ignore the issue seemed likely to succeed. "One year of Watergate," he had said in the 1974 State of the Union message, "is enough."

The Road to Resignation

The lumbering momentum of congressional machinery prevented the question of Nixon's culpability from simply drifting away. Capitol Hill insiders speculated that the Judiciary Committee might approve a bill of impeachment; press leaks interspersed tidbits of gossip with hints of presidential wrongdoing. Yet all the testimony and talk confused more than it clarified. No one knew exactly what the Constitution meant when it mandated that the President be removed from office if he were found guilty of "high crimes and misdemeanors." Just what was an impeachable offense? Nixon's accusers found only complicated, technical violations of arcane rules of law, which the President's supporters insisted were only errors in judgment. A comic strip summed up the problem, "If only he'd rob a bank!"

Then, quite suddenly in mid-summer, the Nixon presidency disintegrated. It began on July 8, 1974, when Jaworski and St. Clair argued two historic cases before the Supreme Court. In *United States* v. *Richard Nixon*, the issue seemed straightforward: whether or not the President must turn over additional tapes subpoenaed by the special prosecutor. "No man is above the law," Jaworski insisted, "and no man can sit as judge in his own case." The Court must order Nixon to release the tapes, thus preserving "the rule of law, not of men." St. Clair countered vigorously with legal precedents concerning the separation of powers and executive privilege. "The President," he emphasized, "had acted to protect national security." Within the restraints imposed on him by law and Constitution, Nixon had cooperated fully. If the Court collaborated in Jaworski's "fishing expedition for more evidence," the justices might permanently tilt the checks and balances system. In a second, less heralded case, *Richard Nixon* v. *the United States*, the

President asked the judges to set aside an action by the Watergate grand jury that had named him as an "unindicted co-conspirator" in covering up the burglary. St. Clair argued that the move had "no standing in law" when applied to an incumbent President; Jaworski pointed out that only his office had protected Nixon from formal charges. Eight justices—former Deputy Attorney General William H. Rehnquist voluntarily disqualified himself—took up the two cases, so legalistic to millions, so momentous for a President.

The public found another show in town much more intriguing. The House Judiciary Committee allowed its final debates at the end of July to be televised, and for almost a week Americans tuned in to the ten-hour-a-day talkathon. Most of them heard only a fraction of the argument, but since committee rules alternated proponents with opponents of impeachment, the viewers at least heard both sides. Citizens began to understand the issues; many argued at lunchtime or over the backyard fence about complicated testimony, specific grounds for impeachment, or larger constitutional principles. Anxious to appear serious and fair-minded, the twenty-one Democrats and seventeen Republicans on the committee scrupulously maintained a high level of debate. Nixon's defenders argued that, although probably unethical or even illegal, his actions did not deserve impeachment. Others thought the proposed articles of impeachment too general or too political. Where, they asked, was "the smoking gun" that would unquestionably establish presidential guilt? But many citizens realized that the representatives were talking of the extent, not the existence, of Nixon's wrongdoing. Nixon's credibility sagged dangerously.

The fragile public faith in the man elected so overwhelmingly in 1972 cracked irretrieveably during the three successive days when a coalition of Democrats and liberal Republicans approved formal articles of impeachment. The first article charged the President with obstructing investigations of the Watergate break-in and covering up evidence that implicated himself. Nine separate counts accused Nixon of lying, withholding criminal evidence, interfering with the FBI and CIA, and condoning hush money for the Watergate burglars. "For all these reasons, and others," the article read, "there is no recourse but to impeach Richard Nixon, President of the United States." On July 29, the committee adopted this "Watergate article," 27 to 11. Thomas Railsback of Illinois, one of six Republicans voting for it, emotionally explained his vote against his long-time political friend: "I have to live with myself for the rest of my life. I want to do the right thing." Another Republican, Lawrence J. Hogan of Maryland, was more direct: "The President is guilty: I must do my duty." Then the legislators turned to a second article, which accused the President of "abusing power." Nixon and his staff had illegally wiretapped for purposes "unrelated to national security," organized a secret unit in the White House that "engaged in covert activities," and misused executive power by interfering with the special prosecutor, the Justice Department, and the Internal Revenue Service. This time seven of the seventeen Republicans joined with the Democrats to favor indictment of the President, 28 to 10. The committee also considered three other articles. Two of them—charges of tax fraud and unlawful bombing in Cambodia —were dismissed for lack of evidence. But they did approve the last, charging that Nixon "acted in a way subversive of Constitutional government" when he refused to comply with committee subpoenas for additional records. And so, on July 30, 1974, for only the second time in American history, a President stood charged with high crimes and misdemeanors, for which, the Representatives recommended to the full House, "there is no remedy but impeachment."

The lopsided votes in committee almost ensured that the lower house would easily achieve the simple majority needed to force trial in the Senate. Six days of televised debate had reconciled many citizens to the need for impeachment while reassuring them about the workability of constitutional government. Polls indicated that the people no longer feared that Nixon's removal would harm the nation. Even as congressional and public opinion swung against the President, events elsewhere, in the chambers of the Supreme Court and in secret meeting places in the White House, soon made his ouster inevitable. Nixon had always insisted that only actual crimes justified removal, and, quite unexpectedly, a tortured legal process uncovered "the smoking gun."

On August 1 the Supreme Court by a vote of 8 to 0 ordered the White House to turn over additional tapes to Jaworski. The President wanted to refuse this command, but certain of his advisers, especially St. Clair and Chief of Staff Alexander Haig, threatened to resign unless he complied. Then on Monday, August 5, Nixon surprised the nation not only by agreeing to turn over tapes to the courts, as he had been commanded to do, but by voluntarily making public those conversations he had had with Dean and Haldeman just after the Watergate break-in. They proved that on June 23, 1972, the President had planned to cover up White House connections with the burglary and, therefore, had lied repeatedly to the American people. His legal maneuvers were not in defense of national security or executive privilege, but only ruses to hide evidence of personal wrongdoing. Nixon seemed strangely unaware of the implications: he admitted to "a serious act of omission for which I take full responsibility," but he argued that "the record, in its entirety, does not justify the extreme step of impeachment."

Many citizens and Nixon loyalists had had enough; for them, presidential culpability was no longer in doubt. All eleven members of the Judiciary Committee who had supported the President now announced that they favored impeachment. After House Minority Leader James Rhodes of Ohio and Nixon defender Representative Charles Wiggins of California publicly called for resignation and, barring that, his removal from office, only a handful of Representatives still backed the President. With indictment a foregone conclusion, attention shifted to the Senate. Republican leaders Hugh Scott of Pennsylvania and Barry Goldwater of Arizona conferred with their party colleagues on Tuesday and then visited Nixon the next day; they informed him that at least eighty-five Senators—well over the necessary two-thirds—were ready to convict him on the Watergate article. "We didn't urge him to resign," Goldwater said. "We just told him the facts." Nixon had earlier told his cabinet that he would never quit, but the President realized that without the support of his own party he could not remain in office. The White House announced that Nixon would speak to the nation on Thursday evening. Tourists saw him walking the grounds of the executive mansion, alone. Vice-President Gerald Ford canceled a scheduled trip to the Far West.

"I am not a quitter," Nixon told the nation on August 8. But, for the good of the country, he would resign. Admitting only to "errors of judgment," the President reviewed the five and a half years of his tenure, emphasizing his innovations in foreign affairs. Yet people would remember more than this dignified speech, for the next morning television captured his emotional farewell to the White House staff. His usual control gone, the President rambled on, his comments revealing his compulsions and tears.

Then he left for California, a lonely man who, some thought, was mentally distraught or, others said more kindly, was mismatched for the presidency. The new chief executive, Gerald Ford, sadly spoke of the former leader, "May the man who brought peace to millions find it for himself."

EPILOGUE

RICHARD NIXON was the second consecutive President to see his administration dissolve around him. Commentators speculated that the modern presidency had become too large for any single man to fill, that its overweening grandeur had cut it off from sources of information and from political currents, that it had attained "imperial" proportions. The President no longer seemed to possess the common humanity that Americans demand of even their highest leaders. Nixon's successor, Gerald Ford, vowed to decentralize and demythologize the office to which he had never aspired and to effect a "marriage" with Congress.

Ford's personality and style seemed well suited to the realization of such goals. A modest man, fundamentally conservative and old-fashioned, the former college football star from Grand Rapids, Michigan, symbolized the national mood of relief that ensued from the evaporation of the constitutional crisis. His brief and unassuming inaugural address, so appropriate to the first man to assume the presidency without the sanction of a national election, reassured the American people that "our long national nightmare is over. Our Constitution works." In subsequent weeks, the nation became accustomed to a President who seemed comfortable with people, who was open to criticism and argument, and who was anxious to be a partner rather than a master in his relations with the other branches and institutions of government. Ford's earliest moves—calling a national summit meeting on the economy, nominating former New York governor Nelson Rockefeller for Vice-President, retaining Henry Kissinger as Secretary of State and continuing the foreign policy of the Nixon administration, seeking a middle ground between the welfare spending ideas of the Democratic Congress and his own conservative leanings—breathed reassurance and consensus, a pleasant change from the immediate past.

Yet the options of a latter-day Calvin Coolidge were not Ford's, even had he wished them to be. President Coolidge had been able to keep things low-key and comfortable in a world that allowed more of the luxury of respite from hard decisions and political conflict. In 1974 this world no longer existed. The President had to make fundamental choices, and, as he did, divisions once more appeared. Seeking to "bind up the internal wounds of Watergate," as he had promised to do in his inaugural address, Ford, without consultation outside his own and the former President's staff, granted an unconditional pardon to Richard Nixon covering all his actions while President. Coming at a time when Vietnam War resisters were being offered a complicated, partial, and—for most of them—impractical mechanism to gain "amnesty" and when coconspirators of the pardoned ex-President were being tried for alleged crimes committed at his behest, the pardon renewed rather than quieted the arguments over Watergate. Similarly, the nomination of Nelson Rockefeller for Vice-President, at first generally well received, stirred controversy when investigations showed that Rockefeller had made astonishingly large cash gifts to his subordinates and had approved the publication, as well as his brother Laurence's financial underwriting, of a defamatory biography of his 1970 gubernatorial opponent, the widely respected former Supreme Court Justice Arthur J. Goldberg. Ford's main problems, however, were in the closely related areas of the economy and foreign policy.

Inflation was worldwide, and international economic relations were in a state of extreme perturbation due to major shifts in the economic balance of power. Led by the Arab oil countries, nations that export raw materials had organized to control prices and get what they considered their fair share of the profits from their products—a dramatic reversal of roles after the long era of Western imperialism and exploitation. In addition, the Arab nations had directed their economic pressures to a specific diplomatic objective: the creation of an independent state for the Palestinian Arabs. Some among this bloc had gone even further and demanded the destruction of the state of Israel, the main ally of the United States in the Middle East and an object of solicitude for millions of Jewish-Americans. With his typical efficiency and smoothness, Henry Kissinger moved back and forth among the Arab and Israeli leaders, working to calm the Israelis and, by taking advantage of divisions among the Arab states, to head off the renewed Middle Eastern war that many observers thought inevitable. Meanwhile, Ford and Kissinger continued to seek support in these efforts among old enemies. The Nixon Administration's policies of encouraging détente with the Soviet Union, through the extension to that country of the status of "most favored nation" and through the grain deal and the SALT agreements of 1972, were promoted by the Ford Administration in a summit meeting at Vladivostok in the Soviet Union in November of 1974. Whether Ford could successfully use those policies, as Nixon had done, to work toward solutions in the troubled areas of the world remained to be seen.

The domestic repercussions of these international economic shifts came mostly in the form of inflation. Oil prices had already leapt ahead, and food prices shortly followed suit. This was partly because the price of petroleum-based fertilizers had risen and partly because poor crops and outbreaks of famine in many parts of the world had increased the demand for available food. Then inflation inevitably produced consumer resistance to purchasing large and increasingly expensive items like automobiles and appliances. Interest rate curves paralleled the use of "double-digit" inflation, slowing business activity, while the housing market suffered disaster as mortgage money disappeared. Even the Administration began to concede, late in 1974, what many economists had known for months: the United States economy was clearly in a recession. Numerous local and state governments, as they ran out of money, initiated job freezes and cutbacks in services. New York City even took the extreme step of firing or forcing to retire almost 8,000 city employees in November-December 1974. Some of the large automobile manufacturers closed nearly all of their production lines; by January 1975, 141,000 workers were laid off and 76,000 were affected by temporary plant closings.

The President's summit conference of businessmen, labor leaders, and economists was a disappointment. No single and persuasive answer, no consensus on policy, emerged from it, and the President had pointedly ruled out price and wage controls prior to the meeting. The economic policy that finally evolved seemed weak: a tax surcharge and incentives both for business to spend and for the public to limit its consumption. Such programs were largely voluntary and promised little relief from the spiraling inflation. Many Americans therefore prepared for a considerable period of economic difficulty.

In the troubled autumn of 1974, the outcome of the Congressional elections was hardly a surprise. Despite strenuous speech-making by the President—and Gerald Ford had always been an effective campaigner—the results were heavily Democratic. The new governors of the two largest states, New York and California, were now relatively young and very vigorous Democrats rather than aging Republicans. The new Congress was even more overwhelmingly Democratic than the previous one. The possibility of two years of political stalemate between Congress and the Executive threatened a renewal of some of the conflicts of the Watergate era, which Ford's aggressive campaigning against a "veto-proof" Democratic Congress had made all too likely. Watergate was gone, but all of its attendant problems were not. And the deeper dilemmas— particularly the nation's position in a shifting world economy —became more dramatically apparent, once the distraction of the constitutional crisis had been removed.

In the modern world, the present has almost always seemed a moment of crisis. If problems are solved (or, as is more frequent, passed over and forgotten), the sense of crisis fades with them, only to reappear with the next troubled situation. This sense of crisis derives both from our awareness of our strength and from our uncertainty about how to use it. Power always has its ambiguities, and, because it is almost never absolute, its wielders are never confident that it is sufficient to their tasks. In this sense, the present is not very different from the recent past; all that has changed, perhaps, is that the magnitude of our hopes has been diminished. The United States cannot keep the world in order—yet thirty years ago we did not know that. Because we now realize that we cannot control everything that happens in the world, we find it easier to understand that none of our adversaries can control it either, and so our fears of a Communist conspiracy capable of dominating the world have diminished. The international dreams of all the powers have become less vivid, but we recognize that this is scarcely a development to be deplored.

In our domestic life as well, the past thirty years have been a time for sober education. We have watched the future—the world of affluence—become the present, and we know now that wealth does not solve all human problems. We have seen the thorough institutionalizing of the welfare state, and still some people are hungry. We have seen extensive regulation of the economy, and still the fears of serious depression persist. We have educated a greater proportion of the American population than anyone a generation ago thought possible, and yet our culture is far from entering its Periclean age. Furthermore, we have learned the narrowness of our official views of American norms; we have come to accept the fact that we are a heterogeneous people, despite the often thin veneer of our conformities. One reason we are less imperialistic in our world outlook is that we are no longer certain of the model of living we would like to impose on other cultures.

The history of twentieth-century America has been, in a sense, a history of the United States joining the rest of the world, and paying at last the costs of those benefits through the increasing regimentation of society, our growing involvement in the world's common problems, and our now total commitment to a world future that is threatened—militarily, ecologically, economically—in ways that the rest of the Western world has been quicker than we to recognize. While many people are discouraged by the disillusionments of the era since 1945, at least a few of them will say that the death of some of our most pervasive illusions is not to be regretted, and that the years since the Second World War have been a time, however costly, of national education.

INDEX

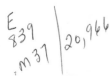

Date Due

APR 7 1982		
MAR 2 1 1986		
MAR 0 8 1990		
Mar 23		
SEP 1 5 1999		
JUL 2 6 1999		
JAN 2 9 2002		
FEB 1 8 2003		
MAR 1 1 2003		
MAR 1 1 2003		
APR 1 3 2003		
APR 0 7 2003		

FORM 109